Marzi *a memoir*

VERTIGO

Marzi a memoir

Marzena Sowa

with art by Sylvain Savoia

Translated by Anjali Singh

Introduction by Marzena Sowa

In my life, I've always been a fugitive.

If I don't like something, I leave.
I scatter my photos, give away my clothes,
get rid of my books, sell my shoes.

I move.
I change boyfriends, haircuts, countries.

I learn a new language.

I trample my past deliberately.

While avoiding mirrors I repeat to myself
that only the future matters.

Making a tabula rasa of my life is my way
of becoming someone else, or rather, of
trying my best to become someone else.

No need to spell out that it's a clash
of Titans I'm engaging in. My flawless
memory won't let me recast everything.
I fail miserably.

I was born in Poland at a time when it
was undergoing some big changes.
I watched it rebel. I watched it dream.
And saw its dreams come true. This
allowed me to believe that through
perseverance, stubbornness and force
of character, you could change the world.

The Poland of my childhood found itself
under the communist regime imposed by
the USSR at the end of the Second World
War. The Polish people rebelled because
they wanted Poland to become itself, to be
Polish, to not depend on others, to be free.

In those days, Poles were looking for
their own identity. They needed to define
themselves as a nation. But I had the
feeling that in looking for an "us," they
forgot the "I."

Without choosing it, I was a witness to all
these changes, to all these aspirations.
A mute and insignificant witness perhaps.
Children don't count for much. Like fish,
they don't have voices. This is the motto I
was raised with.

So I contented myself with observing. My memory recorded everything my eyes took in. I didn't know that one day I was going to talk about it, that I was going to share my experiences, to describe the Poland of that time. I just thought I'd get away quickly, as I later did, without turning back.

I didn't want to carry the weight of my nation, nor search for our identity. In truth, I didn't care. I had no desire to settle History's accounts, to try to figure out who was good and who was bad. I wanted to get away from all that. Maybe it was a selfish gesture, but for me, then, it was vital.

I dreamed of choosing my own life, of choosing the way I wanted to live and where I would live.

I wanted to be free, independent, a unit, an individual, an island.

Now I tell myself that I'm the spitting image of my country, a rebellious dreamer.

You might ask me: So why would someone who runs away suddenly decide to talk about what she ran away from, what she doesn't want to face?

Maybe because I realize that I'm wasting my energy at a task I will never succeed at, because what I am fleeing is none other than myself. Maybe because, quite simply, I'm growing older and wiser. I'm less scared. All the monsters of the past aren't as monstrous as I always thought they were.

Maybe because I haven't lived in Poland for some time, and together the distances of geography and time are allowing me to put into perspective many things, to revisit my history with more serenity and objectivity.

Maybe because Sylvain, my partner and the illustrator, to whom I told the stories of my childhood, asked me, "Why don't you write them down? You had an unusual childhood, it would be a shame to forget it. It's an experience you should share."

Probably all of the above.

I am Marzi, born in 1979, ten years before the end of communism in Poland, an only child who lives in a small industrial city. My father works at a factory, my mother at a dairy. I have family in the country, aunts and uncles, neighbors, friends, a guinea pig and then a dog.

I hate shots, getting my hair cut, milk skin, and a lot of other things besides. I'm scared of spiders, and the world of adults doesn't seem like a walk in the park.

Social problems are at their height. Empty stores are our daily bread. The people rebel, the government cracks down. A state of war sets in. And even when it's over, the situation doesn't improve. But the Poles don't lower their arms. Little by little, they manage to get what they want more than anything, their Freedom. And the life of a little girl passes half-unnoticed in the Poland of the 1980s drowning in politics and problems.

Poland. Writing this word, I wonder what it might evoke for you. Perhaps the tragedy of the Second World War? Pope John Paul II? Vodka? Perhaps you have a neighbor who answers to Kowalski or Nowak? Or perhaps nothing at all. It's a country in central Europe, where the Baltic Sea is always cold and gray, where men still kiss the hands of ladies, where, in front of the American embassy, there are always enormous lines of Poles hoping to get visas for the United States. A country where people still dream immoderately.

You might turn the question on me:

What do I know about your country? Or better yet, what did I know when I was little Marzi? I dreamed of Barbie dolls. I loved Donald's chewing gum. We always knew someone with a relative in the United States, someone who had something American: a perfume, a hair elastic, a sweater, socks. Something which amazed us, something which made us dream. I remember gorging myself on an American cream that claimed to be toothpaste.

I can't forget the first English words I learned (badly), thanks to a friend who had heard them from another friend: She taught us that to greet someone, you should say, "How do you do?" And in response, you should answer, "Do you how how." How many times did we repeat these precious words religiously, words from another world, a better world?

I don't live in Poland anymore. I don't have any more Polish clothes. I've already cut off my Polish nails. The ones growing now are entirely French. The same is true of my hair.

I don't dream in Polish anymore. I've changed many things. I've evolved the way I choose to.

But I am not scared anymore of facing the person I used to be. I am who I am because I was Marzi. And she continues to live in me.

If someone had asked me what my specialty was, a while ago, I would have said that I'm a burner of bridges. Marzi is the first bridge I haven't destroyed. Quite the opposite. I've strengthened it deliberately, out of a desire to face myself and to show you, through my experience, the daily life of the Polish people close to me during the final years of communism. It's a pretty solid bridge. Don't be scared to stand on it. Welcome.

EVERY YEAR, THERE'S A SPECIAL DAY WHEN WE BUY SOMETHING SPECIAL...

SOMETHING WE EAT ONLY ONCE A YEAR...

A CARP...

MY DAD GOES TO THE MARKET IN THE CITY CENTER VERY EARLY ON SATURDAYS. THERE, YOU CAN BUY ANYTHING YOUR SOUL DESIRES (THAT'S WHAT WE SAY IN POLISH ...)

DEAD FOOD, BUT ALSO LIVE FOOD, CLOTHES, FURNITURE, RUGS... EVEN CARS...

BUT HE JUST GOES FOR THE FOOD. HE WOULD NEVER BUY A CAR THERE. IT'S NOT THE MOST RELIABLE PLACE...

YOU DON'T KNOW WHERE THEY CAME FROM, THERE'S A LOT OF DANGER AND NO GUARAN-TEES. HE DOESN'T WANT TO TAKE ANY RISKS.

AND, HE DOESN'T HAVE ANY MONEY... TO BE HONEST.

THAT'S THE REAL REASON HE WOULDN'T.

ON THE DAY OF THE CARP, CARP'S THE STAR OF THE MARKET. IT'S ALL ANYONE TALKS ABOUT.

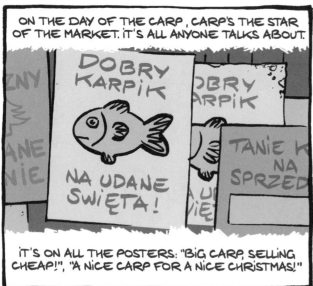

DOBRY KARPIK

NA UDANE ŚWIĘTA!

DOBRY KARPIK

TANIE K NA SPRZED

IT'S ON ALL THE POSTERS: "BIG CARP, SELLING CHEAP!", "A NICE CARP FOR A NICE CHRISTMAS!"

A LOT OF PEOPLE ARE CARRYING PLASTIC BAGS THAT MOVE. INSIDE IS A FISH WHO'S STRUGGLING, CONFUSED, IN NEED OF WATER.

THOSE HEADING BACK FROM THE MARKET STOP AND CHAT WITH THEIR NEIGHBORS ON THEIR WAY THERE—THEY GIVE THEM A LINE ON THE GOOD CARPS.

THE CARP SWIM AROUND IN BIG TUBS WHILE THEY WAIT TO BE ADOPTED BY A HUMAN FAMILY. THEY HOLD MAYBE 20, I DON'T KNOW...

I'M STILL SLEEPING WHEN MY DAD'S HAGGLING OVER THE PRICE.

NO MATTER WHERE HE GOES, HE WANTS TO NEGOTIATE. IT'S IN HIS BLOOD.

IT'S COLD OUTSIDE. FROM MY WARM SNUGGLY BED, I HEAR THE APARTMENT DOOR OPEN. HE'S BACK AND TALKING LOUDLY.

HA HA! HERE IT IS, I GOT ONE!

DAD! I'M SLEEPING!!

HE ALWAYS FORGETS ABOUT ME.

SORRY!

I WAS SLEEPING...NO NEED TO WHISPER NOW.

HE'S MOVING AROUND IN THE BATHROOM.

I FACE THE CARP... SHE'S SWIMMING...

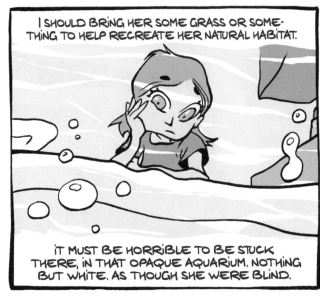

IT MUST BE HORRIBLE TO BE STUCK THERE, IN THAT OPAQUE AQUARIUM. NOTHING BUT WHITE. AS THOUGH SHE WERE BLIND.

BUT HONESTLY, THERE'S NOTHING MORE ANNOYING THAN FISHBONES!

I'D LIKE TO STICK MY HAND IN THE WATER, BUT WHAT IF SHE BITES ME? TOO BAD SHE'S NOT A DOG. I LIKE DOGS, PLUS YOU CAN PET THEM, AND ROLL IN THE GRASS WITH THEM...

WHEREAS WITH A FISH...I'M NOT SURE WHAT WE COULD DO TOGETHER. SHE'S NOT MOVING VERY FAST.

MAYBE I SHOULD NAME HER. MY MOM SAYS YOU SHOULDN'T GIVE AN ANIMAL A HUMAN NAME... TOO BAD, I'M GOING TO CALL HER HONORATA, SOMETHING LIKE THAT.

IF I NAME YOU, IT'LL PROVE I'M GETTING ATTACHED TO YOU!

MY AUNT NIUSIA ALWAYS NAMES HER PIGS, THEN SHE KILLS THEM AND TELLS US WHO WE'RE EATING.

ONCE, I SAW HER IN TEARS AFTER THE MOTHER PIG CRUSHED A LITTLE ONE.

SHE LIFTED THE LITTLE ANIMAL'S FRAIL BODY AND CRIED AS SHE GAVE HIM MOUTH-TO-MOUTH.

AFTER THAT, I HAD A VERY HARD TIME KISSING MY AUNT...

SHE TALKS TO ALL HER ANIMALS-PIGS, COWS, CHICKENS, TURKEYS, DOGS, CATS...

SHE TELLS THEM WHAT SHE'S FEEDING THEM, AND THAT IT'LL MAKE THEM GROW...GROOOWWW AS TALL AS THE SKY...

IT'S SILLY... WHEN WE EAT TOGETHER (I DON'T LIKE EATING MUCH), SHE TELLS ME THE SAME THING.

COME ON, ONE MORE SPOONFUL AND YOU'LL GROW SO TALL! AS TALL AS THE SKY!!

I BROUGHT SOME BREAD, I DON'T KNOW WHAT FISH EAT... PLANTS? WELL ANYWAY, I'M NOT GIVING HER MY MOM'S PLANTS!

LAST YEAR, I SPIT SOME TOOTHPASTE INTO THE BATHTUB TO SEE WHAT WOULD HAPPEN, BUT THE CARP DIDN'T TASTE LIKE MINT AT CHRISTMAS DINNER.

WHAT SHOULD I FEED THE CARP?

NOTHING, SHE'S NOT HUNGRY, SHE'S FAT, AND ANYWAY, I'M KILLING HER TOMORROW!

... AND HE'S SO HAPPY... YOU'D THINK MY DAD LIKED KILLING. LIKE AUNT NIUSIA, IT MUST BE IN THEIR GENES.

WE DON'T HAVE MUCH IN COMMON; MAYBE I'M MORE LIKE MY MOM'S FAMILY?... NO, ANYTHING BUT THAT!

I LIKE TO KILL TOO! SEE...

BUT I DON'T NEED TO.

I'M GOING NEXT DOOR TO PLAY, THE TIME HAS COME FOR MY DAD TO "DO WHAT NEEDS TO BE DONE!"

IN ALL 80 APARTMENTS IN OUR BUILDING, ONE OR TWO CARP ARE GOING TO DIE.

ONCE A YEAR OUR COMPLEX BECOMES A GIANT SLAUGHTERHOUSE ECHOING WITH SILENT SCREAMS.

THE FISH IS IN THE FRIDGE, IT DOESN'T FEEL THE COLD, IT'LL NEVER FEEL THE COLD AGAIN. ONE CARP IS A LOT FOR THREE. WE USUALLY EAT IT ONCE A DAY FOR THREE DAYS.

MAYBE MORE OFTEN IN MY MOM'S CASE. THERE MUST BE SOME LOGICAL EXPLANATION FOR HER OBESITY.

BY DAY THREE, THE CARP ISN'T VERY FRESH ANYMORE SO WE HAVE TO KEEP IT IN THE OVEN A LITTLE LONGER TO KILL WHATEVER BACTERIA MIGHT BE RUNNING RAMPANT.

THE BATHROOM STINKS DESPITE THE CLEANING MY DAD GAVE IT. I DON'T WANT TO BE THE FIRST ONE TO USE IT, I'LL PEE AT THE NEIGHBORS'.

MY DAD IS ANNOYED, THE BATHTUB IS PLUGGED UP BY SOMETHING SPONGY...

THE CARP DIDN'T WANT MY BREAD.

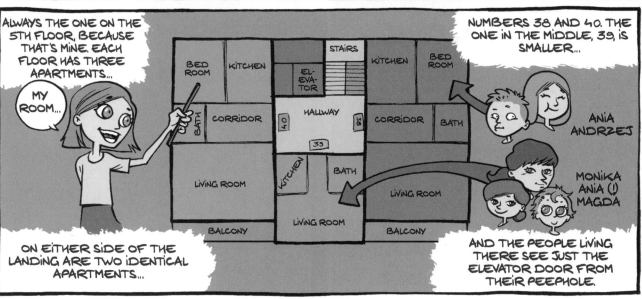

SO WE MEET ON FIVE TO HAVE FUN AND ... MAKE TROUBLE!

WE PLAY WITH THE ELEVATOR, THOUGH WE DON'T RIDE IT. WE GO TO EVERY FLOOR...

AND PUSH ALL THE CALL BUTTONS.

PEOPLE HAVE TO WAIT A LONG TIME FOR THE ELEVATOR...

THOSE ON THE LOWER FLOORS GET IMPATIENT AND TAKE THE STAIRS

PSIAKREW!!

CHOLERA JASNA!

CHRYSTE PANIE!

EVERYONE ELSE IS LAZY. THEY SWEAR, BUT STILL WAIT.

OUR ELEVATOR IS REALLY NOISY AND WE CAN HEAR IF SOMEONE IS CALLING IT FROM THE LOBBY.

THEN, WE HAVE TO BE EVEN FASTER...

ah ah ah ah ah

AND PUSH THE BUTTON OF THE FLOOR WHERE WE WANT THE ELEVATOR TO GO BEFORE THEY CAN. SOMETIMES ALL THE FLOORS!

WE ALSO EXERCISE OUT HERE. WE BRING OUR OWN JUMP ROPES AND COMPETE TO SEE WHO CAN JUMP THE LONGEST.

ANDRZEJ DOESN'T REALLY LIKE THIS GAME BECAUSE HE ALWAYS LOSES, BUT SINCE HE'S THE ONLY BOY, HE DOESN'T HAVE MUCH CHOICE.

HE CAN EITHER OBEY, OR NOT BE PART OF OUR (MOTLEY) CREW ANYMORE!

BUT JUST TO MAKE EVERYONE HAPPY, WE GO DOORBELL HUNTING.

BRINNG!

WE TAKE OFF. WE DASH UP A FEW FLOORS BECAUSE PEOPLE ARE BEGINNING TO RECOGNIZE US.

THEY ALL REALLY LIKE US, BUT THERE'VE ALREADY BEEN A FEW COMPLAINTS.

ANIA AND ANDRZEJ'S MOM IS A NURSE. THESE DAYS, SHE'S WORKING AT A NURSERY WITH VERY TINY BABIES.

ONE DAY SHE BROUGHT HOME A BUNCH OF SYRINGES AND BOTTLES FILLED WITH A CLEAR FLUID.

HEY KIDS!

WHO WANTS PRETTY EARS?

APPARENTLY, MY MOM WAS IN THE KNOW BECAUSE SHE HAS A PAIR OF GOLD EARRINGS FROM RUSSIA FOR ME.

MONIKA'S DAD WORKS ABROAD AND EVERY TIME HE COMES BACK HE BRINGS US LOTS OF THINGS.

I DON'T LIKE BEING PRICKED, BUT I'D REALLY LIKE TO WEAR EARRINGS...

WHO'S FIRST?

ME !

MONIKA'S ALWAYS TRYING TO PROVE SHE'S THE STRONGEST... ONE DAY SHE TRAPPED ME IN THE ELEVATOR.

THE ONE TIME I WAS BRAVE ENOUGH TO TAKE IT BY MYSELF.

I COULDN'T OPEN THE DOOR. I DON'T LIKE ELEVATORS, AND SHE KNOWS IT!

I DIDN'T KNOW MONIKA WAS ON OUR FLOOR.

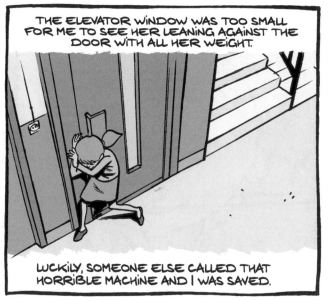

THE ELEVATOR WINDOW WAS TOO SMALL FOR ME TO SEE HER LEANING AGAINST THE DOOR WITH ALL HER WEIGHT.

LUCKILY, SOMEONE ELSE CALLED THAT HORRIBLE MACHINE AND I WAS SAVED.

WHEN I CLIMBED BACK UP IN TEARS, SHE WAS ROLLING ON THE FLOOR LAUGHING.

...THAT'S MY BEST FRIEND.

THERE, IT'S DONE. SHE DOESN'T EVEN RUN TO LOOK IN THE MIRROR. I DON'T UNDERSTAND HER SOMETIMES.

DOES IT HURT?

NO!

I WAS EXPECTING THAT ANSWER.

IT'S ANIA'S TURN NEXT...

Hee Hee

ANIA IS ALWAYS LAUGHING, AT ANYTHING. YOU CAN TORTURE HER AND SHE'LL STILL LAUGH.

THE ELEVATOR GOES BY, THE PEOPLE TAKING THE STAIRS LOOK BEWILDERED, WE LAUGH... ME NOT TOO HARD, IT'S MY TURN.

I HEAR A DOG BARKING... IT GRATES ON MY NERVES, I NEED QUIET.

I ASK IF I CAN LOOK AT THE NEEDLE ANOTHER MINUTE AND MONIKA MAKES FUN OF ME.

WANTING TO LOOK AT THE NEEDLE AND BEING SCARED ARE NOT THE SAME...BUT ANYWAY, THEY'RE ALL LAUGHING!

HUMPF!

MY EARS ARE RED, BUT THERE ARE TWO LITTLE GOLD BALLS HANGING FROM THEM.

THEY CHANGE ME...THEY MAKE ME FEEL DRESSED UP.

MONIKA'S SISTER GOES LAST. SHE'S ALL EXCITED. SHE RUSHES OVER TO THE CHAIR, IMPATIENT!

ANDRZEJ WON'T SIT DOWN, MAYBE HE'S A LITTLE JEALOUS. I'VE SEEN BOYS WITH PIERCED EARS, BUT ANDRZEJ'S MOM DOESN'T WANT HER SON TO BE ONE.

MAGDA, MONIKA'S BABY SISTER, IS TOO YOUNG. IT'LL NO DOUBT BE HER TURN NEXT YEAR.

IN THE MEANTIME, WE GO BACK TO MAKING PEOPLE WALK UP AND DOWN TEN STORIES.

A CARPET FOR LIFE

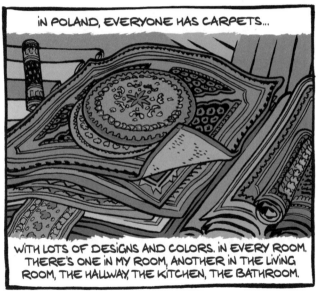

IN POLAND, EVERYONE HAS CARPETS...

WITH LOTS OF DESIGNS AND COLORS. IN EVERY ROOM. THERE'S ONE IN MY ROOM, ANOTHER IN THE LIVING ROOM, THE HALLWAY, THE KITCHEN, THE BATHROOM.

WE OFTEN DECORATE THE WALLS WITH EMBROIDERED CARPETS.

WITH ALL THE TURKISH CARPETS, PATTERNED RUGS, FLOWERED BEDSPREADS AND OTHER RANDOM ITEMS IN A SIMILAR VEIN, OUR HOUSES LOOK MORE LIKE FOLK LIFE MUSEUMS THAN HOMES!

THE REASON I LOVE THEM IS THAT THEIR PATTERNS PROVIDE ME WITH INSPIRATION.

THEY CAN BE MAZES FOR MY MODELING CLAY CHARACTERS TO GET LOST IN. MY MOM SAYS THEY LEAVE MARKS, BUT THE CARPETS ARE SO DARK YOU WOULDN'T EVEN NOTICE SPILLED INK.

I ALSO HAVE SOME SMALL CARS THAT MY OLDER COUSIN JACEK, FROM WARSZAWA, GAVE ME.

THE PATTERNS BECOME ROADS.

ALL THE CARPETS IN OUR HOUSE COME FROM CZECHOSLOVAKIA. UNCLE CZESIEK, MONIKA'S DAD, BRINGS THEM BACK ON THE ROOF OF HIS LITTLE CAR.

MY PARENTS BOUGHT AN EXTRA ONE THAT THEY'RE STORING IN MY ROOM, BEHIND THE CURTAIN.

THEY SAY IT'S FOR ME...

IT'LL BE PART OF MY WEDDING DOWRY!

MY MOM DOES THE GROCERY SHOPPING. ONE MORNING, SHE ARRIVES HOME ALL OUT OF BREATH AND WAKES ME AND MY DAD UP...

WE JUST SPLASH SOME WATER ON OUR FACES AND WE'RE OFF.

THE LINE IS ALREADY LONG AND IT'S COLD OUT. LUCKILY, IT MOVES FAST.

MY MOM HAS GONE IN SEARCH OF OTHER PROVISIONS.

MY DAD IS TALKING TO THE PEOPLE AROUND US, THEY MUST BE DISCUSSING POLITICS BECAUSE I DON'T UNDERSTAND A WORD.

THE LINE SPILLED OUT OVER THE SIDEWALK AGES AGO — THE STORE ITSELF IS PACKED.

WE'RE ENTITLED TO A KILO OF SUGAR EACH, SO WE BUY TWO, ENOUGH TO SWEETEN OUR TEA FOR AWHILE. MAYBE EVEN TO BAKE A CAKE!

WHEN WE EMERGE, THE SUGAR LINE HAS GOTTEN MIXED UP WITH THE MEAT LINE, WHERE MY MOM IS.

WE GO SAY HI. SHE ONLY HAS ENOUGH RATION CARDS FOR HALF A KILO AND ASKS MY DAD WHAT HE WANTS HER TO GET.

SHE DIDN'T HEAR ME. SHE'LL MAKE ME EAT WHATEVER SHE BUYS, WITHOUT GIVING A THOUGHT TO WHETHER OR NOT I LIKE IT. I WOULD'VE LIKED SAUSAGES...

THERE ARE MAYBE THIRTY PEOPLE IN FRONT OF HER. SHE'S COLD, HER NOSE IS ALL RED, SHE LOOKS LIKE A CLOWN. WE'RE FROZEN TOO.

WE MARCH IN PLACE TO KEEP OUR FEET WARM AT LEAST.

STEAM RISES FROM PEOPLE'S OPEN MOUTHS AND NOSES. LITTLE CLOUDS OF HOPE THERE WILL BE SOMETHING LEFT TO BUY.

JUST A LITTLE SOMETHING TO FEED THEIR FAMILIES. A BIT OF SUGAR TO SWEETEN THEIR LIVES. TO FORGET THE STRESS OF LIVING IN THIS COUNTRY.

I'M GOING TO GET BREAD WITH MY DAD. IT'S THE ONE THING THAT'S EASILY AVAILABLE, BUT THERE'S STILL A LINE BECAUSE IT'S THE ONLY BAKERY IN THE NEIGHBORHOOD.

ON THE WAY BACK, WE RUN INTO OUR NEIGHBORS WHO ARE HURRYING TO BUY SUGAR TOO.

MY MOM KNOCKED ON THEIR DOOR TO LET THEM KNOW.

OUR HOUSE IS WARM. WARMER THAN OUTSIDE. I CAN FINALLY DRINK MY TEA... WITH PLENTY OF SUGAR!

MY MOM GETS HOME SOMETIME AFTER WE DO. SHE'S PLEASED BECAUSE SHE GOT SOME PORK. THERE'LL BE BEEF TOMORROW, BUT WE WON'T HAVE MORE RATION CARDS UNTIL THE END OF THE MONTH.

I LOVE SWEETS, BUT I DON'T EAT THEM A LOT BECAUSE MY MOM ONLY BAKES CAKE EVERY OTHER WEEK AND IT'S SPLIT THREE WAYS...

...EVEN MORE IF WE HAVE NEIGHBORS OR GUESTS OVER.

I ALSO LIKE THE RAISINS THAT MY COUSIN JANUSZ SOMETIMES BRINGS FROM ABROAD.

ONCE HE BROUGHT CHOCOLATE AND IT WAS THE MOST DELICIOUS THING I'D EVER EATEN.

I KEPT THE WRAPPING PAPER, IT STILL SMELLS LIKE CHOCOLATE. I ONLY HAD A TINY PIECE, THERE WAS BARELY ENOUGH TO GO AROUND... BUT OH HOW GOOD IT WAS!

SNIF
SNIF

IF I GET TO TRAVEL ONE DAY, I'LL BRING BACK TONS FOR ME AND FOR MY PARENTS, MY GRANDMOTHER, OUR NEIGHBORS...

IN THE SUMMER, WE EAT A LOT OF APPLES, PLUMS, STRAWBERRIES... IN THE WINTER, THERE ISN'T MUCH FRUIT, JUST THE APPLES WE STORE IN BAGS ON THE BALCONY OR IN THE BASEMENT.

I DON'T LIKE WINTER BECAUSE YOU HAVE TO EAT FAT TO PROTECT YOURSELF FROM THE COLD AND THERE'S NOTHING ELSE GOOD. NOTHING I LIKE ANYWAY.

THE APPLES ARE COLD TOO. THEIR SKIN SHRIVELS UP AND THEY LOSE THEIR TASTE. BUT I EAT THEM ANYWAY...

AS I WAIT FOR THE WARMTH OF SPRING AND THE BUDS PROMISING BRAND NEW FRUIT.

OCCASIONALLY WE EAT OTHER FRUIT, VARIETIES WE CAN'T GROW IN THE GARDEN BECAUSE THEY DEMAND SPECIAL CONDITIONS.

BUT IT DOESN'T HAPPEN OFTEN. ONCE AGAIN, JANUSZ IS THE ONE WHO BRINGS BACK THESE WONDERS!

IT'S EVEN RARER TO FIND THEM IN THE STORE. THE SHELVES ARE ALMOST ALWAYS EMPTY.

EXCEPT FOR THE JARS OF MUSTARD AND VINEGAR, THEY'RE ALWAYS THERE!

HOWEVER, ONCE IN AWHILE...

POMARAŃCZE!!!

KIDS! THE STORE JUST GOT IN ORANGES!!!

QUICK, GRAB THE BAGS AND SOME MONEY!!

ORANGES!!

WE HAVE TO GET THERE FAST, BEFORE ANYONE ELSE CAN BUY OUR ORANGES, I CAN ALREADY FEEL THEIR TANGY TASTE IN MY MOUTH.

WE HAVE CASH AND WE RUN FAST, ALL EXCITED!

I HAVE A NET BAG, PEOPLE WILL SEE THAT I'M CARRYING ORANGES, THEY'RE ALL GOING TO BE JEALOUS !

THEY'LL COME OVER TO ASK WHERE I GOT THEM.

MY DAD WILL PEEL MY ORANGES AND THE WHOLE ROOM WILL BE FILLED WITH THEIR REFRESHING SCENT. I JUST HAVE TO BE PATIENT.

STAND IN LINE...WAIT MY TURN...

BEHIND ME, THERE ARE ADULTS, NO OTHER CHILDREN, BUT WOMEN ABOUT MY MOM'S AGE. WE'RE EACH ENTITLED TO A KILO, NO MORE.

I CAN SEE THEIR BRIGHT COLOR FROM A DISTANCE!

THERE ARE TWO SALES LADIES. ALWAYS THE SAME ONES. THEY'RE LUCKY BECAUSE AS SOON AS THE PRODUCTS ARRIVE, THEY CAN KEEP THE BEST FOR THEMSELVES.

THEY'RE NOT FRIENDLY, THEY ACT LIKE YOU'RE BOTHERING THEM EVEN WHEN YOU'RE BEING VERY POLITE.

THEY DON'T RESPOND OR SAY HELLO OR GOODBYE. THEY DON'T EVEN ASK "WHAT WOULD YOU LIKE?"; THEY'RE LIKE MACHINE GUNS, FIRING WORDS AT THEIR CUSTOMERS.

I ONLY...

OF COURSE WE'RE NOT KILLED, BUT IT STILL LEAVES YOU FEELING BAD.

MONIKA IS AHEAD OF ME AND THERE IS LESS AND LESS FRUIT. ANIA ALREADY GOT SOME, SHE'S VERY HAPPY, HER BROTHER GOT A KILO TOO. THEY'RE WAITING OUTSIDE.

THE SALES LADIES ACT LIKE THEY'VE HAD IT. THEY DON'T LIKE HECTIC DAYS.

MONIKA GETS HER ORANGES. IT'S MY TURN!

BUT WHAT'S GOING ON? I'M RIGHT HERE! THIS CAN'T BE HAPPENING! THE CLERKS ARE ACTING LIKE I'M INVISIBLE. I START TO CRY.

THEY'RE SERVING THE WOMAN WHO WAS BEHIND ME. SHE PUSHED ME. I COULDN'T DO ANYTHING. NO ONE'S PAYING ANY ATTENTION TO ME...

THE WOMAN'S DELIGHTED. SHE LEAVES WITH MY ORANGES. THERE AREN'T ANY MORE. I WOULD HAVE BEEN THE LAST TO GET SOME...

I AM ONE BIG TEAR. IF I FELL INTO A PUDDLE, YOU WOULDN'T SEE ME ANYMORE. IF IT RAINED, I'D DISAPPEAR.

MY TEARS FORM THE PATH OF MY INVISIBLE EXISTENCE...

MY MOM IS ANGRY. FOR ONCE, NOT AT ME. HER EYES SHINE WITH FURY, HER FACE IS ON FIRE. I'M STILL CRYING.

SHE'S GOING TO BURN DOWN THE STORE TO AVENGE ME!

MY MOM MAKES MONIKA TESTIFY. SHE'S SCREAMING HER HEAD OFF! SHE'S GOING TO PUT WHAT SHE THINKS OF THOSE CLERKS IN THE STORE'S COMPLAINT BOOK.

THE SALES LADIES AREN'T PLEASED BUT FOR THE FIRST TIME, THEY SEEM MORE HUMAN TO ME. AN EMOTION PASSED OVER THEIR FACES...FEAR.

THEY APOLOGIZE AND SAY WE CAN WAIT, THERE MIGHT BE ANOTHER DELIVERY, THAT'S WHY THE STORE IS STILL FULL OF PEOPLE. THEY REMAIN HOPEFUL...

OUR FRIENDS SHARED THEIR ORANGES WITH ME. WE ATE THEM CRACKING UP IN THE STAIRWELL WHILE MY MOM TOLD THE STORY TO OUR STUPEFIED NEIGHBORS.

THE WHOLE BUILDING MUST HAVE HEARD ABOUT IT!

LATER THAT NIGHT WHEN I WAS IN BED, I HEARD HER IN THE KITCHEN WITH MY DAD. THEY WERE REPEATING THAT "IT" COULDN'T LAST, THAT "IT" WOULD HAVE TO END...

WHATEVER « IT » MEANS, I CAN TELL IT HAS SOMETHING TO DO WITH WHAT HAPPENED TO ME. I WANT « IT » TO STOP TOO. I FALL ASLEEP ... THE ORANGES FEEL GOOD IN MY STOMACH.

I'M STILL ASLEEP WHEN MY MOM GETS ME DRESSED IN THE MORNING. WE GET UP EARLY, SHE STARTS WORK AT 7 O'CLOCK.

I WAKE UP SOME WHEN SHE DOES MY HAIR.

IT HURTS, BUT SHE TELLS ME SHE DOESN'T HAVE TIME TO BE CAREFUL...SHE'S NOT VERY CAREFUL IN GENERAL.

FOR EXAMPLE, MY DAD'S THE ONE WHO ALWAYS CUTS MY HAIR. THANKFULLY!

I DON'T EAT AT HOME, SHE TAKES ME TO SCHOOL WHERE I HAVE MY BREAKFAST. THEN SHE GOES TO WORK. SHE'S SOME KIND OF BOOKKEEPER AT A DAIRY.

THE COOKS ALL KNOW I DON'T LIKE THE MILK SKIN, SO THEY POUR MY MILK THROUGH A SIEVE.

THE TRIP TO SCHOOL AND THE FIRST FEW HOURS THERE FEEL UNREAL TO ME.

I'M STILL ASLEEP AND DREAMING...

I REALLY LIKE MY CLASSROOM BECAUSE IT'S FULL OF TOYS. I'VE NEVER IN MY SHORT LIFE SEEN SO MANY.

THE BOYS AND GIRLS ALL PLAY TOGETHER.

WE HAVE SOME VERY BIG DOLLS, BABY-SIZE ONES, BUT THEY'RE COLD AND STIFF. I LIKE STUFFED ANIMALS BETTER.

EXCEPT FOR THE ONES HERE BECAUSE THE LITTLE KIDS DROOL ALL OVER THEM WHICH I FIND A LITTLE DISGUSTING. SO I WAIT TILL I GET HOME TO PLAY WITH THE YELLOW RABBIT MY GRANDMOTHER GAVE ME.

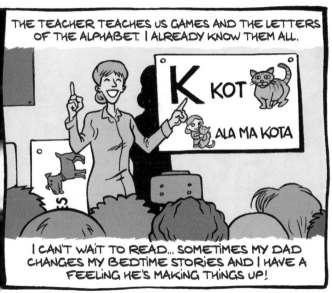

THE TEACHER TEACHES US GAMES AND THE LETTERS OF THE ALPHABET. I ALREADY KNOW THEM ALL.

K KOT
ALA MA KOTA

I CAN'T WAIT TO READ... SOMETIMES MY DAD CHANGES MY BEDTIME STORIES AND I HAVE A FEELING HE'S MAKING THINGS UP!

AFTER LUNCH, WE LIE ON THE GROUND AND REST OUR TUMMIES WHILE THE TEACHER TELLS A STORY. SHE ASKS US TO CLOSE OUR EYES TO IMAGINE IT BETTER.

RRFLLBL RFLLBLL

SOME KIDS FALL ASLEEP THEN.

BUT IN FACT, THERE'S A ROOM FOR THAT. IT'S FULL OF BEDS! I PUT ON MY PAJAMAS WITH THE "M" FOR MARZI AND MY LAST NAME THAT MY DAD EMBROIDERED.

SOME KIDS CRY, OR ARE RESTLESS, SOME WET THE BED... I GO RIGHT TO SLEEP.

WHEN WE GET UP, WE GO PLAY. WE SING TOO, WITH OUR TEACHER AT THE PIANO.

THEN WE WAIT FOR OUR PARENTS. IT'S USUALLY MY MOM WHO COMES TO GET ME. SHE LEAVES WORK AT 3 O'CLOCK.

SINCE HER MOM WORKS LATER, MONIKA OFTEN COMES HOME WITH US. WHEN THIS HAPPENS, WE CAN KEEP PLAYING.

IF NOT, I GIVE LESSONS TO MY RABBIT WHO HAS BEEN SO PATIENTLY WAITING FOR ME ALL DAY.

I SHARE EVERYTHING I'VE LEARNED WITH HIM. I SHOW HIM MY SPELLING BOOK AND SOUND OUT ALL THE LETTERS. HE HAS TO BE SMART TOO AFTER ALL!

UNFORTUNATELY, HE'S NOT ALLOWED TO COME WITH ME...BUT ANYWAY I'D BE TOO SCARED THE LITTLE ONES WOULD CHEW ON HIS EARS!

WHEN WE GO SLEDDING, AN ADULT ALWAYS COMES WITH US BECAUSE THE BIG HILL IS A LITTLE FAR AWAY.

YOU HAVE TO CROSS SEVERAL VERY WIDE AND BUSY STREETS.

IT'S OFTEN MY DAD WHO COMES. SOMETIMES, IT'S "UNCLE" ZDZICH (ANIA AND ANDRZEJ'S DAD).

MY DAD PULLS EACH OF US IN TURN UNTIL WE GET TO THE BOTTOM OF THE HILL.

I DON'T THINK IT'S FAIR BECAUSE HE'S MY DAD AND I DON'T SEE WHY HE HAS TO PULL THE OTHERS TOO...

BUT I DON'T SAY ANYTHING, WE HAVE A LOT OF FUN!

WE PUT MY DAD ON THE SLED AND ALL TRY PULLING HIM, BUT IT'S HARD!!

WE EVENTUALLY GIVE UP.

IT'S CROWDED, SLEDS ARE COLLIDING ON THEIR WAY DOWN. I DON'T WANT TO BE RUN OVER BY SOMEONE ELSE'S SLED. I HESITATE...

SO, WHAT? ARE YOU SCARED OF THE SNOW?

HE GETS ON MY NERVES!

ONCE IN AWHILE, HE RIDES DOWN THE SLOPE TOO, BUT NOT OFTEN BECAUSE WE ONLY HAVE THREE SLEDS, AND NONE OF US REALLY WANTS TO GIVE UP OUR TURN.

I USUALLY GO DOWN WITH LITTLE ANIA. MONIKA TAKES UP ALL THE ROOM, SO IF I RIDE WITH HER I DON'T STAY ON THE SLED.

HEY!

ANIA, WHO IS SO LIGHT, AND I ALWAYS PASS MONIKA.

SHE DOESN'T COMMENT, BUT I KNOW IN HER HEART, SHE'S ALREADY PLANNING HER REVENGE.

MY LEAST FAVORITE PART IS HAVING TO PULL THE SLED BACK UP ONCE YOU'VE GOTTEN TO THE BOTTOM...

IN THE COUNTRY, AT SKOWIERZYN (GRAND-MOTHER JADZIA'S VILLAGE), THERE ARE MORE SMALL MOUNTAINS AND NOBODY TO BOTHER ME.

THE SNOW IS IMMACULATE, EVERYWHERE!

AND I MAKE MY SLED MYSELF. AUNT NIUSIA GIVES ME A BIG PLASTIC BAG THAT I FILL WITH STRAW AND TIE WITH A STRING. AND VOILA, IT'S READY TO GO!

IT'S MORE COMFORTABLE AND SLIDES REALLY FAST!

MY GRANDMOTHER'S NEIGHBOR ORGANIZES SLEIGH RIDES FOR THE CHILDREN. WE TIE THE SLEDS TOGETHER AND A BIG TRACTOR PULLS US AROUND THE WHOLE VILLAGE.

I LIKE IT BETTER WHEN HE USES A HORSE, IT'S LESS NOISY AND SMELLY...

IN SKOWIERZYN, I SLEEP WITH MY GRAND-MOTHER. SHE HAS TWO ENORMOUS BEDS, SIDE BY SIDE, WITH COVERS THAT SWALLOW ME UP.

DAWNO, DAWNO TEMU, ZA GÓRAMI...

BEFORE GOING TO SLEEP, SHE TELLS ME STORIES SHE PULLS UP FROM HER DISTANT CHILDHOOD, OR THAT SHE MAKES UP.

THE SUN WAKES ME. MY GRANDMOTHER'S USUALLY ALREADY BEEN UP FOR A WHILE.

I LOVE THIS ROOM.

THERE ARE THREE MIRRORS YOU CAN SEE YOURSELF IN AT THE SAME TIME, BUT YOU DON'T LOOK EXACTLY THE SAME IN ALL THREE!

WHEN I ARRIVE IN THE KITCHEN, MY BREAKFAST IS WAITING. TWO BIG PIECES OF TOAST WITH BUTTER, CHEESE AND HAM.

IN THE SUMMER, GRANDMA ADDS SLICES OF TOMATO AND A FEW NEW ONIONS. I WASH IT DOWN WITH VERY HOT, SUGARY TEA.

THERE'S NOT A LOT TO DO IN THE COUNTRY IN THE WINTER. BESIDES SLEDDING, I CAN SKATE ON A LITTLE POND WHERE THE COWS DRINK WHEN THEY'RE AT PASTURE.

OTHERWISE, I STAY HOME. I LOOK THROUGH THE DESIGNER CATALOGS THAT MY COUSIN JANUSZ BRINGS BACK FROM FRANCE OR GERMANY FOR AUNT NIUSIA.

MY AUNT IS A SEAMSTRESS. SHE SEWS MY CLOTHES. SHE MAKES THEM FOR THE WHOLE FAMILY, AND FOR OTHER PEOPLE WHO PAY HER.

SHE HAS ALL DIFFERENT KINDS OF FABRIC OF EVERY COLOR AND TEXTURE. SHE HAS BIG SCISSORS AND A MACHINE THAT MAKES AN INFERNAL RACKET.

I HAVE A HONEY-COLORED VELOUR DRESS WITH LOTS OF LITTLE TRACTORS ON IT THAT'S MY FAVORITE. IT'S WARM AND COMFORTABLE.

THE ONLY PROBLEM IS MY AUNT ALWAYS MAKES MY DRESSES A LITTLE TOO NARROW FOR MY HEAD!

IT THROWS ME INTO A PANIC. THE DRESS GETS STUCK, I CAN'T SEE ANYTHING, I HAVE TROUBLE BREATHING AND MY ARMS ARE TRAPPED. IT'S REALLY ANNOYING...

MMMH!!

MY DAD USUALLY HELPS ME GET THEM ON AND OFF.

AUNT NIUSIA IS ALWAYS LOOKING FOR IDEAS IN THESE THICK CATALOGS. NOBODY ELSE HAS CLOTHES LIKE MINE!

THE WOMEN'S CLOTHES BEGIN THE CATALOGS. I STUDY THEM VERY CAREFULLY.

THEN COME THE CHILDREN'S CLOTHES, THEN THE SHOES (I LOVE THE HIGH HEELS) AND FINALLY THE MEN'S CLOTHES.

I IMAGINE HOW I'D LIKE MY DAD TO DRESS.

FINALLY COME THE SHEETS, NAPKINS AND FURNITURE. IN MY HEAD, I REDECORATE MY ROOM WITH ALL THESE BEAUTIFUL THINGS.

THEY ALSO HAVE SOME THINGS I DON'T RECOGNIZE, WHICH I LOOK AT ANYWAY. SOMETIMES GRANDMA PUTS ON HER GLASSES AND READS WITH ME.

BUT SHE CAN'T UNDERSTAND ANYTHING EITHER, IT'S NOT IN OUR LANGUAGE...

I STUDY THE GIRLS' CLOTHES AND WITH SCRAPS OF CLOTH FROM MY AUNT, GRANDMA AND I CREATE OUTFITS FOR MY PLASTIC DOLL.

WHEN SHE ISN'T SEWING, AUNT NIUSIA TAKES CARE OF HER SMALL FARM ALL BY HERSELF. MY UNCLE ADAM WORKS IN A FACTORY...

THEY HAVE TWO CHILDREN. JANUSZ OFTEN GOES ABROAD EITHER TO WORK OR TO BUY OR SELL THINGS. HE BRINGS BACK PIECES OF JEWELRY TO RESELL IN POLAND.

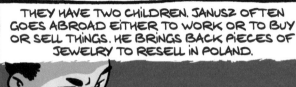

IT'S AGAINST THE LAW. SO BEFORE CROSSING THE BORDER, HE PUTS THE RINGS, EARRINGS AND NECKLACES IN TINY PLASTIC BAGS.

AND THEN SWALLOWS THEM! THAT WAY, HE WON'T GET CAUGHT...

TOALETA

BUT ONCE HE'S IN POLAND... EEEK! I'D RATHER NOT THINK ABOUT IT.

HIS SISTER BASIA'S QUITE A BIT YOUNGER. SHE'S BEAUTIFUL, WITH A VOICE LIKE AN ANGEL AND A VERY TALL BOYFRIEND WHO PLAYS THE ACCORDION.

HE LIVES IN ANOTHER VILLAGE NEARBY.

THE THREE OF US ARE HOME FOR LUNCH. WE COOK TOGETHER. MY AUNT IS IN CHARGE, WHILE I JUST WATCH, ENJOYING THE DELICIOUS SMELLS.

I DON'T REALLY LIKE SOUP, IT'S OILY. THE BIG CIRCLES ON THE SURFACE LOOK LIKE EYES. I'D SAY THIS SOUP LOOKS A LITTLE FAT!

I TRY TO MAKE THE EYES GO AWAY, BUT THEY COME BACK.

ATOS IS OUTSIDE. HE'S ALWAYS HAPPY TO SEE ME. HE'S CHAINED TO HIS DOGHOUSE.

HAU! HAU!

I CONVINCED MY AUNT TO LENGTHEN HIS LEASH A LITTLE SO NOW HE HAS MORE SPACE TO ROAM IN.

HE JUMPS ON ME. HE'S ALL EXCITED AND PRACTICALLY KNOCKS ME OVER BECAUSE I'M CARRYING LEFTOVERS.

HE'S LUCKY I DON'T REALLY LIKE MEAT.

ACCORDING TO MY MOM, A DOG ON A CHAIN IS A DANGEROUS DOG. SHE DOESN'T LIKE HIM. SO I HIDE IN HIS DOGHOUSE WHENEVER SHE'S MEAN TO ME.

SHE DOESN'T DARE COME NEAR.

I'D LOVE TO TAKE HIM EVERYWHERE WITH ME. HE WOULD PROTECT ME... AND HE COULD BE OF USE.

IF I HAD HIM, I WOULDN'T NEED TO STRUGGLE UP HILLS ANYMORE!

MY DAD'S USUALLY THE ONE TO GO WAIT IN LINE.

WE JUST LEARNED TODAY THERE'LL BE A MEAT DELIVERY ON MONDAY MORNING.

PEOPLE START LINING UP ON SUNDAY NIGHT. IT'S COLD...

THE GROUND IS COVERED WITH SNOW AND ICE.

MY DAD MAKES HIMSELF A THERMOS OF HOT TEA AND A SALT AND BUTTER SANDWICH.

SOMETIMES, WHEN WE HAVE IT, HE ADDS THE HOMEMADE PATÉ THAT MY AUNT MILA IN KAMIEŃ CANS FOR US. THOSE DAYS ARE SPECIAL.

HE AND UNCLE ZDZICH GO OUT INTO THE FREEZING NIGHT. THEY'RE ALL BUNDLED UP AGAINST THE COLD.

I'M JUST GETTING READY TO GO TO BED.

I'M LEAVING FOR SCHOOL BY THE TIME HE COMES BACK IN THE MORNING. HIS NOSE IS ALL RED.

HE TELLS US HE AND SOME OF THE OTHERS MADE A FIRE SO THEY WOULDN'T DIE OF COLD.

MY MOM SERVES HIM A SOUP OF MILK AND PASTA, IT'S VERY HOT, THE WAY HE LIKES IT.

HE DID GET SOME MEAT. SO THAT WINTER NIGHT SPENT OUT IN THE OPEN WASN'T IN VAIN.

WHEN THE STORE GETS A DELIVERY, IT'S USUALLY OF A SINGLE ITEM.

EVERYONE COMES TO BUY THE SAME THING IN THE SAME QUANTITY, MEANING AS MUCH AS POSSIBLE.

IT'S BECAUSE EVERYONE'S AFRAID WHATEVER PRODUCT WILL RUN OUT. AND IF THEY HAPPEN TO HAVE TOO MUCH, THEY CAN GIVE IT AWAY, OR TRADE IT FOR A SERVICE. NO MATTER WHAT IT IS, THEY'RE SURE IT'LL BE OF USE ONE DAY.

THIS TIME, IT'S TOILET PAPER.

I GO WITH MY PARENTS... TOGETHER THE THREE OF US CAN GET A LOT.

THE ROLLS ARE TIED SIX TO A STRING, FORMING A KIND OF NECKLACE.

THEY'RE SO BULKY WE CAN'T FIT THEM IN A BAG. WE HAVE TO CARRY THEM IN OUR HANDS, OR AROUND OUR NECKS.

MY DAD HANGS THEM FROM HIS HANDLEBARS.

A LOT OF PEOPLE DO THIS. IT HAS THE BENEFIT OF LETTING EVERYONE IN THE CITY KNOW PRETTY QUICKLY THE TOILET PAPER IS IN - THAT IT'S TIME TO RUN OUT AND BUY SOME.

I DON'T LIKE IT...

I FIND THIS WHOLE SITUATION EXTREMELY EMBARRASSING. I DON'T WANT ANYONE TO KNOW I POOP.

BUT BEARING THIS GARLAND, IT'S A LOST CAUSE! EVERYONE KNOWS! I HATE BEING EXPOSED LIKE THIS. I FEEL HUMILIATED.

I MIGHT AS WELL BE WEARING A SIGN SAYING: "I'M ON MY WAY HOME TO LOCK MYSELF IN THE BATHROOM." I'M RED AS A BEETROOT, WHICH ATTRACTS EVEN MORE ATTENTION.

I'D LIKE MY DAD TO CARRY MY SHARE, BUT IT WOULD COME DOWN TO THE SAME THING: "OH YEAH, I'M CARRYING MARZI'S TOILET PAPER...OH YES, SHE POOPS...(A SILENT "UNFORTUNATELY" HANGS IN THE AIR)

WHAT'S WRONG WITH YOU?

WHY ARE YOU ALL RED?!?

HOW CAN I EXPLAIN TO MY MOM? "MOM, LISTEN, I'M ASHAMED TO BE CARRYING THIS...OR RATHER, I'M ASHAMED OF... I MEAN, OF GOING TO...UHH..."

ALSO SHE TALKS VERY LOUDLY, I CAN JUST SEE HER SHOUTING IN THE MIDDLE OF THE STREET...

WHAT?!

YOU'RE ASHAMED OF GOING TO THE BATHROOM?

BUT IT'S HUMAN!!

EVERYONE DOES IT!!

MAYBE, BUT I DON'T WANT TO BE LIKE EVERYBODY ELSE!!

WHAT DOES SHE WANT? FOR ME TO BE PROUD OF THIS PURCHASE?

LOOK AT ME, EVERY-ONE!

TAKE A GOOD LOOK!

I HAVE TOILET PAPER AND IT'S GREAT!

I CAN FINALLY POOP!

YIPPEE!

THAT ABOUT SUMS UP MY MOM'S ATTITUDE.

WITH OUR THREE ROLL NECKLACES, THEY PROBABLY ALL THINK WE SPEND ALL OUR TIME ON THE TOILET...

DEEP DOWN, I HOPE I'M THE ONLY ONE WHO THINKS THIS WAY. I CAN'T WAIT TO GET HOME...

INTERESTINGLY, IN POLISH TOILET PAPER IS ALSO KNOWN AS "PAPIER SZCZĘŚCIA"...

THE PAPER OF HAPPINESS!

A VERY WET EASTER

THIS YEAR, WE'RE GOING TO SPEND EASTER WITH MY MOM'S FAMILY IN KAMIEŃ. I DON'T PARTICULARLY WANT TO, BUT I DON'T REALLY HAVE A CHOICE...

MY MOM, HOWEVER, IS COMPLETELY OVERJOYED.

KAMIEŃ MEANS STONE IN ENGLISH. WE SAY THE PEOPLE WHO LIVE HERE HAVE HEARTS JUST AS HARD.

THEY WORK ALL THE TIME. THEY GO TO THE FIELDS IN THE MORNING, WITH THEIR LARD SANDWICHES AND THERMOSES OF SWEET, STRONG TEA, AND STAY THERE UNTIL EVENING.

I GO CRAZY THERE. ALL YOU SEE IS FIELDS EVERYWHERE. OPEN SPACES WHERE THE PEOPLE PAY TRIBUTE TO THEIR SUN-GOD.

THEIR FACES ARE LIGHTER THAN THEIR BACKS BECAUSE THEY ALWAYS WORK WITH THEIR HEADS DOWN.

THEY HAVE THICK SKIN AND LOTS OF WRINKLES ON THEIR HANDS AND FACES. THEIR EYES ARE PALE AND GO BAD QUICKLY.

THEY ARE STRONG AND SPEAK LITTLE, AND IN A KIND OF RAPIDFIRE DIALECT THAT ONLY MY MOM CAN INTERPRET.

MY DAD AND I HAVE TO MAKE AN EFFORT. HE'S SLOWLY GOTTEN USED TO IT. BUT I DON'T WANT TO.

THE MEN IN THIS BIG FAMILY REALLY LIKE VODKA. MY POOR DAD CAN'T HANDLE ALCOHOL AND THEY GET HIM DRUNK.

HIS EYES SHINE AND HE TALKS EVEN MORE LOUDLY THAN USUAL!

THE MORE HE DRINKS, THE MORE THE WORDS GET LOST IN HIS THROAT, THEY BECOME UNCERTAIN, LIKE A DRUNK WALKING DOWN A STRAIGHT ROAD.

WE ALWAYS GO THE HOUSE OF MY MOM'S MOM, WHO LIVES WITH HER SON (MY GODFATHER). I'M SCARED OF HIM.

HE HAS A BIG NOSE POINTED LIKE IN THE PICTURES IN THE BOOK OF ANDERSEN'S FAIRY TALES MY DAD READS ME ALMOST EVERY NIGHT.

HE ALSO HAS A POINTY CHIN SO IT'S LIKE HE HAS TWO NOSES POINTING IN DIFFERENT DIRECTIONS. HIS THINNING HAIR MAKES HIM LOOK LIKE A CRAZED MUSICIAN.

ARH! ARH!

HE LOOKS LIKE A MADMAN AND HE'S MISSING TEETH. NO MATTER WHETHER HE'S TALKING, EATING, OR LOOKING AT ME, HE SCARES ME.

I DON'T THINK THE CATS LIKE HIM EITHER. ONE DAY WHEN HE WAS SLEEPING ON THE COUCH, A CAT JUMPED ON HIM AND SCRATCHED HIS TEMPLE.

IT DREW BLOOD. EVER SINCE THEN, I'VE BEEN SCARED OF CATS TOO.

HIS WIFE'S AN EXCELLENT COOK. SHE'S NICE, EVEN THOUGH SHE ACTS WEIRD WHENEVER SHE TALKS TO ME.

I THINK SHE PROBABLY DOESN'T KNOW HOW TO TALK TO KIDS. HER VOICE GOES ALL HIGH AND SHE USES VOCABULARY FOR A BABY, EVEN THOUGH I'M ALREADY BIG!

HAPPILY, SHE MAKES GOOD PIEROGIS (THEY'RE LIKE RAVIOLIS). ONE IS ENOUGH FOR ME. IT TAKES UP THE WHOLE PLATE.

IT'S STUFFED WITH POTATOES AND COTTAGE CHEESE. ADD A LITTLE MELTED BUTTER ON TOP AND I'M IN HEAVEN!

HERE WE ARE ON OUR WAY TO THE VILLAGE. IT'S STILL SNOWING AND I'M SURE I WON'T BE ABLE TO GO PLAY OUTSIDE.

I THOUGHT WE WOULDN'T LEAVE AT THE LAST MINUTE BECAUSE I'M SICK. I CAUGHT A ZAPALENIE USZU, AN EAR INFECTION!

BUT MY MOM HAS BEEN PLANNING THIS TRIP FOR SO LONG, THERE WAS NO QUESTION OF CANCELLING IT.

WHAT AM I GOING TO DO INSIDE ALL DAY? WATCH THE MEN DRINK TOO MUCH OR PRAY ALONG WITH THE WOMEN?

THERE ARE NO CHILDREN, THERE'S NO ONE TO TALK TO OR PLAY WITH. I ONLY HAVE MY RABBIT.

TOGETHER, WE WATCH THE SNOW FALL OUT THE WINDOW, WHILE AWAITING OUR RETURN TO THE CITY. I LIKE TO PRESS MY NOSE UP AGAINST THE GLASS.

I BREATHE ON IT AND DRAW OR WRITE. I TEACH MY RABBIT LETTERS. EVERY SO OFTEN ONE OF MY RELATIVES WALKS BY, NOTICES ME AND SMILES STRANGELY WHILE TAPPING HIS FINGERS ON HIS FOREHEAD.

THEY'VE NEVER UNDERSTOOD ME. I WONDER WHAT THEY DID WHEN THEY WERE YOUNG? IN MY OPINION, THEY WERE ALL BORN OLD!

THE WORST THING ABOUT BEING HERE IS I HAVE TO SLEEP IN THE SAME ROOM WITH MY PARENTS AND MY GRANDMOTHER.

MY BED IS A BIG WICKER THING THEY SET UP AT BEDTIME.

IT SITS IN THE MIDDLE OF THE ROOM. I'M TOO TALL FOR IT AND CAN'T STRAIGHTEN OUT COMPLETELY.

ZZZ!
ZZZZ!
ZZZ!

ALSO, WHENEVER THEY BRING IT IN, IT'S ALL COLD AND HALF-COVERED IN SPIDER WEBS.

WE GO TO CHURCH A LOT IN THIS FAMILY. AND NOW THAT IT'S EASTER, WE REALLY GO THERE ALL THE TIME.

WE GO ON WEDNESDAY, ALL AFTERNOON...

WE GO ON THURSDAY AFTERNOON TOO...

WE GO ON FRIDAY...

FRIDAY IS AN IMPORTANT DAY. JESUS HAS DIED AND WE KEEP VIGIL OVER HIS BODY, LAID OUT ON THE CROSS JUST IN FRONT OF THE ALTAR.

MOST PEOPLE KNEEL DOWN AS SOON AS THEY ENTER AND APPROACH ON THEIR KNEES TO KISS JESUS' BODY.

MY MOM AND MY AUNT KISS HIS FEET, HANDS, FOREHEAD, AND MOUTH.

I JUST KISSED HIS FEET BECAUSE I DIDN'T DARE APPROACH HIS HEAD. I WAS SCARED OF THE EXPRESSION ON HIS FACE.

I DON'T LIKE DEATH. MY MOM DIDN'T INSIST WHEN SHE SAW THE EMOTION WASHING OVER ME.

YOU CAN SPEND THE WHOLE NIGHT AT CHURCH ON FRIDAY, IT'S THE DAY OF LAMENTATION.

I HAVE TO HAVE TEARS IN MY EYES AND BE VERY UPSET IN ORDER TO LEAVE, OTHERWISE IT'S ALMOST IMPOSSIBLE TO GET MY MOM OUT OF THERE.

BUT I LOVE SATURDAY. WE ONLY GO TO CHURCH IN THE MORNING. MY MOM FIXES A BASKET WITH HARD BOILED EGGS, SAUSAGES, BREAD, STALKS OF HORSE-RADISH... AND LITTLE SHEEP IN SUGAR OR WAX.

I LIKE THE ONES IN SUGAR. THEN WE HAVE A FEAST!

I FEEL PROUD CARRYING THIS BIG, CHIC BASKET. IT'S BRIMMING WITH OUR SUNDAY LUNCH.

THE PRIEST COMES AND BLESSES IT WITH HOLY WATER.

HE DOES IT SO FERVENTLY HE ALSO SHOWERS THE PEOPLE A LITTLE...

SUNDAY, WE GO TO THE SIX O'CLOCK MASS. IT'S THE RESURRECTION, BUT WE ARE FROZEN TO DEATH.

THERE ARE SO MANY PEOPLE ALL I CAN SEE IS A SEA OF COATS PACKED TIGHTLY TOGETHER.

I'M ON THE LEFT WITH MY MOM ON THE SIDE RE-SERVED FOR WOMEN. MY DAD IS SOMEWHERE ON THE RIGHT.

SOMETIMES I BEG TO GO WITH HIM BECAUSE I'M SURE HE LEAVES A BIT EARLY. HE'S ALWAYS WAITING FOR US OUTSIDE FIRST.

AT SOME POINT, THE PRIESTS AND THE CHILDREN'S CHOIR START A PROCESSION WE ALL FOLLOW AROUND THE CHURCH.

DONG DONG DONG DONG

WE CIRCLE IT THREE TIMES WITH THE BELLS RINGING VERY LOUDLY AND THEN WE GO BACK INTO THE CHURCH. I'M FROZEN SOLID.

MY JAWS ARE SO CLENCHED I CAN'T EVEN SING. SO I GAZE UP AT THE CEILING. IT'S BEAUTIFUL AND FAR AWAY.

THE LIGHTS ARE SUSPENDED FROM IT. JUST ONE WOULD FILL UP MY WHOLE BEDROOM.

I SHIFT FROM ONE FOOT TO THE OTHER TO GET A BETTER VIEW OF THE WINDOWS. BUT THE MINUTE I CATCH A GLIMPSE OF MY MOM'S FACE, I KNOW I HAVE TO SETTLE DOWN.

I DON'T MOVE ANYMORE...

I LIFT MY HEAD DISCREETLY. I CAN SEE THE NOSTRILS OF THE PEOPLE AROUND ME AND THEIR FALSE TEETH GLINTING!

IT MAKES ME LAUGH.

MASS LASTS AROUND TWO HOURS. IT'S ALWAYS LONGER IN THE COUNTRY BECAUSE THE PRIEST SPEAKS TO THE PARISHIONERS ABOUT DONATIONS AND ARRANGEMENTS FOR CLEANING THE CHURCH.

WE HAVE TO WAIT FOR THE BENEDICTION. WITHOUT IT, IT'S LIKE YOU DIDN'T GO TO MASS.

WHEN IT'S OVER, WE FINALLY GO HOME. BUT IT'S NOT THAT EASY BECAUSE THERE ARE LOTS OF PEOPLE WALKING OR BICYCLING HOME PRETTY MUCH IN THE MIDDLE OF THE ROAD.

DON'T BE IN SUCH A HURRY!!

WHAT ARE YOU DOING?

WATCH OUT!

MY DAD HAS TO BE CAREFUL... WE'RE GOING 15 KILOMETERS AN HOUR AND COULDN'T HURT A FLY BUT MY MOM IS STILL SCARED.

I'M SQUEEZED IN THE BACK BETWEEN MY GRAND-MOTHER AND HER TWO FRIENDS, THEIR PERFUME IS SUFFOCATING ME AND THEIR SCARVES TICKLE.

I CAN'T WAIT TO GET HOME!

WHILE THE ADULTS ARE TALKING, I CHECK OUT THE NAILS AND OTHER MYSTERIOUS METAL THINGS MY UNCLE HAS IN HIS WORKSHOP. SOME OF THEM LOOK LIKE LITTLE MEN OR STRANGE ANIMALS.

YOU CAN TAKE SOMETHING IF YOU'D LIKE.

WHAT LUCK!

I FILL THE POCKETS OF MY ANORAK. I BEGIN TO FEEL VERY HEAVY.

MY MOM'S NIECE HAS JUST ARRIVED. HER KIDS ARE MY AGE: JUSTYNA, JAREK AND JOASIA.

THEY REALLY LIKE PLAYING OUTSIDE. UNFORTUNATELY, I'M NOT ALLOWED TO BE OUTSIDE MUCH WITH MY INFECTED EARS.

STILL, WE SOMEHOW MANAGE TO SLIP AWAY TO PICK BAZIE (CATKINS). THEY'RE SMALL BUSHES WITH A LITTLE FLUFFY BALL FOR A FLOWER.

IT'S VERY SOFT, BUT THE BRANCHES ARE HARD TO BREAK. THEY'RE CLUSTERED AROUND THE POND.

IT'S AN OLD QUARRY FULL OF WATER. WE LIKE TO SKIP STONES ON IT BUT IT'S NOT EASY TO FIND THEM. EVEN THOUGH WE'RE IN KAMIEŃ!!

THE GROUND IS HARD BECAUSE OF THE ICE, AND EVERYTHING IS REALLY STUCK TO IT.

I DON'T KNOW HOW BUT, PROBABLY THANKS TO MY HEAVY POCKETS, I LOSE MY BALANCE AND FALL INTO THE WATER.

JAREK HOLDS OUT HIS HAND BUT HE'S TOO LITTLE. VERY SLOWLY, THE POND SUCKS ME IN...

ALL THREE OF THEM LOOK AT ME WIDE-EYED, WITHOUT SAYING A WORD.

GO GET HELP!!

DON'T LEAVE ME ALL ALONE!

NOT ALL OF YOU!!

BUT THEY DON'T HEAR ME. I FEEL MY ANORAK SWELLING UP WITH WATER. I'M GETTING FATTER AND FATTER.

THE LITTLE METAL CREATURES ARE SLIPPING OUT OF MY POCKETS AND FALLING AROUND ME.

I TRY TO SAVE THEM BUT MY HANDS ARE ICE CUBES, INCAPABLE OF OBEYING ME. TOO BAD, I REALLY WANTED THEM...

JUST AS I BEGIN TO COMPLETELY GO UNDER, I SEE EVERYONE ARRIVE, MY DAD AND MY UNCLE IN FRONT, IN SWEATERS AND SOCKS!

LITTLE BY LITTLE I LOSE CONSCIOUSNESS.

THEY QUICKLY PULL ME ONTO THE SHORE. MY MOM AND MY AUNTS ARE CRYING AND PRAYING.

MY DAD AND UNCLE SMELL STRONGLY OF ALCOHOL, I THINK THAT, MORE THAN ANYTHING, IS WHAT BRINGS ME BACK TO EARTH.

THEY CARRY ME TO THE HOUSE. I FEEL LIKE I'LL BE FROZEN FOREVER.

I CAN'T MOVE.

THE NEXT NIGHT A BIG FEVER TAKES HOLD OF ME. WE LEAVE FOR HOME IMMEDIATELY, EARLIER THAN PLANNED.

THE DOCTOR PRESCRIBES SHOTS AND A WASHING-OUT OF MY EARS.

USING A TUBE, HE POURS SOME WATER IN AND AFTERWARDS IT RUNS OUT ALL YELLOW. I TRY TO REMEMBER THE LAST TIME I WASHED MY EARS. I'M A LITTLE ASHAMED.

APPARENTLY, IT'S A NORMAL COLOR. BUT THAT DOESN'T STOP ME FROM FEELING ASHAMED...

AUNT MARYSIA, OUR NEIGHBOR, COMES TO GIVE ME THE SHOTS TWO TIMES A DAY. NOTHING UNEXPECTED EVER COMES UP FOR HER?! SHE CHATS, LAUGHING WITH MY DAD WHILE PATTING MY BUTTOCKS.

I EXPECT THE WORST. SHE TALKS, JOKES AND ALL AT ONCE BETWEEN LAUGHS, THERE IT IS, THE SHOT! IT'S OVER, YAY! HMMPF... AT LEAST UNTIL TOMORROW MORNING.

A FEW DAYS LATER, MY MOM BRINGS ME THE NEWSPAPER, ALL EXCITED. THERE'S A SHORT ARTICLE IN IT ABOUT A LITTLE GIRL WHO ALMOST DIED ON EASTER SUNDAY.

THEY DON'T SAY MY NAME BUT I KNOW IT'S ABOUT ME.

YIKES...I DIDN'T REALIZE HOW SERIOUS THIS ACCIDENT WAS. I DIDN'T KNOW MY LIFE WAS AT STAKE.

JUST THE LIVES OF MY LITTLE MEN THAT REST AT THE BOTTOM OF THE POND.

ONCE I'VE RECOVERED FROM THIS EPISODE, I PROUDLY BRING THE NEWSPAPER TO MY TEACHER TO SHOW OFF.

BUT SHE IS MORE SHOCKED THAN ANYTHING! FOR ONCE, I WASN'T THAT BORED IN KAMIEŃ.

WE'RE LUCKY BECAUSE MY DAD WORKS AT HUTA STALOWA WOLA, THE CITY'S FACTORY...

AND THE WORKERS ARE ALWAYS GETTING COOL THINGS BECAUSE OF THEIR JOBS.

THE SAME GOES FOR UNCLE ZDZICH. THOUGH HE'S NOT IN THE SAME SECTOR AS MY DAD, HE WORKS AT THE FACTORY TOO.

A LITTLE WHILE AGO, FRIDGES WERE DELIVERED TO THEIR WORKPLACE. EACH WORKER COULD BUY ONE IF HE WANTED.

MY DAD DID, AND SO DID ZDZICH.

THE NEW FRIDGE IS THREE TIMES BIGGER THAN THE OLD ONE...AND FIVE TIMES EMPTIER.

EVEN THOUGH IT'S MADE IN RUSSIA, IT'S PRETTY, AND IT HAS A SEPARATE FREEZER...

IN FACT, ALL THE FRIDGES ARE IDENTICAL. ZDZICH'S IS EXACTLY THE SAME, EXCEPT THAT THEY HAVE EVEN LESS FOOD TO PUT IN IT.

THEY DON'T HAVE FAMILY IN THE COUNTRY LIKE WE DO.

IF YOU WALK THROUGH THE APARTMENTS IN MY CITY AND SEE THIS MACHINE, IT MEANS THE RESIDENT WORKS AT THAT FACTORY AND BOUGHT IT ON THE SAME DAY AS MY DAD.

I'VE SEEN IT IN COUNTLESS HOMES.

MY PARENTS BOUGHT ME A SLIDE PROJECTOR. SEVERAL TIMES A WEEK THE WHOLE FLOOR ASSEMBLES AT MY HOUSE IN THE EVENING.

WE PARK OURSELVES IN THE ENTRYWAY AND WATCH THE IMAGES MY DAD PROJECTS ONTO THE FRONT DOOR.

I PARTICULARLY LIKE ONE STORY ABOUT A YOUNG BOY WHO LIVES IN THE MOUNTAINS. HIS NAME IS ONDRASZEK.

HE'S A THIEF, BUT HE'S A GOOD THIEF BECAUSE HE STEALS FROM THE RICH (THE VERY, VERRRRY RICH, THE "DISGUSTINGLY" RICH) TO GIVE TO THE POOR.

THE STORY ENDS BADLY. HE'S BEHEADED!

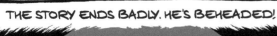

MY DAD KNOWS I DON'T LIKE THE LAST THREE SLIDES. I DON'T LIKE SEEING ONDRASZEK KILLED BY THE RICH.

SO HE TAKES THE SLIDES OUT BEFOREHAND AND TELLS US THE STORY'S OVER.

EVEN THOUGH WE KNOW IT'S NOT TRUE, WE DON'T MIND STOPPING THERE. WE'D STILL LIKE TO BELIEVE IT HAS A HAPPY ENDING.

THE ADULTS TALK AND DRINK TEA IN THE LIVING ROOM, WHILE ANOTHER STORY BEGINS IN THE FRONT HALL...

IT'S THE ONE ABOUT THE FROGS WITH RED HATS. I KNOW IT BY HEART. MY DAD OFTEN READS IT TO ME BEFORE BED.

THE YOUNGER ONES LIKE THIS STORY BETTER. THEY DON'T REALLY UNDERSTAND ONDRASZEK. HE'S MORE FOR THE BIGGER KIDS.

MY MOM GAVE ME ANOTHER STORY IN SLIDES: THE POPE'S TRIP TO POLAND. IT'S A LITTLE BORING. THE TEXT DOESN'T REALLY SAY ANYTHING SPECIAL.

"AND NOW, THE POPE IS EXITING THE AIRPLANE AND GREETING THE ASSEMBLED CROWD AT THE AIRPORT." IT DOESN'T ADD ANYTHING, WE CAN SEE THAT QUITE CLEARLY IN THE PHOTO.

THIS TIME, OUR PARENTS WATCH THE PROJECTION WITH US.

MY MOM IS MOVED, SHE LOOKS LIKE SHE'S GOING TO CRY ANY SECOND. I THOUGHT I WAS THE ONLY ONE WHO MADE HER CRY, BUT APPARENTLY NOT! THERE'S STILL THE POPE.

BUT ANYWAY, NOT FOR THE SAME REASONS.

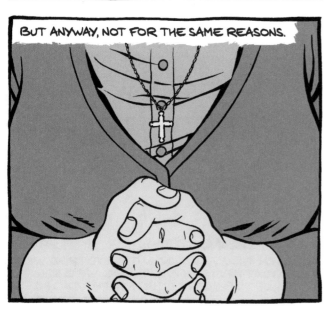

SO OUR NEW GAME CONSISTS OF ACTING OUT HIS VISIT TO POLAND. ONE OF US IS THE POPE. THE OTHERS PLAY THE BISHOPS, PRIESTS, OR PEOPLE WHO GREET THE POPE WHEN HE ARRIVES.

THE ELEVATOR IS THE AIRPLANE...

I OVERCOME MY FEAR OF THIS SUSPENDED BOX BECAUSE BEING THE POPE IS REALLY GREAT.

MONIKA USUALLY PLAYS THE BISHOP WHO WELCOMES ME.

IF WE'RE PLAYING WHEN THE OTHER RESIDENTS GET HOME FROM WORK, WE DON'T USE THE ELEVATOR...

CZEŚĆ!

I WOULDN'T WANT ANYONE IN THE LOBBY TO SPY ME IN MY MOM'S WEDDING DRESS.

SO I EXIT FROM THE GARBAGE AREA BETWEEN TWO FLOORS AND DESCEND THE STAIRCASE AS THOUGH I WERE DISEMBARKING FROM A REAL AIRPLANE AND GREETING THE PEOPLE FROM ON HIGH.

THE PEOPLE (THAT IS TO SAY MONIKA AND THE OTHERS) SING HYMNS IN MY HONOR.

MY MOM HEARD US ONCE AND GOT ANGRY, SAYING THAT IT WAS BLASPHEMY TO SING PSALMS IN PLAY...

AND THEN WHEN SHE SAW WHAT WE WERE PLAYING, SHE TURNED RED AND PURPLE. SPARKS FLEW OUT OF HER EYES!

WE THOUGHT SHE WAS GOING TO BURN US ALIVE, ALONG WITH THE STAIRWELL. I WAS REALLY SCARED TO GO HOME THAT DAY...

BLAM

SHE FORBADE US FROM PLAYING POPE. WE DIDN'T LISTEN. (IN FACT, WE DON'T REALLY KNOW WHAT THE WORD BLASSFAMEE MEANS...) WE SUSPECT IT'S NOT GOOD... BUT NOT THAT SERIOUS EITHER.

SO THEY SING PSALMS, I DESCEND, I KNEEL DOWN AND KISS THE GROUND, JUST LIKE THE POPE DID IN THE SLIDES.

AFTERWARDS I VISIT WITH THE PEOPLE AT WHOSE HOMES I CELEBRATE MASS.

MOST OFTEN, WE GO TO MONIKA'S HOUSE BECAUSE AUNT STASIA IS AT MY HOUSE, DRINKING TEA WITH MY MOM.

WE HOST MASS IN THE BATHROOM. THERE'S A SMALL ECHO LIKE IN A REAL CHURCH.

I GET INTO THE BATHTUB WHICH STANDS FOR NOAH'S ARK. MONIKA IS ON THE TOILET, IT'S THE HOLY SEE. THE OTHERS, THE PEOPLE, STAND WHERE THEY CAN, WHICH ISN'T VERY EASY...

TODAY I'M BAPTIZING PEOPLE BY DUNKING THEM IN THE BATHTUB. BUT NO ONE VOLUNTEERS. SO WE DECIDE TO USE MAGDA, MONIKA AND ANIA'S LITTLE SISTER.

SINCE SHE CAN'T SPEAK, SHE CAN'T PROTEST. QUITE THE OPPOSITE, SHE'S THRILLED TO BE INCLUDED IN OUR GAME.

UNFORTUNATELY, HER MOM GETS BACK TO THE APARTMENT JUST AS I'M SUBMERGING HER IN THE BATHTUB WHICH IS FULL OF WATER THAT'S A BIT TOO CHILLY...

AUNT STASIA IS VERY TOLERANT... BUT NOT THIS TIME!!

LUCKILY, I'M NOT THE ONLY ONE SHE POUNCES ON. IN EVERY SENSE OF THE WORD...

SHE IS SO ANGRY SHE AIMS JUST ABOUT EVERYTHING IN ARM'S REACH AT US. A DAMP SPONGE (YUCK!), TOWELS AND A BAR OF SOAP THAT HITS ANDRZEJ FULL ON THE HEAD!

POOR BOY, HE'S ALWAYS THE ONE WHO GETS IT THE MOST EVEN THOUGH HE'S DONE THE LEAST. I HAVE TO SAY WE DON'T TREAT HIM VERY FAIRLY. THE POWER BELONGS TO THE WOMEN ON THIS HALLWAY.

ANYWAY, WE'RE STOPPING THE BAPTISMS...

AFTER MASS, I HAVE TO RETURN TO THE VATICAN. BUT BEFORE THAT, THE POLES OFFER ME GIFTS. ACTUALLY, ONLY ONE GIFT. AN OLD RUG FROM MONIKA'S BATHROOM.

THEN I CLIMB THE STAIRS AND SHUT MYSELF IN THE GARBAGE AREA TO AWAIT TAKEOFF.

44

PLAYING POPE, WE FIGURED OUT THAT WE COULD SING INTO THE TRASH CHUTE.

OUR VOICES TRAVEL UP AND DOWN THE BUILDING'S CHUTE.

WE KEEP AN EYE ON THE CHUTE AND AS SOON AS SOMEONE COMES TO DROP A BAG OF TRASH, ONE OF US SPEAKS VERY LOUDLY IN A DEEP VOICE!

I'M GOING TO GET YOU!

YOU WON'T ESCAPE!!

THOSE ARE THE LAST WORDS WE MANAGE TO GET OUT BECAUSE WE'RE DOUBLED UP LAUGHING BY THEN.

AT FIRST, WE ALL COVER OUR MOUTHS TO KEEP FROM MAKING A SOUND.

OH!

BUT WHEN WE SEE EACH OTHER LIKE THAT, WITH OUR HANDS OVER OUR MOUTHS AND OUR EYES LAUGHING, WE CAN'T TAKE IT ANYMORE! THE PERSON WHO'S SHOUTING INTO THE HOLE HAS TO HAVE A LOT OF SELF-CONTROL... IT'S MONIKA!

TO KEEP FROM DISTRACTING HER, WE GO INTO A DIFFERENT GARBAGE AREA AND LISTEN EXCITEDLY!

IT WOULD REALLY SCARE ME...

BUT THE VICTIMS OF THE JOKE DON'T REACT THE WAY WE WOULD...

WHAT IS THIS NON-SENSE?

IT'S THOSE KIDS FROM THE 5TH FLOOR MAKING TROUBLE AGAIN!?!

ONE DAY MONIKA ENDED UP WITH POTATO SKINS AND DAMP TEA LEAVES ON HER HEAD!!

SHE WENT HOME IMMEDIATELY, ANGRY AT THE REST OF US WHO WERE ROLLING ON THE FLOOR AND CRYING WITH LAUGHTER.

WE TRIED TO HOLD OURSELVES IN AT FIRST, BUT SHE WAS BEING SO MELODRAMATIC WE COULDN'T RESIST!

AFTER THAT, SHE DECIDED TO ONLY TALK INTO THE CHUTE FROM THE TOP FLOOR.

BUT WE FIGURED OUT SOMETHING EVEN BETTER...

WE TAKE OVER A BUNCH OF THE OPENINGS WHERE PEOPLE DUMP THEIR GARBAGE AND PRETEND LIKE THEY'RE OUR APARTMENTS, CALLING TO EACH OTHER UP AND DOWN THE CHUTE.

WHAT? YOUR HUSBAND GOT SOME CHOCOLATE?!

YES, HE BROUGHT SOME BACK FOR THE KIDS!

GREAT! THEY'RE GOING TO BE HAPPY.

IT'S OUR TELEPHONE AND IT WORKS REALLY WELL. BUT IT'S NOT VERY CONFIDENTIAL.

ONE DAY SOMEONE SURPRISED ANDRZEJ WITH HIS HEAD AND SHOULDERS IN THE CHUTE.

HE TAPPED HIM ON THE BUTT AND I'M SURE HIS CRY OF TERROR COULD BE HEARD AS FAR AS THE BASEMENT!

HE BANGED HIS HEAD ON THE GARBAGE CHUTE AND CAME TO FIND US WITH TEARS IN HIS EYES.

HE TOLD ME THAT'S HOW THEY LOADED CHILDREN INTO THE OVENS OF HELL!!!!

I DON'T KNOW IF WE EVER SCARED THE OTHER RESIDENTS, BUT THEY SURE FIGURED OUT HOW TO SCARE US.

I HOPE, IN SPITE OF ALL OUR SILLY GAMES, WE'LL STILL GO TO HEAVEN...

SUNDAY MORNINGS BEFORE CHURCH, MY PARENTS ALWAYS HAVE THE TELEVISION ON.

FRRRK!

EVEN THOUGH THEY'RE NOT WATCHING IT, THEY'RE LISTENING TO WHAT'S GOING ON WHILE TAKING CARE OF THEIR SUNDAY CHORES...

CHOOSING CLOTHES FOR MASS, IRONING, PREPARING OUR LUNCH, WASHING THE TUB OUT AFTER SATURDAY NIGHT'S BATHS.

A FEW YEARS AGO, ON A MID-DECEMBER SUNDAY, THE SCREEN STAYED BLANK... THERE WAS NO PICTURE OR SOUND, ONLY SNOW.

HUH?

MY DAD KNOCKED ON THE TOP, THINKING THERE MUST HAVE BEEN A BAD CONTACT OR SOMETHING LIKE THAT, BUT NOTHING CHANGED.

MAYBE THERE'S DUST.

PFFF

HE DISCONNECTED ALL THE CABLES AND BLEW ON THEM, THEN HE PLUGGED EVERYTHING IN AGAIN, TO NO EFFECT... IT WAS SNOWING ON THE TV!

ALL OF A SUDDEN AROUND TEN, THE IMAGE CAME BACK. GENERAL WOJCIECH JARUZELSKI, THE HEAD OF STATE, APPEARED IN PLACE OF THE USUAL ANCHOR AND HE WAS ADDRESSING ALL THE CITIZENS.

STARTING TODAY...

POLAND IS IN A STATE OF WAR!

TATO?

MAMUŚ?!

FLBLBLB!!

IT WAS DECEMBER 13, 1981... I WAS TWO AND A HALF.

MAYBE THE REGULAR NEWS CAME ON AFTER-WARDS, BUT I DON'T THINK ANYBODY CARED.

THERE WAS COMPLETE PANIC IN OUR BUILDING.

WE WEREN'T THE ONLY ONES TO HAVE SEEN THE NEWS. MY DAD WENT OUT TO THE STAIRWELL WHERE THE NEIGHBORS HAD ALREADY BEGUN TO GATHER.

THEY DIDN'T KNOW IF THEY SHOULD GO TO CHURCH, IF GOING OUTSIDE WOULD MEAN RISKING THEIR LIVES.

MY MOM WAS CRYING, SHE WAS REALLY SCARED, WE DIDN'T KNOW WHAT WAS GOING ON WITH OUR RELATIVES BECAUSE NO ONE HAD A TELEPHONE.

OUT OF OUR WHOLE BUILDING THERE MIGHT BE ONE APARTMENT THAT HAD A TELEPHONE, BUT YOU COULDN'T BE SURE!

SO EVERYONE STAYED HOME, NO ONE DARED TO VENTURE OUT OF THE COMPLEX.

AT 6 AM THE NEXT MORNING, TANKS ROLLED BY ON THE AVENUE BELOW OUR BUILDING, ALL SIRENS WAILING. (THIS HAPPENED SEVERAL TIMES A WEEK FOR MORE THAN A YEAR!)

THE HORRIFIC NOISE WOKE US CHILDREN UP WITH A START!

LOTS OF FACTORIES WENT ON STRIKE. BUT THE "ZOMO" CAME TO DRIVE OUT THE STRIK-ERS. THEY WERE ARMED WITH RIFLES AND BILLY CLUBS.

THEY KEPT TABS ON THE WORKERS' COMINGS AND GOINGS AROUND MY DAD'S FACTORY.

SOMETIMES THE TV WOULD SHOW THE DEMON-STRATIONS IN THE BIG CITIES AND THE MINES THAT THE ZOMO PACIFIED WITH BRUTALITY.

THE STRIKERS WERE THROWN IN JAIL OR KILLED.

CHRISTMAS WAS COMING, BUT WE DIDN'T HAVE ANY NEWS OF OUR RELATIVES IN KRAKÓW OR WARSZAWA, OR POJEZIERZE.

NOT ONLY DID THE TELEPHONES NOT WORK ANYMORE BUT THE POST OFFICE NO LONGER DELIVERED ANYTHING.

LATER, THE TELEPHONES STARTED WORKING AGAIN, BUT EVERY TIME YOU DIALED A NUMBER, A VERY SOFT AND GENTLE VOICE WOULD WARN YOU:

"YOUR CONVERSATION IS BEING MONITORED"!

WE COULDN'T GO VISIT OUR FAMILIES EITHER, BECAUSE EVEN THE SMALLEST TRIP REQUIRED THE AUTHORITIES' PERMISSION, WHICH TOOK TIME.

AND ONCE YOU ARRIVED, YOU NEEDED TO PRESENT YOURSELF TO THE LOCAL AUTHORITIES IMMEDIATELY!

EVEN TO GO CHRISTMAS SHOPPING AT NISKO, A TINY CITY THREE KILOMETERS AWAY, YOU NEEDED A PASSPORT AND AUTHORIZATION.

THEY HAD A "PEWEX" THERE, A STORE WITH BEAUTIFUL PRODUCTS THAT ONLY TOOK DOLLARS.

BUT THERE WASN'T ANY GAS AT THE STATIONS ANYWAY. WE STAYED HOME AND EVEN THOUGH MEETINGS WERE FORBIDDEN, WE VISITED WITH OUR NEIGHBORS.

THAT'S HOW WE SPENT OUR FIRST CHRISTMAS IN THE STATE OF WAR.

NOW MY COUNTRY ISN'T IN A STATE OF WAR ANYMORE BUT MY PARENTS STILL TALK ABOUT IT A LOT.

AND FOR THE 100TH TIME...

THE TATARS PILLAGED KRAKÓW!

I'M SCARED THE WAR THEY'RE ALWAYS TALKING ABOUT IS AROUND THE CORNER.

SOMETIMES I DREAM THAT THE TATARS ARE STORMING OUR STAIRWELL AND MY DAD HAS TO GO FIGHT THEM, LEAVING ME ALONE WITH MY MOM. I HATE THIS DREAM...

ESPECIALLY THE END, WHEN THE TATARS CARRY US OUT OF THE CITY TO CUT OFF OUR HEADS!

WHEN MY PARENTS LAUNCH INTO POLITICAL DEBATES WITH THE NEIGHBORS, I FORCE MYSELF TO TRY TO UNDERSTAND WHAT THEIR WORDS MEAN...

COMMUNISM MUST FALL! PEOPLE CAN'T TAKE IT ANYMORE!

THERE'LL BE A REVOLUTION OR A WAR...

THAT'S WHAT'LL HAPPEN.

MY MOM IS KIND OF A PROPHET OF DOOM; ACCORDING TO HER, THE FUTURE IS ALWAYS CATASTROPHIC.

SHE'S CONSTANTLY WARNING MY DAD TO BE MORE CAREFUL ABOUT WHAT HE SAYS. HE'S VERY CHATTY.

I KNOW A GUY WHO HAS CONTACTS ABROAD WHO CAN PRINT UP RATION CARDS!

HA HA! INCREDIBLE, NO? PRETTY SOON, WE WON'T BE HUNGRY ANYMORE?!

I DON'T UNDERSTAND WHAT THEY MEAN WHEN THEY SAY "IT HAS TO END SOON." WHAT'S THIS "IT"? THE WAR? THEY TALK ABOUT IT ALL THE TIME! WHAT WAR?

ASIDE FROM IN MY DREAMS AND ON THE TELEVISION NEWS, I HAVEN'T SEEN ANY DEAD, OR EVEN ANY VIOLENCE.

I'M SCARED BECAUSE NO ONE TALKS TO ME.

THESE ARE ADULT AFFAIRS. GO ON AND PLAY, STOP CLINGING TO ME!

IS THERE A WAR, MOM? BUT WHERE?

OH, TAKE A LOOK OUTSIDE, SEE WHAT'S GOING ON!

OUTSIDE!? OUT THE WINDOW? IN THE STAIRWELL?

HMPH! YOU WON'T UNDERSTAND IT ANYWAY.

OF COURSE I WON'T UNDERSTAND ANYTHING IF NO ONE EXPLAINS ANY OF IT TO ME! THEY IGNORE ME...

I MAY LIVE IN IGNORANCE, BUT I'M A HUMAN BEING AFTER ALL! I LIVE HERE, I HAVE THE RIGHT TO KNOW!

I DON'T WANT TO BE LITTLE ANYMORE!

I WANT TO BE BIG! LIKE MY COUSIN BASIA!

BUY A COLOR TELEVISION

DRIVE A CAR

WEAR HIGH HEELS

KOLOROWY TELEWIZOR

AND RAISE CHILDREN SOMEDAY. I WOULD EXPLAIN EVERYTHING TO THEM SO THEY'D KNOW WHAT WAS GOING ON. SO THEY WOULDN'T HAVE TO LIVE IN FEAR, IMAGINING THINGS FROM EVERY OVERHEARD SNATCH OF CONVERSATION!

IT'S NOT FAIR THAT I DON'T HAVE ANYONE TO TALK TO! MONIKA AND ANIA HAVE EACH OTHER, THEY EVEN HAVE LITTLE MAGDA. ANIA AND ANDRZEJ ARE ALSO TOGETHER! EVERYONE ELSE LIVES IN TANDEM.

BUT I'M ALONE WITH THE STORIES MY MIND DREAMS UP, WITH MY RABBIT WHO LOOKS AT ME WITH PITY!

IT'S EASIER WHEN YOU'RE TWO. YOU CAN REASSURE EACH OTHER AND LAUGH, YOU CAN SOUND OUT YOUR IDEAS AND GET ANSWERS...

AS IT IS, I LAUGH AT AND CRY OVER MY OWN IDEAS, I'M INSECURE, I'M SCARED...

WHEN I TALK TO MY PARENTS, THEY DON'T LISTEN. AT FIRST IT'S FINE, THEY'RE THERE IN FRONT OF ME, THEY FOCUS ON ME FOR A WHILE...

AND THE TEACHER TOLD US WE NEED TO BRING A PLANT TO SCHOOL! I THOUGHT IF I PLANTED A SEED NOW, THE PLANT WOULD GROW AND AFTER VACATION, I COULD BRING IT IN. IT WOULD BE GREAT IF I HAD A FERN SEED! SO...

BUT THEN, SUDDENLY, RIGHT IN THE MIDDLE OF MY SPEECH, MY MOM WILL SAY SOMETHING TO MY DAD AS IF I WEREN'T THERE! IT COULD BE ANYTHING:

I'M GO A/W HO

OHH! MY BACK HURTS, IT'S GOING TO RAIN!!

OOM ER BED

YES, THE AIR IS HEAVY, THERE'S GOING TO BE A STORM.

I...

...

I BECOME INVISIBLE TO MY PARENTS.

AM I ONLY VISIBLE TO MY OWN EYES?

IT'S BIZARRE, BECAUSE AS SOON AS I DO SOMETHING BAD, IT'S IMPOSSIBLE TO DISAPPEAR...

THEY SEE ME WHEN THEY WANT TO SEE ME... NOT OFTEN. I'M SCARED IT WON'T END, THAT I'LL BECOME INVISIBLE TO THE WHOLE WORLD.

I WAS TAKING A BATH...

DO I HAVE TO KEEP BEHAVING BADLY TO REASSURE MYSELF THEY KNOW I'M HERE? IS IT THE ONLY WAY I CAN AFFIRM MY EXISTENCE?

MAYBE THE UPCOMING STRUGGLE WILL BE A GOOD WAY FOR ME TO GET NOTICED...

A HEROIC ACTION THAT WILL SAVE MY COUNTRY!

MONIKA TOLD ME THAT EVEN IF THERE IS A WAR IT WON'T BE A BIG DEAL BECAUSE CHILDREN CAN BE REALLY USEFUL.

THEY'RE SMALL AND FAST. SOLDIERS DON'T PAY ANY ATTENTION TO THEM, SO THEY CAN TAKE ON SECRET MISSIONS FOR THE ADULTS.

I WILL FINALLY BE RECOGNIZED!

AHHHHH!!!

BUT AT THE SAME TIME I DON'T REALLY WANT TO SLIP UNDER RUSSIAN TANKS OR THROUGH WATER PIPES...

I'D RATHER NOT HAVE A WAR... TOO BAD NO ONE PAYS ATTENTION TO ME!

I'LL BE A GROWN-UP TOO ONE DAY.

MY PARENTS ARE ALWAYS COMPLAINING WE DON'T HAVE ENOUGH MONEY, THAT WE'RE LIVING IN STRANGE TIMES. THEY TELL EVERYONE IN FACT.

WE DON'T HAVE ENOUGH MONEY.

THESE ARE STRANGE TIMES!

THEY DON'T TRUST BANKS, THEY KEEP THEIR MONEY IN A SAFE PLACE, AT HOME.

MY MOM HIDES IT IN HER LINGERIE, WITH HER PANTIES THAT ARE SO BIG I COULD FIT MY WHOLE BODY IN ONE OF THEM.

WHICH IS TO SAY THAT MY MOM IS FAT AND NOT THAT WE HAVE SO MUCH MONEY.

I KNOW WE'RE NOT WELL OFF BECAUSE WE HAVE A REALLY SECOND-RATE CAR. MY DAD SAYS IT'S BETTER THAN NOTHING, BUT DEEP DOWN I'M SURE HE DREAMS OF A BEAUTIFUL, COMFORTABLE CAR FROM THE WEST.

I LIKE OUR FIAT 126. WE'RE THE SAME AGE! THE ONLY PROBLEM IS THE MOTOR IS SO LOUD WE CAN'T HEAR EACH OTHER TALK WHEN WE'RE DRIVING.

MY MOM COUNTS THE MONEY EVERY EVENING. SHE SORTS IT AND THEN PUTS IT BACK IN WITH HER UNDERWEAR. ONCE WHEN I WAS HOME ALONE, I TOOK IT OUT TO LOOK AT.

BESIDES THE POLISH MONEY, THERE WERE SOME DOLLARS... FOR WHEN THINGS LOOK REALLY BLEAK.

I DON'T KNOW WHEN THEY PLAN TO SPEND IT, BUT IT'S CLEAR THEY'RE NOT USING IT FOR A NEW CAR OR TELEVISION.

DINNER!

THEY DON'T SEEM TO BELIEVE A GOOD TELEVISION IS VITAL TO OUR EXISTENCE. THE MOST IMPORTANT THING IS TO NOT GO HUNGRY.

BUT I NEVER CLEAN MY PLATE. SO IF THEY JUST BOUGHT A LITTLE LESS TO EAT, THEY COULD SAVE SOME MONEY...

AND USE IT TO BUY A COLOR TELEVISION.

THAT'S WHAT MY COUSIN BASIA DECIDED TO DO. SHE'S GROWN UP AND DOESN'T WANT TO LIVE WITH HER PARENTS ANYMORE. I'D LIKE THAT TOO. SHE'S WORKING VERY HARD NOW, SO SHE CAN SAVE ENOUGH MONEY TO MOVE OUT.

SHE'S BUYING THE THINGS SHE'LL NEED TO FURNISH HER APARTMENT. WHICH MEANS SHE COMES TO OUR PLACE IN THE CITY PRETTY OFTEN. PARTICULARLY TO GET A TELEVISION SET.

SO MANY PEOPLE WANT TELEVISIONS.

THAT TO GET ONE, MY COUSIN HAD TO PUT HER NAME ON A WAITING LIST. NOW SHE GOES EVERY WEEK BECAUSE THE SALES PEOPLE READ OUT THE NAMES IN FRONT OF THE STORE BEFORE IT OPENS.

THEY'RE CHECKING THAT EVERYONE ON THE LIST STILL WANTS A TELEVISION.

I WENT WITH BASIA ONCE. IT WAS VERY COLD. LOTS OF PEOPLE WERE WAITING BUT THE EMPLOYEES WEREN'T THERE FOR THE ROLL CALL. EVERYONE LOOKED FROZEN, BUT THEY WERE ALL AFRAID TO LEAVE.

ANOTHER TIME, BASIA COULDN'T COME. SHE LIVES IN THE COUNTRY AND IT'S NOT ALWAYS EASY TO GET TO THE CITY EARLY IN THE MORNING ON THE BUS, ESPECIALLY IN THE WINTER WHEN THE ROADS ARE ALL SNOWY.

SO WHEN THIS HAPPENED, MY DAD WENT TO HOLD HER PLACE WHEN THE CLERKS CALLED ROLL... HE TOOK ME ALONG.

THE MAN IN CHARGE WASN'T VERY HAPPY TO HEAR A MAN'S VOICE WHEN HE SHOUTED OUT "MS BARBARA L." (BARBARA IS HER REAL FIRST NAME).

IT'S IN YOUR NIECE'S BEST INTEREST TO COME HERSELF IF SHE REALLY WANTS A TELEVISION!

IF NOT, THERE ARE PLENTY OF PEOPLE WHO WOULD HAPPILY TAKE HER PLACE ON THE WAITING LIST!!

THOSE WHO PERSEVERE LONGEST WIN.

IT SEEMS LIKELY MY COUSIN WILL GET HER TV IN TWO MONTHS. SHE'S VERY HAPPY AND SO AM I...

I'LL FINALLY BE ABLE TO SEE MY FAVORITE CARTOON "REKSIO" IN COLOR!!

GOD LOVES ME

I'M GOING TO TAKE MY FIRST COMMUNION THIS YEAR. DURING THE CATECHISM, THE PRIEST TELLS US THAT WE FINALLY HAVE THE REQUISITE MATURITY TO TAKE JESUS INTO OUR HEARTS.

PERSONALLY, I'M NOT SURE I'M READY FOR IT...

TO WELCOME SOMEONE INTO YOUR HEART IS A GREAT RESPONSIBILITY. YOU CAN'T JUST DO IT BECAUSE YOU'RE THE RIGHT AGE.

I'M SCARED IT WILL GO BADLY AND THAT JESUS WILL RUN AWAY OR I'LL HURT HIM AND HIS FATHER, GOD, WILL COME GIVE ME A TALKING TO.

YOU HAVE TO BE KIND AND NICE TO JESUS AND EVERYONE ELSE. I DON'T KNOW IF I'M NICE. MY MOM, ANYWAY, IS ALWAYS TELLING ME I'M MEAN.

BUT WHEN I REMIND HER OF THIS AND ADD THAT MAYBE IT'S TOO EARLY FOR ME, SHE TELLS ME IT'S NOT UP FOR DISCUSSION!

FOR A MONTH, THOSE OF US WHO WILL BE TAKING OUR COMMUNION THIS YEAR ASSEMBLE IN FRONT OF ST. FLORIAN'S CHURCH TO RECEIVE INSTRUCTION.

I'M IN THE LAST ROW BECAUSE I'M TALL; IT'S GREAT BEING BIG BUT I'LL BE ONE OF THE LAST TO COME FORWARD...

THE PRIEST TEACHES US THE SONGS FOR THE EVENT. WE ADVANCE SLOWLY IN THE COOL, DARK CHURCH.

WE REHEARSE THE CELEBRATION SO THAT ON THE DAY ITSELF THE MOMENT WILL BE EVEN MORE SOLEMN.

BUT SOME BOYS DON'T PAY ANY ATTENTION TO THE RULES AND FIGHT INSIDE THE CHURCH IN FRONT OF ALL THE SAINTS!

I DON'T THINK EVERYONE HAS THE REQUISITE MATURITY... EVEN IF THEY ARE THE RIGHT AGE.

I DON'T HAVE MY COMMUNION DRESS YET, I JUST HAVE A KIND OF WHITE HOOD IN CASE IT'S COLD. IT WAS KNIT WITH WOOL THAT MY COUSIN JANUSZ BROUGHT BACK FROM FRANCE.

BUT THE DRESS IS MORE IMPORTANT AND IT'S MISSING. I CAN'T TAKE MY FIRST COMMUNION WEARING ONLY MY HOOD.

THERE'S ONLY ONE STORE IN MY CITY THAT SELLS THEM. ACTUALLY, IT MOSTLY SELLS WEDDING DRESSES.

BECAUSE I'M TALL AND THIN, IT'S NOT EASY TO FIND CLOTHES FOR ME. IT'S ONE OF MY MOM'S BIG PREOCCUPATIONS.

WHY AREN'T YOU LIKE OTHER GIRLS?

LIKE MONIKA FOR EXAMPLE!

WHY DON'T YOU EAT?

WHAT A BAG OF BONES YOU ARE!!

SOMETIMES I TELL MYSELF THAT IF I WERE MONIKA SHE'D SAY:

WHY AREN'T YOU LIKE OTHER GIRLS?

LIKE MARZI, FOR EXAMPLE?

WHY DO YOU EAT SO MUCH?

WHAT A GREEDY PIG YOU ARE!!

FINALLY, ONE SATURDAY, MY MOM COMES BACK FROM THE MARKET WITH A WOMAN. I'M STILL IN MY PAJAMAS AND IT MAKES ME UNCOMFORTABLE TO HAVE THIS STRANGER START EXCLAIMING EXUBERANTLY WHILE LOOKING ME OVER!

OOOOH! SHE'S JUST LIKE MY DAUGHTER!!

THE DRESS WILL FIT HER PERFECTLY. IF YOU'D LIKE, I CAN GO GET IT RIGHT NOW.

MY MOM HAD REVEALED HER PROBLEM AT THE BUTCHER'S...

HER COMMUNION'S IN LESS THAN THREE WEEKS AND MY DAUGHTER STILL DOESN'T HAVE A DRESS!

IT'S NOT MY FAULT SHE'S AS SKINNY AS A BEANPOLE!

NOTHING FITS HER BECAUSE SHE'S SO THIN. SHE DOESN'T EAT!

OH WHY AM I EVEN HERE?

THE WOMEN SMILE AND SYMPATHIZE. A FEW ARE MAYBE THINKING IT'S EASY TO GUESS WHO'S EATING MY SHARE...

THEY NOD THEIR HEADS, ADMITTING THAT IT'S TRUE, I'M A HARD CASE, BUT ONE WOMAN SAID SHE'D FACED THE SAME PROBLEM LAST YEAR AND THAT SHE'D EVENTUALLY FOUND A DRESS.

I COULD RESELL IT TO YOU, JUST FOR THIS YEAR...

MY YOUNGEST DAUGHTER'S TAKING HER COMMUNION NEXT YEAR...

SO I'LL NEED IT BACK.

MY MOM IS HAPPY, AND SO IS THE ENTIRE STORE. BEAUTIFUL THINGS CAN HAPPEN WHILE YOU'RE WAITING IN LINE!

THE SPECIAL "SKIN AND BONES" DRESS FITS ME VERY WELL. IT'S NOT VERY BEAUTIFUL, BUT I DON'T THINK OF MYSELF AS A BEAUTY...

WE SUIT EACH OTHER.

I TRY IT ON WITH MY NEW SHOES. ALL THE COMMUNICANTS HAVE THE SAME SHOES, ASIDE FROM A FEW GIRLS WITH WELL-OFF PARENTS WHO COULD BUY THEM IN ANOTHER CITY OR ABROAD.

ANYWAY, THE DRESS IS SO LONG IT COVERS MY FEET. BUT WHAT I'M WEARING ISN'T THE MOST IMPORTANT THING.

DURING THE CATECHISM, THE PRIEST TEACHES US HOW TO CONFESS BECAUSE OUR FIRST CONFESSION WILL TAKE PLACE THE SATURDAY BEFORE OUR FIRST COMMUNION.

PRAISE BE TO GOD, MY NAME IS TOMEK...

I'M SEVEN AND I GO TO MIKOŁAJ KOPERNIK SCHOOL NUMBER 7.

I HAVE OFFENDED GOD WITH THE FOLLOWING SINS...

AND WE LIST THEM...I THOUGHT CONFESSION WOULD BE ANONYMOUS...

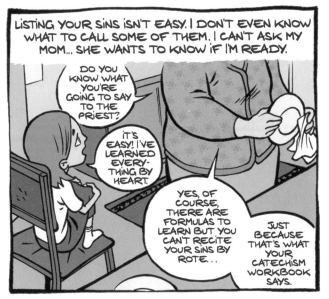

LISTING YOUR SINS ISN'T EASY. I DON'T EVEN KNOW WHAT TO CALL SOME OF THEM. I CAN'T ASK MY MOM... SHE WANTS TO KNOW IF I'M READY.

DO YOU KNOW WHAT YOU'RE GOING TO SAY TO THE PRIEST?

IT'S EASY! I'VE LEARNED EVERYTHING BY HEART.

YES, OF COURSE, THERE ARE FORMULAS TO LEARN BUT YOU CAN'T RECITE YOUR SINS BY ROTE...

JUST BECAUSE THAT'S WHAT YOUR CATECHISM WORKBOOK SAYS.

IT'S SOMETHING YOU HAVE TO FEEL IN YOUR HEART.

WORDS ALONE CAN'T EXPRESS RELIGION.

BELIEVING AND SPEAKING ARE TWO DIFFERENT THINGS. IT'S EASY TO TALK WITHOUT BELIEVING WHAT YOU'RE SAYING.

YOU MUST ALWAYS OPEN YOUR HEART TO GOD'S LOVE.

MY MOM RARELY SPENDS THIS MUCH TIME TALKING TO ME WITHOUT GETTING ANGRY. MY COMMUNION SEEMS VERY IMPORTANT TO HER. THANKS TO IT, I'M RISING IN HER ESTEEM. IF GOD WANTS ME, MAYBE SHE'LL ACCEPT ME TOO.

I DON'T WANT TO DISAPPOINT HER.

DO YOU HAVE A LOT OF SINS?

SEVEN-TEEN... AND YOU?

NINE!

MONIKA IS PROUD, SHE DOESN'T SIN MUCH.

DO YOU REMEMBER WHEN YOU TRAPPED ME IN THE ELEVATOR? THAT'S A SIN TOO, YOU KNOW... I WAS SCARED, YOU MADE ME CRY!

BUT IT WAS A JOKE!

THAT DOESN'T MEAN YOU DIDN'T MAKE ME SUFFER. IT'S A SIN, YOU DID HARM TO OTHERS!

FINE, I'LL WRITE IT IN...

SO NOW I HAVE TEN.

DO YOU THINK IT'S A SIN WHEN WE ANNOY PEOPLE BY RINGING THEIR DOORBELLS OR HOLDING UP THE ELEVATOR?

NO, I DON'T THINK SO, THEY'RE NOT SUFFERING!

YES, BUT THEY GET MAD AND COMPLAIN.

SO WHEN WE SHOUT INTO THE GARBAGE CHUTE THAT'D ALSO BE A SIN?!

MAYBE WE SHOULD COUNT IT... LOOK, I'VE GOT TWENTY NOW!

AND I'VE GOT THIR-TEEN!!

MAKE UP ANOTHER, THAT'S BAD LUCK!!

WAIT, I'M THINKING WHAT ELSE BAD YOU COULD'VE DONE...

I HAVE IT!!

WHAT IS IT?

I CAN'T SAY, IT'S PERSONAL.

COME ON!

DON'T PRESSURE ME!

DO YOU THINK GOD WILL FORGIVE US? TWENTY SINS IS A LOT...

IF YOU REPENT AND PROMISE TO NEVER DO THEM AGAIN, FOR SURE!

NEVER RING DOORBELLS AGAIN?!

DO YOU WANT HIM TO FORGIVE YOU OR NOT?

I DON'T KNOW...BUT MY MOM SAID YOU CAN REPEAT SINS...

YES, BUT OH, WHAT ARE WE GOING TO DO NOW?

I THINK WE JUST HAVE TO REPENT EVERY TIME...

HERE WE ARE, IT'S SATURDAY NIGHT. A LINE FORMS BESIDE EACH CONFESSIONAL... BUT THIS TIME NOT TO BUY ANYTHING.

MONIKA AND I CHOOSE A PRIEST WE DON'T KNOW. THAT WAY, HE WON'T REMEMBER US AND OUR SINS IF WE MEET HIM AGAIN.

THERE ARE A LOT OF GIRLS WEARING HAIR ROLLERS, THEY WANT TO HAVE BIG CURLS TOMORROW, SO THEY'RE HIDING THEM UNDER BABUSHKAS.

WE MAKE FUN OF THEM. MY MOM SIGNALS US FROM A DISTANCE THAT CHURCH IS NO PLACE FOR JOKING AROUND. ALL DISCONCERTED, WE WONDER IF WE SHOULD ADD ANOTHER SIN TO OUR LIST.

THANKFULLY MY MOM DIDN'T INSIST I PUT IN CURLERS TONIGHT TOO. I WOULD HAVE LOOKED A LITTLE RIDICULOUS BEFORE GOD... MONIKA GOES FIRST.

SHE DISCREETLY TAKES OUT THE LITTLE PIECE OF PAPER WHERE SHE WROTE EVERYTHING DOWN.

SHE'S QUICK, SHE'S ALREADY DONE. IT'S MY TURN. I LIST MY SINS IN MY HEAD, I MUSTN'T FORGET ANY OF THEM.

THE PRIEST IS VERY OLD AND REASSURING. HE SAYS GOD WILL FORGIVE ME. I JUST HAVE TO TRY TO BE KINDER TO HIM...

IT'S TRUE, SOMETIMES I'M VERY LAZY AND DON'T SAY MY PRAYERS BEFORE BED. I PROMISE TO BE BETTER.

IT'S OVER! I GO COLLECT MYSELF NEAR THE ALTAR WHERE MONIKA'S WAITING FOR ME.

SO? DID HE FORGIVE YOU?

YES, AND YOU?

MMM. DID YOU ASK ABOUT THE DOORBELLS?

I DIDN'T DARE...

NOW WE HAVE TO WAIT FOR OUR PARENTS. THEY HAVE A LOT TO SAY TO THE PRIEST. I WONDER WHAT SINS ADULTS CAN HAVE?

BACK AT HOME, EVERYONE SETS TO WORK PREPARING SUNDAY DINNER. WE HAVE A LOT OF GUESTS. SINCE SOME OF THEM LIVE IN THE COUNTRY AND DON'T HAVE A CAR, AND SINCE THE BUSES OFTEN DON'T RUN ON SUNDAYS, THEY CAME SATURDAY.

I'M VERY HAPPY THAT ALL THESE PEOPLE HAVE COME JUST FOR ME... AND THAT THERE'LL BE LOTS OF GOOD THINGS TO EAT!

WE CAN'T FIT EVERYONE IN OUR LITTLE APARTMENT. AUNT DZIDZIA AND UNCLE MIETEK HAVE TO SLEEP AT ANIA AND ANDRZEJ'S BECAUSE THEY DON'T HAVE A COMMUNION HAPPENING THIS YEAR.

EVERYONE ELSE WILL FIND SPACE WHERE THEY CAN.

IT'S EVEN WORSE AT MONIKA'S! THEIR APARTMENT IS MINUSCULE AND THEY HAVE TONS OF GUESTS. SO THEY DECIDED TO PUT MATTRESSES ON OUR BALCONY AND ON ANIA AND ANDRZEJ'S FOR PEOPLE TO SLEEP ON.

WE GIVE THEM PIERZYNA (A VERRRRY THICK QUILT THAT MY MOM PUTS ON MY BED WHEN I'M SICK SO THAT I SWEAT AND THE FEVER BREAKS QUICKLY). THAT WAY, THEY WON'T BE COLD!

THAT EVENING, MY COUSIN TERENIA PUTS CURLERS IN MY AND MONIKA'S HAIR. WE LAUGH A LOT.

YOU LOOK LIKE A COUPLE OF OLD GRANNIES!

YOU SHOULD BE RECEIVING THE LAST RITES INSTEAD OF YOUR FIRST COMMUNION!

PEOPLE ARE EVERYWHERE, CHATTING IN THE CORNERS, IT'S FESTIVE! BUT THE BATHROOM IS ALWAYS FULL!

THAT NIGHT, MY DAD SLEEPS IN MY BED WITH ME. UNCLE JASIEK (MY GODFATHER) AND AUNT MILA SLEEP IN MY PARENTS' BED, MY MOM IS ON "THE AMERICAN" (AN ARMCHAIR THAT PULLS OUT INTO A BED), TERENIA IS ON TWO ARMCHAIRS PUSHED TOGETHER AND DZIDZIA AND MIETEK ARE AT THE NEIGHBORS'...

THAT'S NOT COUNTING MONIKA'S GUESTS ON THE BALCONY.

IT FEELS LIKE I'M SLEEPING ON A BAG OF POTATOES WITH ALL THESE CURLERS IN MY HAIR.

IT'S LIKE THEY'RE TRYING TO BURROW INTO MY BRAIN!

ON SUNDAY MORNING, I FINISH GETTING READY AS THE LAST GUESTS ARRIVE... I'M PRETTY IN A SHEEP-Y KIND OF WAY.

I FEEL PROUD GOING TO CHURCH SURROUNDED BY MY WHOLE FAMILY.

MASS GOES QUICKLY, WE'RE ALL CONCENTRATING ON THE PRIEST'S WORDS. EVERYONE IS MOVED BY THIS SOLEMN MOMENT.

HE SAYS THAT COMMUNION SYMBOLIZES OUR BELONGING TO GOD'S FAMILY. WE REJOIN IT BY ACCEPTING JESUS INTO OUR HEARTS.

HE ENTERS US THROUGH OUR MOUTHS IN THE FORM OF A LITTLE ROUND WAFER (OPŁATEK) THAT WE INGEST DURING THE CEREMONY.

IT DOESN'T TASTE LIKE ANYTHING BUT MY HEART STILL BEATS VERY HARD. SO HARD I'M SURE JESUS MADE HIS WAY IN.

THE WHOLE CHURCH VIBRATES WITH THE SOUND OF THE ORGANS. WE ARE IN A ROCKET RISING TO HEAVEN. OVERCOME WITH EMOTION, A GRANDMOTHER FAINTS. A FEW PEOPLE NEARBY CARRY HER OUTSIDE TO REVIVE HER.

THE PRIEST IS HAPPY WITH US. AFTER MASS, WE TAKE PHOTOS NEXT TO THE CHURCH AND GO HOME TO EAT LUNCH... AND OPEN PRESENTS!

MY GODMOTHER GIVES ME A THIN GOLD CHAIN AND I GET A LOT OF BOOKS.

AN ILLUS-TRATED BIBLE FOR CHILDREN

THE BIBLE (STANDARD)

GRIMM'S FAIRY TALES!

THE GOSPELS

THE OLD AND NEW TESTA-MENTS

AND AN ENCYCLOPEDIA THAT'S SO HEAVY I CAN BARELY LIFT IT...

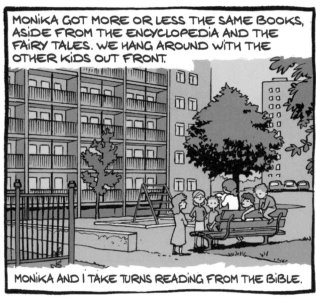

MONIKA GOT MORE OR LESS THE SAME BOOKS, ASIDE FROM THE ENCYCLOPEDIA AND THE FAIRY TALES. WE HANG AROUND WITH THE OTHER KIDS OUT FRONT.

MONIKA AND I TAKE TURNS READING FROM THE BIBLE.

IN OUR CATECHISM COURSE, THE PRIEST TOLD US THAT IF WE CONFESSED EVERY FIRST FRIDAY OF THE MONTH FOR NINE MONTHS, OUR SINS WOULD BE COMPLETELY ABSOLVED.

BUT IF WE WANTED TO, WE COULD OFFER THIS ABSOLUTION TO ANOTHER PERSON, LIVING OR DEAD! BUT IF THEY'RE DEAD, HOW CAN WE KNOW WHETHER OR NOT THEY'VE GONE TO HEAVEN?

IF THEY'RE ALREADY THERE AND I GIVE THEM MY ABSOLUTION, IT'LL BE WASTED... AND IF I GIVE IT TO SOMEONE ALIVE WHO TURNS MEAN OR HURTS PEOPLE, THEY'LL GET TO GO TO HEAVEN ANYWAY, IN SPITE OF THEIR SINS?!

AND IF I KEEP ON RINGING PEOPLE'S DOORBELLS AS A PRANK AND THEN CONFESS FOR NINE MONTHS, CAN I KEEP DOING IT?

I WOULD LIKE JESUS TO APPEAR. MAYBE HE NEEDS SOME TIME TO SETTLE IN AND GET TO KNOW ME...

I STILL HOPE MY QUESTIONS WILL BE ANSWERED.

THERE ARE SO MANY THINGS I DON'T UNDERSTAND ABOUT RELIGION...

BUT MY FIRST COMMUNION DID MAKE ME FEEL MORE IMPORTANT BEFORE THE ALTAR OF GOD, BEFORE HIM, AS IF MY LIFE WAS MORE SIGNIFICANT.

WHAT'S BRED IN THE BONES COMES OUT IN THE FLESH

I'M GOING TO KILL MY MOM ONE OF THESE DAYS...

WE'RE SPENDING THE WEEKEND WITH HER FAMILY IN KAMIEŃ. SHE DRESSED ME IN A PRETTY WHITE OUTFIT BEFORE CHURCH.

MY AUNT SUGGESTED I COME FEED THE ANIMALS WITH HER WHILE THE OTHERS WERE GETTING READY.

I LOVE TO WALK AROUND THE STABLE, WHERE MY COUSIN'S RABBITS AND MY UNCLE'S HORSE LIVE.

I GO CLOSE TO THE HORSE. HE'S BIG! SO BIG I DON'T DARE TOUCH HIM. I JUST LOOK AT HIM ADMIRINGLY.

DON'T GET DIRTY... THIS PLACE IS A MESS.

I HAVE TO CLEAN IT AFTER CHURCH.

SUDDENLY THE MARE TWITCHES AND STOMPS THE GROUND WITH HIS HOOF!

STEADY, BAŚKA

BUT IT'S TOO LATE...

SINCE THE GROUND IS COVERED WITH HIS MANURE, IT'S NOW SPLATTERED ALL OVER THE STABLE, AND MOSTLY ALL OVER ME BECAUSE I WAS REALLY VERY CLOSE. MY DAD AND AUNT ESCAPE UNSCATHED.

MY WHITE OUTFIT IS NOW BROWN AND SMELLS AWFUL!

I RUN OUTSIDE, SHAKING MYSELF FURIOUSLY AS I TRY TO DISLODGE THIS STINKY STUFF STICKING TO EVERYTHING--MY CLOTHES, MY HAIR, MY FACE, EVEN MY NOSE IS FULL OF IT.

WAAAH!

TO MAKE THE TRAGEDY PERFECT, MY MOM ARRIVES, LOOKING COMPLETELY STUNNED.

I TRY TO EXPLAIN, BUT IT'S LIKE THE WORDS COMING OUT OF MY MOUTH SMELL BAD TOO.

YOU ALWAYS FIND A REASON NOT TO GO TO CHURCH!

IT WASN'T ME, MOM, IT WAS THE HORSE...

DON'T BLAME THE HORSE!!

SHE DOESN'T LISTEN TO ME, NO ONE DEFENDS ME.

THERE I AM, IN THE MIDDLE OF THE YARD, COVERED IN THIS CRUST OF DUNG THAT, MIXED WITH MY TEARS, IN NOW RUNNING DOWN MY CHIN AND MY NECK AND INTO MY BLOUSE.

LOOK WHAT YOU'VE DONE TO YOUR BEAUTIFUL WHITE BERMUDA SHORTS!!

MY MOM COMES OVER AND STARTS SHAKING ME BY THE ARMS, THE CHICKENS LOOK AT ME WITH CURIOSITY.

I'M CRYING BECAUSE I STINK AND I'M SICK OF IT. I WANT TO GO CLEAN UP, BUT MY MOM INSISTS I STAY THERE, OUT IN THE OPEN AND COVERED IN EXCREMENT, TEARS, AND SHAME, TO TAKE IN HER SPEECH.

ACCORDING TO HER, THE DEVIL ALREADY HAS ME IN HIS CLUTCHES. NO MATTER WHERE I GO, I'LL NEVER BE NORMAL.

I SMELL SO STRONGLY, EVEN MY MOM CAN'T STAND BEING NEAR ME FOR LONG. ONLY THE FLIES STILL FIND ME APPEALING.

MY DAD FINALLY HOSES ME OFF, WHICH MAKES ME VERY HAPPY.

BECAUSE I DON'T HAVE ANY OTHER NICE CLOTHES, I PUT ON MY PAJAMAS AND INSTEAD OF GOING TO CHURCH, I STAY AT THE FARM ALL ALONE AND PLAY IN THE YARD.

...IT'S NOT SO BAD!

MY MOM TAKES WHAT COMFORT SHE CAN FROM CHURCH.

DOES SHE PRAY FOR MY SOUL OR HERS?

BAD GRASS

MY PARENTS HAVE A GARDEN NOT TOO FAR AWAY, IN THE VILLAGE WHERE MY DAD WAS BORN AND WHERE MY AUNT AND MY GRANDMOTHER LIVE.

WE GO THERE AT LEAST ONCE A WEEK IN OUR LITTLE FIAT.

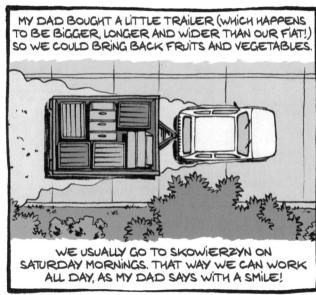

MY DAD BOUGHT A LITTLE TRAILER (WHICH HAPPENS TO BE BIGGER, LONGER AND WIDER THAN OUR FIAT!) SO WE COULD BRING BACK FRUITS AND VEGETABLES.

WE USUALLY GO TO SKOWIERZYN ON SATURDAY MORNINGS. THAT WAY WE CAN WORK ALL DAY, AS MY DAD SAYS WITH A SMILE!

WE DON'T WASTE ANY TIME... I DON'T ALWAYS WANT TO GO BECAUSE ALL WE DO IS WORK AND WORK.

DESPITE ALL THE FACES I MAKE, I STILL HAVE TO GO WITH THEM.

WE USUALLY STOP BY AUNT NIUSIA'S AS SOON AS WE GET THERE. WHILE MY PARENTS DRINK COFFEE, I PLAY OUTSIDE WITH ATOS, THE DOG WHO'S TIED UP.

I BRING HIM WATER THAT I STEAL FROM THE CHICKENS (VERY QUIETLY SO THE ROOSTER WON'T SEE ME). I'M NOT ALLOWED TO GO NEAR THE WELL BY MYSELF.

MY MOM DOESN'T LIKE ATOS. SHE SAYS HE'LL BITE ME AND GET ME DIRTY OR KNOCK ME OVER. IT'S TRUE I'M A LITTLE DIRTY AFTERWARDS. HE ALWAYS LICKS MY CHEEKS AND MY HAIR.

BLEEAH!

BUT HE'S SO HAPPY. THERE ARE SO FEW PEOPLE WHO SHOW HIM ANY AFFECTION.

SOMETIMES, WHEN WE HAVE MORE TIME AT MY AUNT'S, I PLAY WITH THE NEIGHBORS' KIDS. BUT NO ONE CAN PLAY WITH ME ON SATURDAYS BECAUSE IN THE COUNTRY, EVERYONE HAS FIELDS...

AND EVERYONE WORKS IN THEM, INCLUDING THE KIDS!

I USE THE GATE AS MY SWING (IT OPENS ALL BY ITSELF) AND WATCH THE ROAD.

HORSE-DRAWN CARTS GO BY. PEOPLE ARE HEADING OUT TO WORK THEIR LAND, THEIR KIDS ARE SITTING THERE SULKING.

MOM, MARZI'S HERE! CAN WE GO PLAY WITH HER?

NO, SHE'S COME TO HELP HER PARENTS, SHE WON'T BE ABLE TO PLAY WITH YOU.

YOU'LL SEE EACH OTHER NEXT TIME!

PFFF! WE HEAD TO OUR GARDEN TOO...

IT'S MORE LIKE AN ORCHARD BECAUSE IT'S REALLY BIG, WITH VEGETABLES IN THE GROUND AND FRUIT IN THE AIR. I PREFER TO PICK THE FRUIT.

I LOVE CLIMBING THE TREES, IT'S THE FIRST THING I DO WHEN WE GET THERE.

I HAVE A FAVORITE. IT'S THE WALNUT TREE ON THE EDGE OF THE PROPERTY. IT'S VERY LEAFY AND NO ONE CAN SEE ME IN IT.

I CAN SPEND HOURS THERE SINGING, TALKING TO MYSELF, MAKING UP STORIES OR WATCHING THE HORSES AND COWS IN THE PASTURE NEXT DOOR.

AS SOON AS MY PARENTS FORGET ABOUT ME, I GO LOOK AT THEM UP CLOSE, THOUGH I STAY FAR ENOUGH AWAY NOT TO SCARE THEM...

YOU STAY SO FAR AWAY FROM THOSE ANIMALS. I BET YOU CAN'T TELL HORSES FROM COWS.

BUT IT DOESN'T WORK LIKE THAT, I NEVER GET CONFUSED. EVEN THOUGH COWS SCARE ME LESS, I'M MORE FASCINATED BY HORSES.

IF THEY SEE YOU CROUCHED DOWN, THEY'LL THINK YOU'RE A CHICKEN.

AND HORSES DON'T LIKE CHICKENS VERY MUCH!

MY DAD IS TRYING TO MAKE THE HORSES SEEM SCARY TO ME BECAUSE MY MOM ASKED HIM TO GET ME OUT OF THE PASTURE. HE DOESN'T LIKE FORCING ME TO DO SOMETHING, SO HE MAKES ME THINK IT'S MY IDEA.

GET OFF YOUR THRONE, PRINCESS! THERE ARE VEGETABLES TO WEED...

SHE SAYS I'M A PARASITE, THAT I DON'T DO ANYTHING. I LOOK AT THE ANIMALS, I COUNT THE NUTS ON MY TREE, THAT'S NOT NOTHING! TO MAKE HER HAPPY, I'M GOING TO DO SOME WEEDING.

I WORK ON THE ONIONS AND THE CARROTS. MY MOM BATTLES THE POTATOES WHILE MY DAD MOWS THE GRASS AROUND THE TREES.

HE USES A SCYTHE. I LIKE WATCHING HIM AT IT, IT LOOKS SO EFFORTLESS.

COULD YOU TEACH ME TO CUT WITH THE SCYTHE?

BUT THE SCYTHE IS BIGGER THAN YOU ARE!

THAT'S IT, SHE'S ALREADY TIRED OF HELPING ME!

I DON'T MIND...

I'M LOOKING FOR A MORE EXCITING JOB, THAT'S ALL!

HE LETS ME STRUGGLE FOR A WHILE. SCYTHING IS HARD WORK. I CAN BARELY MOVE IT, IT FEELS MORE LIKE IT'S CONTROLLING ME.

WHEW!

PANT!

SOME OTHER TIME!

YOU NEED TO EAT A LOT OF BREAD...

I GO BACK TO THE WEEDS, FEELING BAFFLED...

I WATCH THE LITTLE CREATURES THAT LIVE ON THE GROUND. ESPECIALLY THE ANTS. THERE ARE A LOT IN SOME PLACES. THEY DON'T STOP MOVING.

OTHER PLACES THERE'S ONLY ONE ANT, WHO MUST BE LOST.

I PUT IT ON MY PALM AND BRING IT BACK TO ITS FAMILY. IT'S CARRYING A PIECE OF LEAF BIGGER THAN ITSELF! THE LEAF MIGHT EVEN BE HEAVIER TOO.

A LITTLE LIKE ME WITH MY DAD'S SCYTHE.

IN THE WORLD OF ANTS, I FEEL LIKE A BENEVOLENT GOD WHO WATCHES OVER THEM. I REUNITE THEM. I STUDY THEM FROM ABOVE WITHOUT THEIR SEEING ME.

EVERY SO OFTEN, I PLACE OBSTACLES IN THEIR WAY: A LITTLE TWIG, A STONE. I WATCH HOW THEY HANDLE IT.

USUALLY, THEY CHANGE THEIR ROUTE UNRUFFLED BY THIS APPARITION.

WHEN I TOUCH ONE GENTLY WITH MY FINGER, IT PANICS. IT SENSES MY INTRUSION INTO ITS WORLD AND GETS SCARED. I DON'T THINK IT'S THE SAME WITH HUMANS AND GOD.

AT LEAST, I'D LIKE TO SEE GOD! I WOULDN'T BE SCARED. I'M SURE HE'S AN OLD MAN WHO LOOKS LIKE SANTA CLAUS, EXCEPT NOT WEARING RED.

I HAVE A HARD TIME WRAPPING MY HEAD AROUND HOW HE CAN COMMAND THE ENTIRE UNIVERSE OR SEE EVERYONE AT THE SAME TIME.

HE SEES EVERY MISTAKE I MAKE, HE SEES EVERY CHILD'S EVERY MISTAKE (I HOPE I'M NOT THE ONLY ONE WHO MAKES THEM!), IT'S INCREDIBLE!

MY MOM SAYS HE'S ALWAYS WATCHING ME, THAT HE KNOWS EVERYTHING ABOUT ME...I WONDER WHERE HE MIGHT BE HIDDEN, WHAT SIDE HE'S WATCHING ME FROM. DOES HE HEAR EVERYTHING I SAY?

OH! DOES HE SEE ME WHEN I'M ON THE TOILET? I'M EMBARRASSED JUST THINKING ABOUT IT! NEXT TIME, I'LL TURN OUT THE LIGHTS SO HE DOESN'T SEE ME. BUT MY MOM SAYS HE EVEN KNOWS WHAT I'M THINKING!!

DOES HE GO TO THE BATHROOM TOO? DOES HE TAKE BATHS? AND WHERE ARE HIS PARENTS?

IF IT SO HAPPENS THAT GOD IS JUST THERE TO PUNISH US, WE SHOULD BE SCARED OF HIM. AT LEAST, EVERYONE WHO MAKES MISTAKES SHOULD BE SCARED AT THE THOUGHT OF PUNISHMENT.

WHEN THERE'S A STORM, MOM SAYS IT'S THE VIRGIN MARY THUNDERING BECAUSE WE CHILDREN HAVEN'T BEEN GOOD. THEN I TRY TO REMEMBER EVERYTHING I MIGHT HAVE DONE BAD.

AND I TREMBLE, I LOCK MYSELF IN THE BATHROOM WHERE THERE'S NO WINDOW. I CAN'T SEE THE LIGHTNING AND IF I RUN THE WATER, I CAN BLOCK OUT THE THUNDER.

I EXPERIMENT ON THE ANTS BY SIMULATING RAIN AND THUNDER, BUT THEY DON'T REACT. THEY CONTINUE ON AS THOUGH NOTHING WERE HAPPENING AND MY MOM JUST GIVES ME A STRANGE LOOK.

WHAT'RE YOU WATERING?! THE GRASS?!

THAT WATER'S FOR THE TOMATOES! WHERE'S YOUR HEAD?!

AND WHY ARE YOU SHOUTING LIKE THAT?!

THE PEOPLE ON BICYCLES RIDE BY SPORTING BIG SMILES AND I'M AFRAID EVERYONE THINKS I'M CRAZY!

LATE IN THE AFTERNOON, WE FILL THE CRATES WITH POTATOES, BEANS, AND BASKETS OF RASPBERRIES, RED CURRANTS, PLUMS, APPLES, AND CHERRIES, DEPENDING ON THE SEASON.

THEN WE LOAD UP THE TRAILER. IT'S USUALLY FULL AND OUR POOR CAR HAS A HARD TIME PULLING THE WEIGHT.

WHEN THERE'S TOO MUCH, MY FATHER PUTS SOME OF IT ON MY SEAT AND I GET SQUISHED IN BETWEEN. HE LAYS FLOWERS FROM THE GARDEN ON THE WINDOW SHELF, WHICH MEANS HE CAN'T SEE ANYTHING IN HIS REAR-VIEW MIRROR...

I HAVE TO TURN AROUND TO CHECK THAT THE TRAILER IS STILL THERE AND HOLDING OUT. WHICH ISN'T THAT EASY WHEN YOU'RE TRAPPED BETWEEN TWO ENORMOUS CRATES OF POTATOES!

THIS IS HOW WE RETURN TO OUR 10-STORY BUILDING IN THE CITY. WE PARK OUT FRONT TO UNLOAD.

PASSERS-BY LOOK ON WITH AMUSEMENT. I WANT IT TO GO FASTER. BUT IT'S IMPOSSIBLE BECAUSE THERE ARE ONLY THREE OF US AND I CAN'T CARRY ANYTHING TOO HEAVY.

SO WE TAKE UP A LOT OF THE HALLWAY. MY DAD GOES TO MOVE THE CAR WHILE MY MOM AND I SHIFT THIS HODGEPODGE TO IN FRONT OF THE ELEVATOR. IT TAKES AT LEAST TEN TRIPS.

WHILE MY PARENTS TAKE A LOAD UP TO THE FIFTH FLOOR, I STAY BEHIND TO KEEP AN EYE ON OUR LITTLE HARVEST.

WHAT BEAUTI-
FUL POTATOES!
ARE THEY
FOR SALE?

YES...
YOU CAN
COME BY
OUR PLACE
FOR THEM.

I DON'T POSSESS A SENSE OF SALESMANSHIP. I GET ANNOYED, WHY ARE MY PARENTS TAKING SO LONG? MY FATHER MUST HAVE KNOCKED ON ALL THE NEIGHBORS' DOORS TO LET THEM KNOW THEY COULD COME BUY FRESH PRODUCE FROM THE COUNTRY.

A CROWD HAS ALREADY FORMED BY THE TIME I GET UP TO THE APARTMENT. I CAN'T EVEN MAKE IT TO THE BATHROOM TO PEE. BUT I'D HAVE A HARD TIME GOING WITH ALL THIS ACTIVITY ANYWAY...

AH! MARZI!
COULD YOU
WEIGH THE
VEGETABLES?

EVEN THOUGH IT SOUNDS LIKE A QUESTION, IT ISN'T. I GET RIGHT TO IT. IN FACT, I REALLY LIKE DOING IT!

TWO KILOS FOR
MADAM ZOSIA!
JUST POTATOES?
NO APPLES?

GET A LOAD OF
THESE APPLES, THEY
LOOK SO GOOD IT
WOULD BE A SIN NOT
TO TAKE A FEW!!

COME ON,
TASTE ONE.
PESTICIDE-
FREE, ALL
NATURAL!

EVERYONE LAUGHS, MY FATHER KNOWS HOW TO TALK TO PEOPLE. HE KNOWS HOW TO DRAW PEOPLE IN, BUT HE'S NOT A LIAR. IT'S TRUE THAT OUR APPLES ARE DELICIOUS, AND MRS. ZOSIA LETS HERSELF BE TEMPTED.

THE PEARS GO TOO, AND THE RASPBERRIES FOR MAKING JAM. NO ONE LEAVES WITH EMPTY HANDS. AND CUCUMBERS OF COURSE, AND DILL, FOR PICKLING, AND CABBAGE FOR STUFFING, SO DELICIOUS!

WE EVEN HAVE MILK, WHICH AUNT NIUSIA GAVE US TO SELL. OUR LITTLE APARTMENT IS SOMETHING OF A BLACK MARKET. MY PARENTS' PRICES ARE SIGNIFICANTLY LOWER.

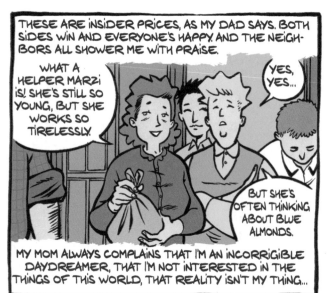

THESE ARE INSIDER PRICES, AS MY DAD SAYS. BOTH SIDES WIN AND EVERYONE'S HAPPY. AND THE NEIGH-BORS ALL SHOWER ME WITH PRAISE.

WHAT A
HELPER MARZI
IS! SHE'S STILL SO
YOUNG, BUT SHE
WORKS SO
TIRELESSLY.

YES,
YES...

BUT SHE'S
OFTEN THINKING
ABOUT BLUE
ALMONDS.

MY MOM ALWAYS COMPLAINS THAT I'M AN INCORRIGIBLE DAYDREAMER, THAT I'M NOT INTERESTED IN THE THINGS OF THIS WORLD, THAT REALITY ISN'T MY THING...

BUT I KNOW SHE'S WRONG. I OBSERVE THE LITTLE CREATURES THAT LIVE IN THE GRASS, I MAKE MUD CAKES, I TEND TO THE GARDEN WHEN NECESSARY. THESE THINGS ARE ALL TIED TO THE EARTH.

AND IF I LIKE CLIMBING TREES IT'S NOT SO I CAN DISTANCE MYSELF FROM THE EARTH, BUT SO I CAN GET A BETTER VIEW OF LIFE UNFOLDING THERE.

MONEY DOES SMELL (GOOD)

THERE'S A GIRL NAMED JUSTYNA IN MY CLASS. HER DAD LIVES IN THE UNITED STATES AND SENDS HER LOTS OF VERY PRETTY THINGS.

SHE HAS BRIGHTLY COLORED CLOTHES THAT ARE MORE BEAUTIFUL THAN ANYTHING THE REST OF US WEARS.. AND SHE'S MORE BEAUTIFUL THAN WE ARE TOO...

ALL THE TEACHERS LOVE HER, ONE OF THEM EVEN BECAME FRIENDS WITH HER MOM. NOW SHE WEARS MAKE-UP AND PAINTS HER NAILS.

NO ONE CALLS HER JUSTYNA, BUT JUSTYSIA, WHICH IS A VERY AFFECTIONATE NICKNAME. SHE'S THE APPLE OF OUR SCHOOL'S EYE.

EVEN HER PAJAMAS ARE PRETTY. THEY HAVE LITTLE BEARS ON THEM.

I DON'T KNOW HER VERY WELL BECAUSE SHE DOESN'T PLAY WITH ME. SHE SEEMS DELICATE AND FRAGILE. SHE'S AN ANGEL WRAPPED IN AMERICAN SCENTS, UNLIKE ME WHO USES MY FAMILY'S NETTLE SHAMPOO. IT GIVES ME DANDRUFF!

MY FAVORITE THINGS OF HERS ARE HER ELASTICS. THEY'RE THICK AND BRIGHTLY COLORED. AND EVEN THOUGH THEY'RE A LITTLE HIDDEN IN HER SUMPTU-OUSLY CURLY HAIR, YOU NOTICE THEM RIGHT AWAY.

IT'S LIKE A BUTTERFLY'S LIVING IN HER HAIR.

MY ELASTICS ARE MADE BY MY DAD. THEY'RE NOT BEAUTIFUL AND THEY PULL ON MY HAIR AND ALWAYS TAKE A FEW HAIRS WITH THEM WHEN THEY COME OFF.

TO MAKE THEM, HE CUTS OFF LITTLE PIECES OF HIS USED BICYCLE'S INNER TUBE... IT'S RUSTIC.

BUT I'M HAPPY HE MAKES THEM FOR ME, I'M ALWAYS HAPPY TO GET SOMETHING FROM HIM.

GIFTS ARE SO RARE THAT WHENEVER I GET ONE, I CHERISH IT, NO MATTER WHAT IT IS.

ONCE A YEAR THERE'S A HOLIDAY WHERE WE ALL DRESS UP AT SCHOOL.

SINCE MY PARENTS DON'T HAVE A LOT OF MONEY, I WEAR THE SAME FOLK DANCE COSTUME EVERY YEAR.

IT CAME FROM ONE OF MY MOM'S SISTERS, IT WAS HER DAUGHTER'S. I'D BE VERY EMBARRASSED IF I WERE THE ONLY ONE WEARING SUCH A THING...

BUT ALL THE GIRLS WHOSE PARENTS DON'T HAVE MUCH MONEY WEAR MORE OR LESS THE SAME THING ON THIS HOLIDAY...

ONLY JUSTYNA IS DRESSED UP AS A REAL PRINCESS. SHE SPORTS A BEAUTIFUL CROWN ON HER HEAD.

WHILE I WEAR A SORT OF HOMEMADE CREPE PAPER HAT WITH SOME BADLY CUT FLOWERS PASTED ON.

IT'S NOT SO BAD BECAUSE MONIKA, ZOSIA AND KINGA WEAR HATS JUST LIKE MINE AND WE CAN'T STOP LAUGHING AT EACH OTHER!

SOME BOYS ARE DRESSED UP AS COWBOYS. OTHERS LOOK MORE LIKE OUR DANCE PARTNERS.

BUT EVEN THEY SEEM ENCHANTED BY JUSTYNA. SHE'S ALWAYS SURROUNDED BY BOYS LOOKING AT HER ADORINGLY, WITH THEIR MOUTHS OPEN... NO ONE LOOKS OVER AT US.

HOW'S EVERY-THING?

ARE YOU THIRSTY?

IS YOUR MOTHER COMING EARLY TODAY?

THE TEACHERS, TOO, WORRY ONLY ABOUT HER. SHE'S THE ONLY ONE WHO'S OFFERED A SECOND PIECE OF CAKE!! AND SHE DOESN'T EVEN WANT IT...

I ENVY HER BECAUSE I WISH MY PARENTS HAD MORE MONEY, I'M SURE IT WOULD EASE A LOT OF OUR WOR-RIES... BUT I WOULDN'T WANT MY DAD TO GO TO THE UNITED STATES.

IT'S VERY FAR AWAY! I'D RATHER WE BE TOGETHER, I'D BE SAD TO HAVE MONEY INSTEAD OF MY DAD.

I'VE ALWAYS WANTED A DOG. SINCE I DON'T HAVE ANY BROTHERS OR SISTERS, I'D AT LEAST LIKE A DOG TO KEEP ME COMPANY.

EVEN THOUGH MY RABBIT IS REALLY NICE, HE'S NOT ENOUGH. IF I DON'T MOVE HIM, HE DOESN'T MOVE. I CAN'T PRETEND ANYMORE!

SO, MY PARENTS GOT ME...

A GUINEA PIG!

SHE (IT'S A GIRL) IS NAMED PEREŁKA. WHICH MEANS LITTLE PEARL IN POLISH.

SHE'S NOT EXACTLY A DOG, BUT SHE'S VERY BEAUTIFUL AND I LOVE HER A LOT.

MY DAD SETS HER UP IN A LITTLE WOODEN CAGE HE MADE.

MY PARENTS THINK SHE SMELLS TOO MUCH TO BE KEPT IN MY ROOM, SO SHE STAYS IN THE KITCHEN.

BUT I PLAY WITH HER ALL THE TIME AND LET HER ROAM ALL OVER THE APARTMENT.

SHE'S NOT USUALLY ALLOWED. EXCEPT WHEN MY PARENTS ARE AWAY, THEN SHE CAN DO ANYTHING!

WHAT GIVES OUR GAMES AWAY IS THE LITTLE POOPS LINED UP (LIKE LITTLE BLACK PEARLS) THAT PEREŁKA PRODUCES REGULARLY AND REALLY EVERYWHERE.

OHHH! NO! YOU LET YOUR PIG OUT AGAIN!

... AND I'M THE ONE WHO GETS IT!

THE WORST IS WHEN PEREŁKA LEAVES HER LITTLE POOPS ON THE LIVING ROOM RUG BECAUSE IT'S VERY DARK AND WE TEND TO SQUISH THEM WITH OUR SHOES.

ARGHH!!

IT'S LIKE BEING ON THE GRASS OUT FRONT!

SQUISH!

SQUISH!

YOU HAVE TO WASH THEM OFF AND THE RUG TOO.

SOMETIMES YOU'RE ONLY WEARING SOCKS...

YUCK!

SQUISH!

AND THEY'RE VERY SOFT...

IT'S REALLY EMBARRASSING WHEN IT HAPPENS TO GUESTS.

SQUISH!
OOPS! I THINK I STEPPED ON SOME- THING?!

MARZI!

PEREŁKA GROWS QUICKLY... AND MOSTLY GROWS FAT.

SHE'S A LITTLE BORING. SHE DOESN'T DO MUCH BESIDES EAT AND RELIEVE HERSELF.

EVERY SO OFTEN SHE RUNS AROUND LIKE CRAZY, SQUEALING.

EEEK!

EEEK!

EEEK!

THOUGH EVER SINCE SHE GOT PLUMP, SHE HASN'T RUN THAT MUCH.

ONCE IN AWHILE I PINCH HER (GENTLY) TO GET A REACTION. SHE'LL GIVE A SMALL JUMP AND IF I HOLD OUT MY FINGER, SHE'LL BITE, BUT THAT'S IT.

SZKRUT

SHE DEFINITELY EATS TOO MUCH.

NOT ONLY DOES SHE DINE ON OUR LEFT-OVERS, BUT ON OUR NEIGHBORS' TOO.

THIS IS FOR PEREŁKA...

SOMEBODY BRINGS SOMETHING FOR HER EVERY DAY.

WHEN I GO INTO THE KITCHEN IN THE MORNING, SHE GETS UP ON HER HIND LEGS AND CALLS ME.

EEK EEK

I CAN'T RESIST, I FEED HER, EVEN THOUGH WHAT SHE NEEDS IS A DIET. THESE DAYS, SHE'S WIDER THAN SHE IS LONG.

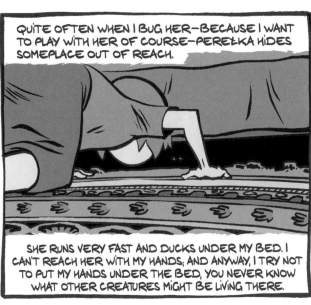

QUITE OFTEN WHEN I BUG HER—BECAUSE I WANT TO PLAY WITH HER OF COURSE—PEREŁKA HIDES SOMEPLACE OUT OF REACH.

SHE RUNS VERY FAST AND DUCKS UNDER MY BED. I CAN'T REACH HER WITH MY HANDS, AND ANYWAY, I TRY NOT TO PUT MY HANDS UNDER THE BED, YOU NEVER KNOW WHAT OTHER CREATURES MIGHT BE LIVING THERE.

MY MOM IS ANNOYED, BUT SHE WANTS TO HELP. HER CHUBBY HANDS DON'T FIT UNDER THE BED, WHICH IS WHY I HIDE THINGS FROM HER THERE.

SO SHE GRABS THE RULER AND TRIES TO CHASE HER OUT.

UNFORTUNATELY, THIS TIME SHE DISLODGES A BIT OF EGG WHITE THAT'S BEEN THERE FOR AGES... SINCE IT'S TURNED COMPLETELY GREEN, SHE DOESN'T RECOGNIZE IT, LUCKILY FOR ME!

FINALLY, ONCE MY MOM HAS HARASSED HER ENOUGH, PEREŁKA COMES OUT FROM UNDER THE BED.

SHE RUNS TO THE LIVING ROOM AND TAKES REFUGE BEHIND A FLOWER POT, WHERE I TRAP HER EASILY. ALL WORKED UP, SHE REWARDS ME WITH A SALVO OF LITTLE POOPS...

PBBT PBBT

THIS ANIMAL FILLS ME WITH DESPAIR.

I MADE HER A LITTLE HOUSE, WHICH I PUT IN HER CAGE. IT'S A BOX MADE OF POSTCARDS.

I CHOSE THE PRETTIEST ONES, THE ONES FROM OTHER COUNTRIES. MY UNCLE ZYGMUNT FROM WARSZAWA, WHO TRAVELS A LOT, SENT THEM FROM LISBON AND ALGERIA.

I CUT A HOLE IN ONE TO MAKE AN ENTRANCE AND EVER SINCE I PUT IT IN, PERELKA WON'T COME OUT.

YOU SHOULD TAKE OUT THE POST-CARDS.

SHE'S MADE IT INTO HER TOILET!

THE PAPER IS DISINTEGRATING AND BEGINNING TO INFILTRATE THE APARTMENT. SOMETIMES YOU CAN SMELL MY LITTLE GUINEA PIG'S EXCREMENT MORE STRONGLY THAN MY MOM'S CULINARY EFFORTS. WE CAN'T EAT IN THE KITCHEN ANYMORE.

I REMOVE PERELKA FROM HER HOUSE. SHE'S VERY UNHAPPY!

I CAN'T SALVAGE ANY OF THE CARDS, THEY'RE SO WET AND STINKY. IT'S TOO BAD BECAUSE I REALLY LIKED THEM.

SHE'S ONCE AGAIN EXPOSED TO PUBLIC VIEW..

DON'T BE SCARED.

I'M TAKING YOU TO THE COUNTRY TOMORROW!

IN KAMIEŃ, SHE CAN GAMBOL IN THE FRESH AIR WITHOUT ANYONE GETTING UPSET ABOUT THE "TRACES" SHE LEAVES.

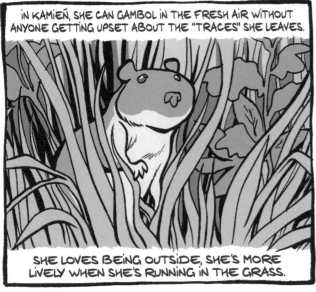

SHE LOVES BEING OUTSIDE, SHE'S MORE LIVELY WHEN SHE'S RUNNING IN THE GRASS.

I JUST HAVE TO BE CAREFUL SHE DOESN'T GET CAUGHT BY A CAT OR RUN AWAY.

THEY'RE DRAWN TO THIS THING THAT SQUEALS AND MOVES IN THE GRASS, BUT THEY DON'T DARE COME NEAR. THEY'VE KNOWN I DON'T LIKE THEM EVER SINCE THAT INCIDENT WITH MY UNCLE.

MAYBE THEY'RE SCARED OF ME TOO... IN ANY CASE, THEY CIRCLE ME AT A DISTANCE.

PEREŁKA IS PREOCCUPIED BY THE FRESH FOOD WHICH SHE CAN FIND FOR HERSELF FOR ONCE!

I GO TO A CATECHISM CLASS NEXT TO THE CHURCH ON MONDAY, AND WHEN I GET BACK...

PEREŁKA IS DEAD!

i PEER ANXIOUSLY INTO HER CAGE.

SHE'S LYING ON HER BACK WHICH SHE'S NEVER DONE. HER LITTLE PAWS ARE STILL AND LOOK LIKE WILTED FLOWERS.

I CRADLE HER IN MY HANDS. MY MOM SHOUTS THAT I SHOULDN'T, THAT IT'S UNHYGIENIC.

I HAVE JUST ENOUGH TIME TO TOUCH MY PEREŁKA WITH MY TEAR-STAINED CHEEK BEFORE MY MOM GRABS HER AWAY AND PUTS HER BACK IN HER CAGE.

SHE SAYS MY DAD WILL TAKE CARE OF IT WHEN HE COMES HOME FROM WORK. I SHUT MYSELF IN MY ROOM. I DON'T WANT ANYTHING.

I FEEL SO POWERLESS IT MAKES ME WANT TO SCREAM, TO CRY SO HARD I'LL BE ABLE TO DRIVE OUT THIS SADNESS INSIDE!

BUT CRYING DOESN'T COMFORT ME AT ALL. MY MOM IS MAKING PIEROGIS IN THE KITCHEN. PEREŁKA IS STRANDED IN HER CAGE. MY DAD IS LEAVING THE FACTORY.

LIFE GOES ON, DESPITE DEATH.

MY DAD IS SAD, BUT AS ALWAYS, HE TRIES TO PLAY IT DOWN.

SHE WASN'T OLD, BUT SHE ATE TOO MUCH...

IT'S NOT FAIR! I KNOW PEOPLE WHO EAT TOO MUCH AND THEY DON'T DIE!

SOMETIMES I EAT TOO MUCH CAKE AND EVEN THOUGH I DON'T FEEL GOOD, I DON'T DROP DEAD IMMEDIATELY!!

SHE MUST HAVE HAD TOO MUCH FRESH GRASS!

DON'T WORRY ABOUT IT, YOU KNOW, GUINEA PIGS DON'T LIVE AS LONG AS PEOPLE...

AND YOU DID SAY SHE WAS A LITTLE BORING...

MONOTONOUS, NOT BORING! SHE WAS MY PIG AND I LOVED HER!

I MISS HER! NOW I'M GOING TO BE ALL ALONE AGAIN.

MY DAD DISPOSES OF THE CAGE AND CLEANS THE CORNER OF THE KITCHEN, FINALLY CONCLUDING THAT AT LEAST THERE WON'T BE ANY MORE STINK. I GO BACK TO MY ROOM. MY RABBIT IS THERE. HE STARES AT ME.

YOU'RE THE ONLY ONE WHO'LL LAST FOREVER. YOU'LL NEVER LEAVE ME. FORGIVE ME, I ABANDONED YOU...

I TAKE HIM IN MY ARMS, I CRY WHILE WHISPERING MY SORROW INTO HIS EAR...

BUT MY RABBIT STAYS IMMOBILE. HE DOESN'T WANT TO PLAY WITH ME ANYMORE. I UNDERSTAND. I PUT HIM ON A TALL BOOKSHELF. FROM NOW ON, WE'LL ONLY LOOK AT EACH OTHER AND REMEMBER OUR TIME TOGETHER.

I'VE GROWN UP.

THIS TIME WE'RE GOING TO SKOWIERZYN BECAUSE AN AUNT FROM FRANCE IS COMING TO VISIT! I DON'T KNOW HER, IT'S HER FIRST VISIT SINCE I WAS BORN.

COME ON, COME ON!

HURRY UP!!

MY DAD HARDLY KNOWS HER, SHE WAS BORN IN FRANCE. HER MOM (A SISTER OF MY LATE GRANDFATHER) LEFT POLAND TO FIND WORK THERE.

WE GET READY AS THOUGH WE'RE ATTENDING A WEDDING. MY MOM WENT TO THE HAIRDRESSERS AND MY DAD PUTS ON HIS SUNDAY SUIT. ON HIS WIFE'S ORDERS, HE GIVES HIMSELF A CLOSE SHAVE.

MY MOM GAVE ME A PRETTY DRESS (UNFORTUNATELY PRETTY DOESN'T MEAN COMFORTABLE). IT'S A LITTLE TIGHT AND DIGS INTO MY NECK.

IN THE COUNTRY, EVERYONE'S EXCITED...

AUNT NIUSIA MADE SPECIAL CAKES AND PREPARED A DELICIOUS MEAL UNLIKE ANY SHE'D EVER MADE FOR US. MY UNCLE SWEPT THE YARD. HE GOT RID OF ALL THE MANURE THAT'D BEEN LYING THERE FOREVER.

MY AUNT IS NAMED HÉLÈNE. I DON'T KNOW FRENCH SO I WRITE IT: ELEN. SHE ARRIVED IN WARSZAWA ON A PLANE YESTERDAY. UNCLE ZYGMUNT MET HER THERE. THEY SHOULD BE ARRIVING TOGETHER BY CAR.

I'M NOT EVEN ALLOWED TO PLAY WITH ATOS WHILE WE WAIT. WE STAND ROOTED TO THE YARD, PRETENDING TO LAUGH AND TALK WHILE KEEPING OUR EARS PEELED FOR THE SOUND OF AN AUTOMOBILE.

MY DAD SMOKES A CIGARETTE, MY MOM COMPLAINS THAT HE'S SMOKING, ALWAYS SMOKING! AND THEN THERE THEY ARE!! AUNT NIUSIA ADJUSTS HER NEW HAIRDO, MY UNCLE EMERGES FROM THE CAR, ALONE...

WHAT HAPPENED? WHERE'S HÉLÈNE?!

SHE WANTED TO WALK THROUGH THE VILLAGE.

SHE'S VERY MOVED TO BE BACK...

WE HEAR DOGS BARKING. IT MUST BE HER.

AUNT HÉLÈNE ENTERS THE YARD. SHE'S TALL AND THIN. HER EYES FILL WITH TEARS WHEN SHE SEES US.

OH LA LA! IT'S SO BEAUTIFUL HERE!

IT HASN'T CHANGED!

SHE HAS A FUNNY WAY OF SPEAKING POLISH. SHE'S ALWAYS REPEATING "OH LA LA!"!! AND SHE SPEAKS VERY FORMALLY, EVEN WITH ME!

MY MOM AND NIUSIA GO INTO THE KITCHEN TO HEAT UP THE DISHES. I FOLLOW THEM (THEY INSISTED I HELP...). THEY'RE LAUGHING AND I LISTEN TO WHAT THEY'RE SAYING. ANYWAY, THEY'RE ACTING AS THOUGH I WEREN'T THERE.

DID YOU SEE HOW SHE'S DRESSED?

SHE SHOULD HAVE AT LEAST DONE HER HAIR!!

AUNT HÉLÈNE WEARS A FASHIONABLE PAIR OF PANTS (MY COUSIN CALLS THEM JEANS), HER HAIR IS DISHEVELED, SHE'S SPORTING BEAT-UP TENNIS SHOES AND A PLAIN T-SHIRT.

IT'S MY FIRST ENCOUNTER WITH FRANCE. WITH A FRENCH PERSON. I'M FASCINATED. EVEN THOUGH HER CLOTHES DON'T IMPRESS THE OTHERS, SHE SEEMS COMFORTABLE IN THEM.

I ENVY HER, WITH MY SCRATCHY DRESS THAT WON'T LET ME JUMP THE WAY I'D LIKE. MY AUNT SEEMS SO FREE WHILE I FEEL COMPLETELY TRAPPED BY FABRIC!

GRANDMOTHER JADZIA IS VERY MOVED. HÉLÈNE GIVES HER NEWS OF HER SISTER-IN-LAW WHOM SHE HASN'T SEEN FOR MANY YEARS. SHE ALSO SHOWS US PHOTOS.

MOM'S HOPING TO COME NEXT YEAR HER HEALTH PERMITTING...

AND HERE ARE MY DAUGHTERS!

WHEN SHE TALKS, IT SOUNDS LIKE SHE'S SINGING... SHE SPEAKS FRENCH WITH ZYGMUNT BECAUSE HE KNOWS THAT LANGUAGE.

FRENCH IS SO BEAUTIFUL! I LISTEN TO THEM, AWESTRUCK. MY FAMILY LAUGHS, THEY TALK ABOUT FRANCE, THE FROGEATERS. THAT'S WHAT WE CALL THEM IN POLAND: ŻABOJADY.

AH AH

THE FRENCH WOULD EAT ANYTHING THAT MOVES.

PFF! IT'S NOT ANY MORE DISGUSTING THAN EATING CHICKEN OR PIG. THEY'RE ALL LIVING BEINGS.

IT'S TIME TO GO. I SAY GOODBYE. O-VWAH (AU REVOIR), IT'S MY FIRST FRENCH WORD...

YOU ABSOLUTELY MUST COME TO FRANCE.

THERE ARE SO MANY THINGS TO SEE!

I'D LOVE TO COME...
AFTERWARDS, IN THE CAR, MY MOM SAYS THAT OUR AUNT INVITED US WITHOUT REALLY INVITING US.

I GET THE FEELING MY MOM DOESN'T REALLY LIKE HER.

OTHERWISE, WE CAN'T GO.

WHAT DOES SHE THINK?

YOU NEED A VISA, A WRITTEN INVITATION FROM SOMEONE WHO WILL HOST YOU, MORE PAPERWORK ON TOP OF THAT!!

IT'S NOT SO EASY FOR A POLE TO LEAVE POLAND!

AT THE LAST MINUTE, AUNT HÉLÈNE GAVE ME A LITTLE GIFT, A SOUVENIR FROM FRANCE, SHE SAID... PAPER TISSUES...

FOR THE FIRST TIME IN MY LIFE, I'M SPENDING FIFTEEN DAYS AWAY FROM MY PARENTS IN A BIG CITY: KRAKÓW. MY GRANDMOTHER JADZIA IS TAKING ME AND WE'LL STAY WITH ONE OF MY DAD'S SISTERS, MY AUNT DZIDZIA.

KRAKÓW IS QUITE FAR AWAY (130 MILES), WE'RE GOING ON A BUS AND THE TRIP WILL TAKE OVER FIVE HOURS. SO MY MOM FIXED US A SNACK AND A THERMOS OF TEA.

AUNT NIUSIA SENT SUPPLIES FOR HER SISTER. WE HAVE STRONG-SMELLING SAUSAGES, MILK, FRESH CREAM, FARMERS CHEESE, FRUIT, AND EGGS WHICH GRANDMA BALANCES CAREFULLY ON HER KNEES.

BESIDES ALL THIS, WE'RE ALSO CARRYING PLASTIC BAGS BE-CAUSE LONG BUS TRIPS DON'T PARTICULARLY AGREE WITH ME...

I DON'T GET BORED EVEN THOUGH IT'S A LONG TRIP. I LOVE LOOKING OUT THE WINDOW. THE BUS GOES THROUGH LOTS OF VILLAGES. I TAKE IN THE HOUSES AND THE PEOPLE IN THE STREET...

THE LEAST PLEASANT MOMENT IS WHEN I GET NAUSEATED. GRANDMA IS READY. SHE HANDS ME A BAG WHICH I FILL UP IMMEDIATELY... THE BUS IS FULL, THE SMELL IS UNAVOIDABLE...

LUCKILY, SINCE IT'S A LONG TRIP WE STOP SEVERAL TIMES. WE HAVE FIVE OR TEN MINUTES TO STRETCH OUT OUR STIFF LIMBS. SOME PEOPLE SMOKE, OTHERS LOOK FOR THE BATHROOM.

MOM, LOOK! SHE'S THE ONE WHO THREW UP!

I THINK I'M A HIT...

MY UNCLE MIETEK COMES TO MEET US AT THE STATION IN KRAKÓW.

HERE, A PRESENT FROM MARZI!!

HA HA!

MY GRANDMOTHER HANDS HIM THE PLASTIC BAG WITH A LAUGH (I THREW UP AGAIN...)

AFTER LONG DRAWN-OUT GREETINGS, MY AUNT SHOWS US OUR ROOMS. I'M GOING TO SLEEP WITH KAROLINA, MY AUNT'S GRANDDAUGHTER WHO'S ON VACATION TOO. THEN WE SIT DOWN TO EAT...

SO?

WHAT WOULD YOU LIKE TO SEE IN KRAKÓW??

I DON'T KNOW... DAD TOLD ME THAT THERE WAS A BIG CASTLE...

KRAKÓW IS A VERY BEAUTIFUL CITY. MY UNCLE WAS BORN THERE, SO HE KNOWS IT REALLY WELL.

MIETEK AND DZIDZIA DON'T LIVE IN KRAKÓW ITSELF, BUT IN A CLOSE SUBURB CALLED NOWA HUTA (WHICH MEANS "NEW FACTORY"). THIS CITY LOOKS A LOT LIKE MINE: STALOWA WOLA (STEEL WILL).

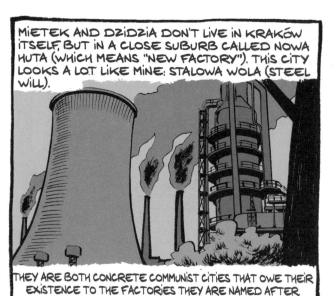

THEY ARE BOTH CONCRETE COMMUNIST CITIES THAT OWE THEIR EXISTENCE TO THE FACTORIES THEY ARE NAMED AFTER

TO GET INTO THE CITY, WE TAKE TRAMS 10, 25, OR 26. SINCE WE GET ON AT THE END OF THE LINE, IT'S EMPTY, BUT IT GETS A LITTLE MORE CROWDED AT EVERY STOP.

SO I HAVE TO GIVE UP MY SEAT BECAUSE THERE ARE ALWAYS A LOT OF OLD PEOPLE WHO GET ON.

I VACATE MY SEAT AS SOON AS I SEE ONE. GENERALLY, IF YOU DON'T, THEY COMMENT VERY LOUDLY AND EMBARRASS YOU.

STAY SEATED, YOUNG-STERS!

HMMPF!

YOU'LL BE STAND-ING WHEN YOU GET OLD!

DON'T GET UP, HE'S NOT THAT OLD! HE'S STILL HOLDING UP...

I TRY TO BE NICE ANYWAY. I DON'T LIKE HAVING OLD PEOPLE HOVERING OVER ME WHILE THEY GET SHAKEN BY THE TRAM'S SPASMODIC MOVEMENTS.

MY GRANDMOTHER SITS ME ON HER LAP.

WE'RE THERE. WE CLIMB UP TO KRAKÓW'S ROYAL CASTLE, KNOWN AS WAWEL.

FIRST, WE VISIT THE CAVE WHERE "SMOK WAWELSKI" LIVED (THE WAWEL DRAGON). HE LIVED UNDER THE CASTLE AND TERRORIZED THE WHOLE COURT AND EVERYONE IN THE SURROUNDING AREAS.

THEY HAD TO APPEASE HIM WITH DOZENS OF ANIMALS—SHEEPS, LAMBS, AND RABBITS—EVERY DAY... HE DESTROYED EVERY-THING AROUND HIM. FINALLY THE KINGDOM COULDN'T SATISFY THE MONSTER ANYMORE.

IN DEEP DESPAIR, THE KING PROMISED HIS ONLY DAUGHTER'S HAND TO THE PERSON WHO COULD FREE THE CITY FROM THE DRAGON'S TYRANNY. SEVERAL KNIGHTS ACCEPTED THE CHALLENGE BUT MET ONLY DEATH IN THEIR ENCOUNTERS WITH THE SMOK.

ONE DAY, A YOUNG COBBLER PRESENTED HIMSELF TO THE KING.

YOUR MAJESTY, LET ME TRY, I KNOW HOW TO MAKE THIS MONSTER DIE.

YOU ARE BUT A YOUNG COBBLER, WHAT CAN YOU DO IN THE FACE OF A DEMON LIKE THAT? DO YOU NOT FEAR LOSING YOUR LIFE?

THE KING WAS DOUBTFUL, BUT SINCE HE HAD FOUND NO OTHER SOLUTION, HE GAVE HIS PERMISSION.

THE YOUNG COBBLER BUILT A FAKE SHEEP AND FILLED IT WITH SULPHUR. THEN HE PUT IT IN FRONT OF THE DRAGON'S DEN. THE UNSUSPECTING SMOK GREEDILY LEAPT UPON IT AND SWALLOWED IT IN A SINGLE BITE!

HE WAS SOON OVERCOME BY A MONSTROUS THIRST! HE WENT DOWN TO THE BANKS OF THE WISŁA, THE BIGGEST RIVER IN POLAND, AND BEGAN TO DRINK.

HE DRANK AND DRANK SO MUCH THAT HE SWALLOWED HALF THE RIVER AND SWELLED UP SO MUCH THAT HE EXPLODED!

JOY RETURNED TO THE CITY AND, AS PROMISED, THE KING GAVE HIS DAUGHTER TO THE COBBLER. THEY WERE MARRIED AND LIVED HAPPILY EVER AFTER!

THE DRAGON'S HOME IS COLD AND BLACK. KAROLINA AND I ARE PARTICULARLY HAPPY TO LEAVE IT... EVEN THOUGH WE KNOW THE MONSTER DOESN'T LIVE THERE ANYMORE...

A BIG STATUE OF THE DRAGON THAT SPITS REAL FIRE STANDS OUTSIDE. I'D LOVE TO BRING MY PARENTS HERE ONE DAY. I'M SURE MY DAD WOULD LIKE IT, HE'S A REAL ADVENTURER...

MY MOM, IN CONTRAST, IS ALREADY SCARED OF FROGS, SO A BIG DRAGON LIKE THIS MIGHT REALLY, REALLY SCARE HER... BUT I'D STILL TRY IT...

A PROFESSIONAL PHOTOGRAPHER IMMORTALIZES THE MOMENT SO WE HAVE A LITTLE SOUVENIR...

THEN WE FINALLY ENTER THE CASTLE COMPOUND.

YOU HAVE TO WEAR BROWN SLIPPERS SO YOU DON'T GET THE FLOOR DIRTY AND THEY'RE HUGE! THERE'S ONLY ONE SIZE - 44. THEY'RE EVEN TOO BIG FOR MY UNCLE.

KAROLINA AND I LOOK RIDICULOUS WITH THESE THINGS ON OUR FEET. SINCE WE CAN'T WALK, WE PRETEND WE'RE WEARING ICESKATES.

WE'RE WAITING FOR A GUIDE SO WE CAN BEGIN OUR TOUR. IT'S AGAINST THE RULES TO WALK THROUGH THE ROOMS ALONE. ANOTHER GROUP BEGINS TO ASSEMBLE BESIDE US.

THEY'RE AMERICAN.

WHAT A FUNNY LANGUAGE! IT SOUNDS LIKE THEIR MOUTHS ARE FULL.

A WOMAN MY MOM'S AGE FINALLY ARRIVES. SHE GIVES THE AMERICANS A BIG SMILE AND BEGINS TALKING TO THEM IN THEIR LANGUAGE, COMPLETELY IGNORING US.

MY UNCLE TELLS HER THAT OUR GROUP WAS HERE FIRST. HER BEAMING EXPRESSION TRANSFORMS INTO A SULLEN GRIMACE AS SHE GLOWERS AT US.

VERY WELL!

FOLLOW ME! THE TOUR WILL LAST AN HOUR. YOU MAY NOT BRING DRINKS OR ANYTHING OF THE KIND WITH YOU!

STAY TOGETHER, AND NO TALKING!!

AND BE SURE TO KEEP A CLOSE WATCH ON YOUR CHILDREN, THEY SHOULDN'T TOUCH ANYTHING!

AND SHE TAKES OFF DOWN THE HALLS AT A RAPID PACE.

WEARING THESE SLIPPERS, WE STRUGGLE TO KEEP UP WITH HER, BUT SHE DOESN'T SEEM THE LEAST BIT CONCERNED.

THE CASTLE IS VERY BIG. MY ENTIRE APARTMENT WOULD FIT INTO A SINGLE ROYAL ROOM!

IN FACT, EVERYTHING IS VERY BIG. THE BEDS, THE TABLES... AS IF GIANTS LIVED HERE. IT FEELS EXCESSIVE. EVEN THE PAINTINGS ARE GIGANTIC AND THE PEOPLE IN THEM ARE RATHER UGLY. THEY'RE SCARY.

EVERYONE WORE WIGS IN THOSE DAYS... IT'S A FASHION THAT CAME FROM FRANCE.

AS A RESULT, OVER TIME, THEIR REAL HAIR FELL OUT. THEY HAD ALMOST NONE LEFT.

WHEN THEY CAME TO, THEY WERE BALD!!

WHERE ARE THE BATHROOMS?

AH, THEY DIDN'T HAVE THEM...

THE KING DIDN'T BATHE? WHAT ABOUT THE QUEEN!?!

YOU KNOW, THEY WORE A LOT OF PERFUME TO CAMOUFLAGE THE SMELL. TAKING BATHS JUST WASN'T THE FASHION THEN.

EXCUSE ME, MA'AM, HOW...?

SAVE YOUR QUESTIONS FOR LATER!

I TOLD YOU AT THE BEGINNING.

PLEASE STOP SO RUDELY INTERRUPTING ME!

WHERE WAS I?... THE ROYAL DÉCOR IS COMPOSED OF A GUIDING SYMBOLIC AND UNIFIED THEME...

WHAT ABOUT THE TOILET?

IT WAS A POT UNDER THE BED...

SO THE KING USED IT IN FRONT OF THE QUEEN?

YES, WHILE SHE WAS SLEEPING, OR HE LEFT THE ROOM WITH THE POT...

THE GUIDE USES STRANGE WORDS. I DON'T UNDERSTAND A LOT OF WHAT SHE IS SAYING.

IT'S BORING. LUCKILY, MY UNCLE IS THERE TO EXPLAIN EVERYTHING TO US. WE'RE GETTING TIRED. I TRY TO SIT DOWN ON A CHAIR.

WE ARE ENTERING A CEREMONIAL ROOM IN A CLASSIC STYLE, MOST LIKELY REDONE BY SIERAKOWSKI IN... REALLY, NOW!

GET OFF THERE IMMEDIATELY, YOU LITTLE SAVAGE! THAT'S AN HISTORIC MONUMENT! A WITNESS TO THE ROYAL PAST! NOT A BENCH AT A TRAIN STATION!!

... IT'S A CHAIR MOST OF ALL, BUT I COMPLY...

AFTER THIS TRYING VISIT, WE COLLAPSE ONTO THE TRAM'S SEATS, PAYING NO ATTENTION TO THE GRUMBLERS.

STAY SEATED, KIDS, WHEN YOU'RE OLD.

THAT'S RIGHT, WE'LL STAND!!

A RITUAL AWAITS US AT HOME...

EVER SINCE I ARRIVED, MY AUNT HAS BEEN SINGING THE PRAISES OF "AMOL" EVERY DAY. IT'S GOOD FOR ANYTHING THAT AILS YOU, SO THEY USE IT WHEREVER IT HURTS.

KAROLINA AND I AREN'T IN ANY PAIN, BUT MY AUNT INSISTS... SHE SAYS IT'S PREVENTATIVE!

SHE FILLS A SOUP SPOON AND MAKES US SWALLOW IT—WE DO, BUT NOT WITHOUT GRIMACING. IT TASTES LIKE LEMON BALM AND IT'S ALCOHOLIC. WHEN I HEAR MY AUNT GOING INTO THE KITCHEN AFTER DINNER, I TASTE AMOL...

NOT TODAY, PLEASE...

JUST A LITTLE SPOONFUL. IT WON'T HURT. COME ON, OPEN UP AND THAT'LL BE THAT!

BUT IT'S NOT TRUE, SHE SAYS THAT EVERY TIME AND THE NEXT DAY, SHE DOES IT AGAIN!

DON'T SCOWL, IT'S NOT SO BAD...IT'S PLANT-BASED, 100% NATURAL!

HERE, I'M GOING TO TELL YOUR PARENTS TO BUY IT. YOUR DAD'S ALWAYS COMPLAINING ABOUT HIS STOMACH...

IN FACT, YOU KNOW WHAT? I HAVE AN IDEA, I'LL BUY A BOTTLE OF AMOL FOR YOUR DAD.

YOU CAN GIVE IT TO HIM AS A GIFT FROM ME.

GREAT... I HOPE THEY AT LEAST WON'T FORCE ME TO DRINK THIS STUFF EVERY DAY WHEN I'M REALLY NOT IN PAIN!

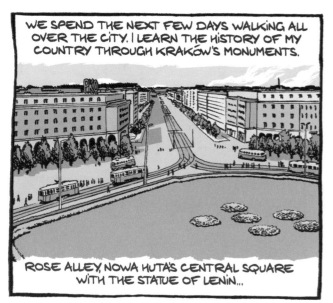

WE SPEND THE NEXT FEW DAYS WALKING ALL OVER THE CITY. I LEARN THE HISTORY OF MY COUNTRY THROUGH KRAKÓW'S MONUMENTS.

ROSE ALLEY, NOWA HUTA'S CENTRAL SQUARE WITH THE STATUE OF LENIN...

"NOAH'S ARK", WHERE WE GO FOR MASS.

THE CLOTH HALL ON RYNEK PLACE... IT'S COVERED IN PIGEONS!

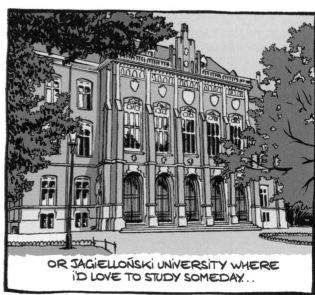

OR JAGIELLOŃSKI UNIVERSITY WHERE I'D LOVE TO STUDY SOMEDAY...

WE COME HOME EXHAUSTED EVERY NIGHT. WHEN KAROLINA AND I BRUSH OUR TEETH WE SEE GRANDMA'S DENTURES SWIMMING IN A GLASS OF WATER.

IT MAKES US LAUGH, BUT AT THE SAME TIME IT STRIKES US AS VERY PRACTICAL TO CLEAN YOUR TEETH OUTSIDE YOUR MOUTH.

AT BEDTIME, GRANDMA COMES TO TELL US STORIES. WITHOUT HER DENTURES, SHE LISPS, AND IT SOUNDS A LITTLE LIKE THE HISS OF A GARDEN HOSE...

AS A RESULT, SHE PUTS US TO SLEEP IN RECORD TIME.

IN THE MORNINGS, MY UNCLE GOES TO BUY THE BREAD. WE GO WITH HIM BECAUSE HE ALWAYS BUYS US LOLLIPOPS.

SOMETIMES WE STOP ON THE SWINGS TO EAT THEM. AUNT DZIDZIA DOESN'T LIKE US EATING TOO MANY SWEETS, SHE SAYS IT'S BAD FOR OUR TEETH.

WE ALSO OFTEN GO SIT ON SOME BOULDERS IN A SMALL WOODS JUST IN FRONT OF THE BUILDING, WHERE WE STRETCH OUT TO WATCH THE CLOUDS. THEY'RE LIKE SNOW SCULPTURES OR GIANT COTTON-CANDIES.

I SEE A POLAR BEAR.

I THINK IT'S YOUR AUNT LOOKING OUT THE WINDOW AND GRUMBLING: "WHERE HAVE THEY GONE THIS TIME!...

I'M SURE HE BOUGHT THEM LOLLIPOPS. THAT MAN'S IMPOSSIBLE!"

IF YOU HOLD YOUR LOLLIPOP OVER IT...

IT LOOKS LIKE A FIRESPITTING DRAGON!

THAT SHOPPING TRIP TOOK YOU QUITE A WHILE!

WE WERE LOOKING AT THE CLOUDS!!

HMM, SHOW ME YOUR TONGUES?!

AH! YOU'VE LICKED THE CLOUDS... AND THEY'RE STRANGELY RED TODAY... COME ON, GO BRUSH YOUR TEETH!

MY AUNT IS A LITTLE OBSESSED WITH HEALTH, BUT SHE'S NOT MEAN.

THE PHOTO WE TOOK IN FRONT OF SMOK'S STATUE CAME IN THE MAIL. I HAVE PROOF I SAW THE DRAGON!

OUR TRIP IS ALMOST OVER AND I HAVE LOTS OF STORIES TO TELL.

I DON'T LIKE GOODBYES, BUT I'M HAPPY TO BE GOING HOME TO MY PARENTS.

Kochani Rodzice!
Kraków to bardzo
ładne miasto.
Szkoda, że Was
tu nie ma.
Do zobaczenia
za tydzień.
Marri
P.s. jem # wszystko i
jestem grzeczna.

Maria i Józef
Sow...
ul. Skora...ki
37-4...
Stalowa...

TWO WEEKS WITHOUT ANY NEWS IS WAY TOO MUCH. AT LEAST I SENT THEM A POSTCARD. SO THEY KNOW I'M DOING WELL AND MISSING THEM.

WE HAVE PLENTY TO EAT ON THE BUS. PLUS, A BOTTLE OF AMOL, A PHOTO, AND SOME PLASTIC BAGS.

YOU KNOW WHY...

BREATHING CAN BE HAZARDOUS TO YOUR HEALTH

NO ONE'S WORKING IN THE FIELDS TODAY. SO WE CAN DO WHATEVER WE WANT!

IT'S A HOLIDAY. I'M PLAYING WITH THE NEIGHBOR KIDS AT AUNT NIUSIA'S IN SKOWIERZYN.

WE'VE GONE TO KALANTO, WHERE A SCHOOL USED TO STAND. THERE'S NOTHING LEFT BUT BRICKS AND PIECES OF WOOD.

WE PLAY HIDE-AND-SEEK OR BLIND MAN'S BLUFF.

WE SOMETIMES COMPETE TO SEE WHO CAN COLLECT THE PRETTIEST FEATHERS. WE GO WHEREVER FEATHERED CREATURES HANG OUT AND WATCH FOR THEM...

THE BRAVEST HAVE NO QUALMS ABOUT CATCHING A YOUNG CHICKEN AND PULLING OUT SOME OF ITS PLUMAGE.

THE BIRD USUALLY LETS OUT A HIGH, HORRIBLE CRY AND THEN HIS OWNER ARRIVES, SHOUTING!

AŁAJ!

GÓWNIARZE ŚMIERDZĄCE!

ANYWAY CHICKEN FEATHERS DON'T GIVE YOU A GOOD CHANCE OF WINNING. THE MOST BEAUTIFUL BELONG TO THE PEACOCKS.

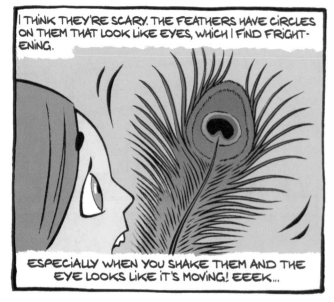

I THINK THEY'RE SCARY. THE FEATHERS HAVE CIRCLES ON THEM THAT LOOK LIKE EYES, WHICH I FIND FRIGHTENING.

ESPECIALLY WHEN YOU SHAKE THEM AND THE EYE LOOKS LIKE IT'S MOVING! EEEEK...

SO I WANDER UNDER THE TREES HOPING A BEAUTIFUL BIRD MIGHT HAVE COME BY AND LOST AT LEAST ONE FEATHER

I FIND SOME BEAUTIFUL ONES, BUT SOMEONE WITH A PEACOCK FEATHER ALWAYS WINS...

WE BRING THINGS TO SHARE TO KALANTO. OFTEN, IT'S FOOD.

THIS TIME ANIA BRINGS A TUBE OF A STRANGE PASTE SHE GOT FROM A DISTANT UNCLE IN AMERICA. WE TAKE TURNS TASTING IT. IT'S VERY GOOD.

SHE TELLS US THERE ARE THREE MORE TUBES AT HOME! SO WE HEAD TO HER HOUSE EAGER TO HAVE MORE... BUT HER MOM CATCHES US IN THE MIDDLE OF OUR FEAST!

WHAT THE...?! STOP STUFFING YOURSELVES WITH TOOTH-PASTE!

YOU'RE ALL GOING TO HAVE STOMACH ACHES!

AMERICAN TOOTHPASTE IS DELICIOUS...

ON OUR WAY BACK FROM KALANTO, WE PASS RIGHT BEHIND MY AUNT'S BARN.

MARZI! WE'RE GOING HOME!!!

HURRY UP!

ALREADY? BUT WE JUST GOT HERE!!

NOT EVEN TIME TO SAY GOODBYE...

IN THE CAR, MY PARENTS LOOK ANXIOUS. MY DAD DRIVES FASTER THAN USUAL AND MY MOM, WHO WOULD NORMALLY ALREADY BE GRUMBLING, IS ENCOURAGING HIM.

FASTER!!

SPEED UP A LITTLE, WHO CARES ABOUT THE MILITIA!

YES, I KNOW! CLOSE THE VENTS!!

THEY'RE TALKING ABOUT A WARNING THEY HEARD ON THE RADIO AT MY AUNT'S BUT, AS USUAL, THEY DON'T EXPLAIN ANYTHING TO ME...

I HOPE IT'S NOT TOO LATE!

THEY COULDN'T CARE LESS ABOUT US!

IN FRONT OF THE BUILDING AT LAST, MY MOM TELLS US TO WAIT. SHE GOES UP QUICKLY AND COMES BACK WITH THE NEIGHBORS' KIDS.

COME ON, TO THE EMERGENCY ROOM!

TO THE HOSPITAL!?!

NO ONE ANSWERS. A GLOOMY SILENCE FILLS THE CAR.

AT THE HOSPITAL, THE CORRIDORS ARE PACKED WITH PEOPLE. THERE ARE A LOT OF CHILDREN. WE'RE ALL A LITTLE CRAMPED, BUT NO ONE WANTS TO WAIT OUTSIDE.

THE DOORS AND WINDOWS ARE ALL CLOSED, EVEN THOUGH IT'S HOT AND WE'RE SUFFOCATING!

WE WAIT WITH MY DAD. MY MOM WENT LOOKING FOR A DOCTOR TO FIND OUT WHAT TO DO.

YOU SHOULD GO GET IN LINE. WE DON'T KNOW IF THERE'LL BE ENOUGH LUGOL'S SOLUTION...

THE MOST RECENT READINGS SHOW RADIOACTIVITY LEVELS 80,000 TIMES WHAT THEY SHOULD BE!

WE'RE GIVING IT TO THE CHILDREN FIRST... THEY'RE THE MOST VULNERABLE...

IT'S THE RUSSIANS' FAULT!

WHO NEEDS A WAR TO DIE IN THIS COUNTRY!

DID YOU SEE WHAT HAPPENED IN HIROSHIMA AND NAGASAKI?

AND WHAT WILL IT MEAN—TOMORROW, IN A YEAR—FOR US?

WELL NOW WE CAN ADD UKRAINE TO THE LIST!

A NEW PANDORA'S BOX...

DAD, WHAT ARE WE DOING HERE?

DON'T WORRY, WE'RE JUST GOING TO TAKE SOME MEDICINE.

A KID WAITING NEXT TO US WITH HIS PARENTS WHO IS APPARENTLY BETTER INFORMED EXPLAINS...

MY DAD SAID THAT A FACTORY EXPLODED IN RUSSIA AND ALL THE SMOKE IS HEADING TOWARDS POLAND...

AND KIND OF GOING EVERYWHERE...

IT'S A SMOKE THAT'S VERY DANGEROUS FOR PEOPLE... AND MUSHROOMS.

LATE THAT NIGHT, AFTER A LONG WAIT, OUR TURN COMES. THE DOCTORS GIVE US A LITTLE GLASS CONTAINER FILLED WITH A YELLOW LIQUID.

HAVE THEY HAD ANY MILK THESE LAST FEW DAYS?

OF COURSE, DOCTOR, THEY'RE CHILDREN. THEY DRINK A LOT OF MILK...

WELL THEY SHOULDN'T ANYMORE. THE GRASS IS HIGHLY RADIOACTIVE... IT'S DANGEROUS.

BLECH...IT'S TERRIBLE!

DRINK THE WHOLE THING...

IT'S IMPORTANT!!

IT FELT LIKE THEY WERE WATCHING US CLOSELY, WE COULDN'T WASTE A SINGLE DROP... THE ADULTS DIDN'T HAVE ANY, IT WAS ONLY FOR THE CHILDREN BECAUSE THERE WASN'T ENOUGH FOR EVERYONE.

WE ARE CONSUMED BY ANXIETY. MY PARENTS DON'T MISS A SINGLE NEWSCAST. THE TOXIC CLOUD IS THE MAIN NEWS ITEM. IT ECLIPSES EVERYTHING ELSE...

THEY SAY THAT SINCE THE EXPLOSION, PEOPLE IN UKRAINE FIRST GO STRANGE, THEN GET SICK--AND VERY OFTEN END UP DYING.

EVEN THOUGH IT'S SPRING, I CAN'T PLAY OUTSIDE AFTER SCHOOL. BESIDES, THERE'S NO ONE TO PLAY WITH.

THE MINUTE IT RAINS, THE STREETS EMPTY OUT. PEOPLE FIND SHELTER.

WATER FROM THE SKY IS POISONED TOO.

IN THE COUNTRY, AUNT NIUSIA CAN'T LET HER COWS OUT. THEY'RE NOT ALLOWED TO EAT THE GRASS, THE GROUND IS CONTAMINATED. MY AUNT HAS TO BUY SPECIAL FOOD FOR THEM.

SHE MILKS HER COWS, BUT THROWS IT AWAY... WE'RE NOT ALLOWED TO DRINK REGULAR MILK, WE HAVE TO USE POWDERED.

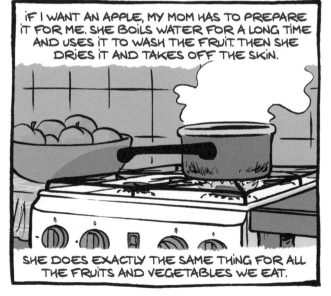

IF I WANT AN APPLE, MY MOM HAS TO PREPARE IT FOR ME. SHE BOILS WATER FOR A LONG TIME AND USES IT TO WASH THE FRUIT. THEN SHE DRIES IT AND TAKES OFF THE SKIN.

SHE DOES EXACTLY THE SAME THING FOR ALL THE FRUITS AND VEGETABLES WE EAT.

WE CAN'T GO MUSHROOM PICKING BECAUSE THEY GOT THE GREATEST DOSE OF RADIATION...

THE ADULTS SEEM ON EDGE. THEY BEGIN TO COMPLAIN OPENLY THE MINUTE SOMETHING BOTHERS THEM. THIS WOULD HAVE BEEN UNTHINKABLE A FEW DAYS BEFORE.

THEY DON'T CARE ABOUT US!

WE WON'T SOON FORGET THIS! THIS WON'T BE THE LAST EXPLO-SION!!

BUT NEXT TIME, WE'LL BE THE ONES WHO EXPLODE!

EVEN MY MOM DOESN'T HIDE HER DISCONTENT IN PUBLIC!

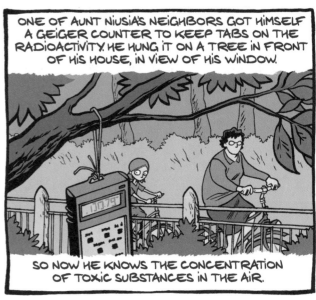

ONE OF AUNT NIUSIA'S NEIGHBORS GOT HIMSELF A GEIGER COUNTER TO KEEP TABS ON THE RADIOACTIVITY. HE HUNG IT ON A TREE IN FRONT OF HIS HOUSE, IN VIEW OF HIS WINDOW.

SO NOW HE KNOWS THE CONCENTRATION OF TOXIC SUBSTANCES IN THE AIR.

MY AUNT SAYS HE'S GONE A LITTLE CRAZY. BUT I'VE NOTICED THAT WHEN WE RIDE BY HIS HOUSE ON BICYCLE, SHE SLOWS DOWN TO CAST A FURTIVE GLANCE AT THE COUNTER.

STOP

DANGER
НЕБЕЗПЕКА

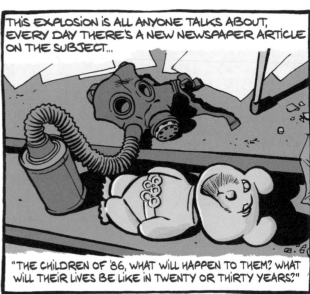

THIS EXPLOSION IS ALL ANYONE TALKS ABOUT, EVERY DAY THERE'S A NEW NEWSPAPER ARTICLE ON THE SUBJECT...

"THE CHILDREN OF '86, WHAT WILL HAPPEN TO THEM? WHAT WILL THEIR LIVES BE LIKE IN TWENTY OR THIRTY YEARS?"

BUT THESE KIDS, THEY'RE MONIKA, ANIA, ANDRZEJ, ME AND MANY OTHERS...

THEY CALL US THE CHERNOBYL GENERATION.

WHAT LIFE AWAITS US?

MY DAD GOT SICK OVER THE WINTER. IT WAS SERIOUS. HE HAD TO GO TO THE HOSPITAL, EVEN THOUGH THE HOSPITAL WAS TO BLAME IN THE FIRST PLACE...

THE FACTORY WHERE HE WORKS REQUIRES ITS EMPLOYEES TO PASS A PHYSICAL EXAM, BUT THEY DREW HIS BLOOD WITH A CONTAMINATED NEEDLE. IT WASN'T PROPERLY DISINFECTED AND HE CAUGHT JAUNDICE.

HE SPENT A LONG TIME IN THE HOSPITAL AND NOW HE'S GOING TO A SANATORIUM IN THE MOUNTAINS FOR TWO WEEKS.

THAT'S HOW THEY'RE FIXING HIM UP. BUT NOBODY GAVE A THOUGHT TO ME! I'M GOING TO HAVE TO SPEND THIS WHOLE TIME WITH MY MOM...I WOULD MUCH RATHER BE ALONE.

SINCE WE DON'T HAVE A TELEPHONE, I CAN'T TALK TO HIM. BUT MY MOM CAN CALL HIM FROM HER OFFICE. SHE BRINGS ME HIS NEWS...

HE'S DOING WELL...

HE'S RESTING AND TAKING LONG WALKS IN THE MOUNTAINS.

WE RECEIVE A POSTCARD WHERE HE SAYS HE SENDS KISSES AND THAT HE'S SORRY THE TIME IS GOING SO FAST. HE'D LIKE TO STAY A LITTLE LONGER BEFORE HAVING TO GO BACK TO THE FACTORY.

AND I READ THIS CARD FEELING SORRY TIME IS PASSING SO SLOWLY, BECAUSE I'D LOVE HIM TO FINALLY BE HOME.

BEFORE LEAVING, HE GAVE ME A MATCH BOX WITH THE SAME NUMBER OF MATCHES AS DAYS HE WOULD BE GONE.

"THIS WAY, YOU'LL KNOW EXACTLY WHEN I'LL BE BACK."

SO EVERY NIGHT I TAKE OUT A MATCH AND LIGHT IT.

IT MAKES MY MOM SMILE...IT'S CERTAINLY THE FIRST TIME SHE HASN'T OBJECTED TO MY PLAYING WITH FIRE!

EVERY MORNING I TELL MYSELF: ONE LESS DAY...

I'M A LITTLE BORED AFTER SCHOOL. MY MOM NOTICES AND MAKES ME HELP HER DO CHORES AROUND THE HOUSE.

SHE IRONS. I HAVE TO FOLD THE CLOTHES, INCLUDING A LOT OF MY DAD'S SHIRTS WHICH I DON'T PARTICULARLY LIKE FOLDING. IT'S METICULOUS WORK AND MY MOM RECHECKS EVERYTHING.

BUT TODAY I'M HAPPY TO BE TAKING CARE OF MY DAD'S CLOTHES. I THINK ABOUT TIMES WE'VE SPENT TOGETHER WHILE I WORK...

QUITE OFTEN AFTER HE GETS HOME FROM WORK, WE GO WAIT IN SOME LINE.

HE GETS ANNOYED SOMETIMES BECAUSE I'LL STAND RIGHT NEXT TO HIM, STICKING TO HIM LIKE GLUE. IT'S EASY TO CRUSH OR STEP ON A LITTLE PERSON LIKE ME.

AS SOON AS WE GET INTO THE STORE, I CAN GO SIT ON THE LOW WALL THAT RUNS THE LENGTH OF THE WINDOW. IT'S A NICE PLACE TO REST YOUR BOTTOM IN THE WINTER BECAUSE IT'S JUST OVER THE RADIATOR.

BUT I'D STILL RATHER BE STANDING NEXT TO MY DAD.

IT DRIVES HIM CRAZY. ONCE, HE PRACTICALLY FORCED ME TO GO SIT ON THE WALL.

IF YOU DON'T GO OVER THERE I WILL AND YOU'LL HAVE TO STAND HERE AND WAIT YOUR TURN!!

SO I GO AND SIT DOWN.

I LOOK AROUND ME, THE LINE IS MOVING VERY SLOWLY BUT EVERYONE STAYS CALM. THEY'RE NOT THINKING ABOUT GETTING HOME AS QUICKLY AS POSSIBLE...

BUT ABOUT GETTING HOME WITH SOMETHING IN THEIR BAG.

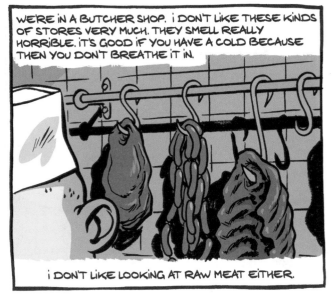

WE'RE IN A BUTCHER SHOP. I DON'T LIKE THESE KINDS OF STORES VERY MUCH. THEY SMELL REALLY HORRIBLE. IT'S GOOD IF YOU HAVE A COLD BECAUSE THEN YOU DON'T BREATHE IT IN.

I DON'T LIKE LOOKING AT RAW MEAT EITHER.

BUT FOR THE PEOPLE IN LINE, YOU'D THINK IT WAS THEIR LIFE'S GOAL: A PIECE OF MEAT AND THEIR FACES JUST LIGHT UP!

HOP HOP

RRHHH

IT'S SURPRISING HOW A SAUSAGE CAN GIVE LIFE MEANING.

THESE PEOPLE ARE ALL ALIKE. THEY'RE MORE PREOCCUPIED THAN SAD. YOU CAN HEAR IT IN THEIR CONVERSATIONS, LINES ARE GOOD PLACES TO EXPRESS YOURSELF...

THEY COMPLAIN OFTEN, BUT JOKINGLY BECAUSE THEY KNOW IT'S RISKY TO SAY ANYTHING HERE. MOSTLY THEY TALK ABOUT THE WEATHER, THEIR FAMILIES, THEIR CHILDREN, WHO'S SICK AND WHO'S HEALTHY.

SO I SIT THERE ON THE WALL, STUDYING PEOPLE, THEIR BEHAVIOR, THEIR CLOTHES... EVERYONE IS BUNDLED UP.

DELIKATESY MIĘSNE

EVEN THOUGH THE STORE IS HEATED, IT FEELS QUITE COLD BECAUSE THE DOOR IS CONSTANTLY OPENING AND CLOSING.

IT'S FULL OF OLD PEOPLE, MOSTLY WOMEN. A FEW OLD FOLKS WHO HAVE TROUBLE STANDING ARE SEATED BESIDE ME ON THE WALL.

BONG

BONG

I'M A LITTLE COLD. I SHAKE MY LEGS AND KICK THEM AGAINST THE RADIATOR THERE'S SO MUCH NOISE IN THE ROOM NO ONE HEARS ME BANGING.

I LOOK AROUND FOR MY DAD... WHERE IS HE?

I FEEL MY PANIC RISING. I STAND UP. I LOOK AROUND MORE CAREFULLY... TOO MANY PEOPLE ARE CROWDED IN HERE... IT'S IMPOSSIBLE TO PICK HIM OUT!

I HAVE TEARS IN MY EYES! WHERE HAVE YOU GONE, DAD? DON'T LEAVE ME ALL ALONE! DON'T ABANDON ME!...ALL OF A SUDDEN, I HEAR A SOUND ON THE GLASS BEHIND ME...

THERE HE IS! IN FRONT OF THE STORE! HE'S CRACKING UP...HE GOT ME. I WAS VERY SCARED, IT'S TRUE. EVER SINCE THEN HE'S CALLED ME DZWONEK (LITTLE BELL) BECAUSE WHEN WE GO OUT I WON'T LEAVE HIS SIDE EVEN FOR A SECOND.

YOU DID A GOOD JOB FOR ONCE!

MY MOM IS PLEASED WITH MY FOLDING.

AT NIGHT WHEN SHE'S WATCHING TELEVISION, I GET OUT OUR OLD TAPE RECORDER AND LISTEN TO THE RECORDINGS THAT MY DAD MADE.

POSZŁA ŻABKA PO WODĘ DO ZIMNEGO ZDROJU...

GO AHEAD, IT'S YOUR TURN...

WHEN I WAS VERY LITTLE, HE WANTED TO RECORD ME SINGING. HE'D START OFF TO GET ME TO JOIN IN, BUT I'D BE SO INTIMIDATED THAT YOU MOSTLY HEAR MY DAD'S VOICE AND IN THE BACKGROUND, I MEAN WAY IN THE BACKGROUND, YOU CAN PICK OUT SOME VERY FAINT PEEPS...THAT'S ME!

SO MY DAD GOT ANNOYED BUT HE FORGOT TO TURN OFF HIS TAPE RECORDER.

ZA NIĄ BOCIEK RACH CIACH CIACH, NIE DAŁ JEJ SPOKOJU...

WHY AREN'T YOU SINGING?!

YOU REHEARSED SO MUCH...WHY DON'T WE DO IT AGAIN? I WANTED YOU TO REMEMBER THIS WHEN YOU GOT OLDER, AND YOU'RE REFUSING TO SING!

I LOVE LISTENING TO THIS TAPE.

DAY AFTER DAY, THE RITUAL UNFOLDS... THIS MATCHBOX FEELS BOTTOMLESS.

I WAIT FOR MY DAD SO IMPATIENTLY THAT IN MY MIND HE'S BECOME A KIND OF GOD, MY EVERYDAY SAVIOR.

SATURDAYS WITH MY MOM AREN'T FUN OR INTERESTING. I HAVE TO DUST OFF THE FURNITURE, POLISH THE FLOORS, WIPE DOWN THE PLANT LEAVES, ETC...

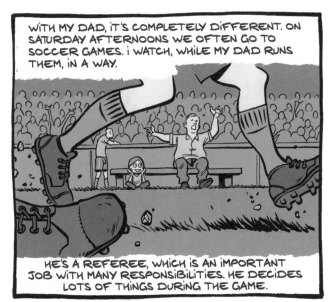

WITH MY DAD, IT'S COMPLETELY DIFFERENT. ON SATURDAY AFTERNOONS WE OFTEN GO TO SOCCER GAMES. I WATCH, WHILE MY DAD RUNS THEM, IN A WAY.

HE'S A REFEREE, WHICH IS AN IMPORTANT JOB WITH MANY RESPONSIBILITIES. HE DECIDES LOTS OF THINGS DURING THE GAME.

AFTER THE GAMES THERE'S USUALLY A PARTY. SO THE MEN DRINK ALCOHOL...

MY MOM LIKES ME TO GO WITH MY DAD BECAUSE THEN SHE'S SURE HE WON'T GET TOO DRUNK OR COME HOME TOO LATE!

EVERYONE IS NICE TO HIM THERE, AND ALSO VERY NICE TO ME.

WHAT'S YOUR NAME?

SHE'S YOUR DAUGHTER, MR JÓZEK?

SHE'S ADORABLE!!

YOU SEE MR. JÓZEK, WE COULD MAKE AN ARRANGEMENT. I COULD SUPPLY YOU PRODUCTS THAT EVEN THE RUSSIANS AT YOUR FACTORY CAN'T OFFER...

YOU'D HAVE WHAT IT TAKES TO FILL UP YOUR SOVIET FRIDGE! HA, HA!

COME ON, PLAY! I CAN'T SCORE GOALS FOR YOU!

BUT YOU COULD DO A LOT MORE!

THINK ABOUT IT! LOLLIPOPS FOR YOUR DAUGHTER, MEAT FOR YOUR WIFE, VODKA FOR YOU...NOT A BAD DEAL!

LISTEN, THAT'S VERY NICE OF YOU, BUT I'VE ALREADY AGREED TO HELP THE OTHER TEAM SO YOU'LL HAVE TO UNDERSTAND, THERE'S NOTHING I CAN DO FOR YOU!

WHAT?!

ARMED WITH HIS WHISTLE, HE OCCUPIES THE CENTER OF THE FIELD AND EVERYONE LISTENS TO HIM. OF COURSE, IT'S THE SOCCER PLAYERS WHO PLAY, BUT IN MY MIND HE'S THE MOST IMPORTANT.

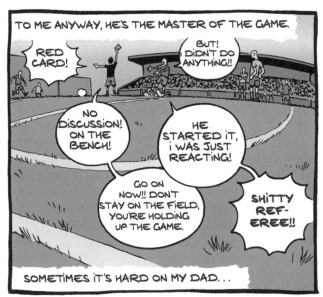

TO ME ANYWAY, HE'S THE MASTER OF THE GAME.

RED CARD!

BUT! I DIDN'T DO ANYTHING!!

NO DISCUSSION! ON THE BENCH!

HE STARTED IT, I WAS JUST REACTING!

GO ON NOW!! DON'T STAY ON THE FIELD, YOU'RE HOLDING UP THE GAME.

SHITTY REF-EREE!!

SOMETIMES IT'S HARD ON MY DAD...

IN THE END, YOU DIDN'T HELP THE OTHER TEAM TOO MUCH...

I DIDN'T HELP ANYONE, I JUST SAID THAT TO GET RID OF YOU!

HA HA! ANYWAY, IT MADE US SO MAD WE WON!

COME HAVE A DRINK WITH US. A VICTORY LIKE THIS SHOULD BE CELEBRATED!!

TO VICTORY!!

TO OUR TEAM!!

TO THE POLISH SOLDIERS!

TO JUREK, THE BEST GOALKEEPER!

TO OUR COUNTRY, TO POLAND!!

TO MR. JÓZEK, THE BEST REFEREE!

TO MIREK, IT'S HIS BIRTHDAY TODAY!!

TO SOLIDARNOŚĆ!!

AND THEY BEGIN SINGING THE NATIONAL ANTHEM... THEIR FACES ARE RED, THEIR BREATH BOOZY, THEY STAY STANDING AND SEEM VERY MOVED...

AHH, WE'RE LEAVING. MY DAD SMELLS LIKE VODKA BUT IS WALKING STRAIGHT. THE PLAYERS GAVE ME A CHOCOLATE BAR! AND A LITTLE HAM TO TAKE BACK TO THE HOUSE.

DO WIDZENIA ♪ PANIE ♫ JÓZKU

SO YOUR WIFE WON'T BE MAD WHEN YOU COME HOME A LITTLE DRUNK...

YOU SEE, HAM CALMS WIVES DOWN AND MAKES THEM HAPPY.

IT'S GREAT BECAUSE THE REFEREE ALWAYS WINS!

BUT ANYWAY, THIS SATURDAY I HAVE TO DO HOUSEWORK. MY MOM IS HAPPY BECAUSE WE'RE FINALLY SPENDING A LITTLE TIME TOGETHER.

I'VE NEVER SEEN YOU APPLY YOURSELF LIKE THIS! WHAT WOULD YOU LIKE TO EAT TONIGHT?

I COULD MAKE SCRAMBLED EGGS?

OH NO! NOT THOSE, PLEASE, I'LL JUST HAVE SOME TOAST...

OK, I WILL MAKE THAT.

SHE'S NOT USUALLY SO EASILY CONVINCED!!

SOON... FINALLY!

SO? TELL ME...

DO YOU HAVE AN ADMIRER AT SCHOOL?

WHAT? YOU'RE A PRETTY GIRL, MAYBE YOU HAVE A BOYFRIEND?

MOM?!?

YOU KNOW, YOU STILL HAVE A LOT OF TIME, YOU'RE YOUNG...

ACTUALLY... THERE'S SEBASTIAN. BUT HE LIKES MONIKA...

OH WELL... HE'S NOT THE ONLY BOY!

YES, HE IS, I LIKE HIM A LOT, I'M WAITING FOR HIM TO STOP LIKING MONIKA...

YES... AND I LIKE GIRLS BETTER ANYWAY.

WHAT?

THEY'RE NOT AS INTIMIDATING AND THEY'RE PRETTIER.

YES, BUT THEY'RE JUST FRIENDS! A BOYFRIEND IS COMPLETELY DIFFERENT!!

I CAN'T PLAY WITH BOYS, THEY ALWAYS WANT TO GO FIRST OR HAVE THE BETTER CAR...

IT'S NOT THE SAME WITH GIRLS. WE DON'T COMPETE WITH EACH OTHER ALL THE TIME, WE HAVE FUN...

IF YOU ASK ME, IT'S NO FUN TO ALWAYS BE THE ONE COMING IN LAST OR LOSING. AND BOYS' GAMES ARE ALWAYS LIKE THAT!

THAT NIGHT, AUNT STASIA (MONIKA'S MOM) COMES OVER FOR TEA. I'M SUPPOSED TO BE ASLEEP.

SHE SAID SHE LIKED GIRLS BETTER!!

HA HA! THAT'S NORMAL AT HER AGE.

BUT I SAW MONIKA AND MARZI KISSING WHEN THEY WERE PLAYING! I DIDN'T KNOW HOW TO INTERRUPT THEM. SO I DROPPED A POT...

YOU'RE PANICKING FOR NOTHING! THEY'RE ALWAYS PLAYING FAMILY AT MY HOUSE AND I DON'T SAY ANYTHING. I THINK IT'S FUNNY. THEY'RE JUST GETTING TO KNOW THEMSELVES.

BUT IT'S COMPLETELY UNHEALTHY! I NEVER DID THAT!!

OH REALLY? I DID IT AND LOOK, I HAVE A HUSBAND, KIDS, A NORMAL LIFE...

I'M STILL SCARED. MONIKA HAS A BOYFRIEND! MARZI DOESN'T!!

LISTEN... LET THEM BE, THEY'RE NOT DOING ANYTHING BAD. YOU KNOW WHAT? CZESIEK BROUGHT BACK SOME COGNAC FROM RUSSIA. I'LL GO GET IT, LET'S HAVE A LITTLE TASTE TO CALM OUR NERVES!

SHE SAW US KISS...SHE SPIES ON ME! SHE PROBABLY READS MY JOURNAL. MY CHEEKS BURN, I WON'T BE ABLE TO SLEEP! I TOO WILL NEED SOMETHING TO CALM MY NERVES.

LUCKILY, MY DAD IS COMING HOME! I'M SO IMPATIENT TO SEE HIM AGAIN. MOM TOO I THINK, SHE WENT TO THE HAIR-DRESSERS AND BAKED A CAKE SPECIALLY FOR HIM.

BIZARRELY, I FEEL INTIMIDATED BY MY OWN DAD. IT'S BEEN SO LONG SINCE I SAW HIM I DON'T KNOW HOW TO ACT...

BUT IT DOESN'T LAST LONG BECAUSE MY DAD KNOWS HOW TO BE WITH KIDS. EVEN THE SHYEST COME OUT OF THEIR SHELLS WHEN HE PLAYS WITH THEM...NO MORE HOUSEWORK ON SATURDAYS!!

HE BROUGHT ME A DOLL. A BABY RAG DOLL WITH BIG EYES AND LONG EYELASHES. SHE'S SO SOFT, I CAN FOLD HER HOWEVER I WANT AND SHE WON'T BREAK...

BUT NOT FOR LONG BECAUSE SHE DISAPPEARS RIGHT AFTER I SHOW HER TO OUR NEIGHBORS. MY GUESS IS THAT ANIA, MONIKA'S SISTER, TOOK HER. SHE'S ALREADY STOLEN LOTS OF THINGS FROM ME, LIKE MY DONALD CHEWING GUM COMICS FOR EXAMPLE.

I CRY AND SEARCH ALL OVER HER HOUSE, BUT EITHER SHE HID HER WELL, OR SHE DIDN'T HAVE HER ANYMORE.. ACTUALLY, GIRLS AREN'T SO GREAT EITHER!

OH WELL, I HADN'T GOTTEN VERY ATTACHED TO THAT DOLL YET. IT MOSTLY REMINDED ME OF MY DAD'S RETURN. OF COURSE I WAS HAPPY TO HAVE IT, BUT I WAS EVEN HAPPIER TO HAVE MY DAD BACK.

ANY GIFT PALES NEXT TO HIM.

ONLY MY PARENTS LIVE IN STALOWA WOLA (MY CITY). SO TO SEE MY GRANDMOTHERS, AUNTS, UNCLES AND COUSINS, WE HAVE TO TRAVEL BY CAR. BUT SOMETIMES WE CAN'T GO AS OFTEN BECAUSE WE'VE USED UP ALL THE GAS RATION CARDS.

WE'RE PERMITTED TEN LITERS THREE TIMES A MONTH FOR OUR FIAT.

ONE TIME MY DAD FORGOT TO BRING THE RATION CARDS. HE ONLY REALIZED IT WHEN HE WAS ALMOST OUT OF GAS.

WE FOUND A SERVICE STATION AND MY DAD DECIDED TO ASK THE ATTENDANT TO PLEASE SELL US THE GAS ANYWAY.

I FORGOT MY RATION CARDS AT HOME AND I DON'T HAVE ENOUGH GAS TO GO GET THEM...

COULDN'T YOU PLEASE ADVANCE ME JUST A LITTLE GAS? I COULD PAY EXTRA IF IT WOULD HELP...

WHAT'S WRONG WITH YOU!?!

WHO DO YOU THINK YOU ARE?!?

THE ATTENDANT GOT ANGRY, CALLING MY DAD A "USURPER" OR SOMETHING LIKE THAT. HE SAID WE'D ALL LIKE TO TRAVEL BUT WE CAN'T BECAUSE WE'RE LIMITED BY THE RATION CARDS THAT COME WITH OUR MONTHLY PAYCHECKS.

HE CALLED HIM A LIAR AND A THIEF WHO THINKS ONLY OF HIMSELF AND HIS OWN FAMILY, WHO MAKES TROUBLE FOR HIS COUNTRY AND EVERYONE ELSE! HE SAID PEOPLE LIKE HIM ARE HOLDING POLAND BACK AND IF MY DAD CONTINUED TO INSIST, HE'D CALL THE MILITIA!!

I WAS VERY SCARED FOR HIM. THE DRIVERS WAITING FOR THE PUMP LOOKED AT US WITH DISGUST...

HUMBLY, MY DAD RETURNED TO THE CAR AND WE LEFT. WE STOPPED AT A PARKING LOT A LITTLE FURTHER DOWN WHERE PEOPLE WERE LEAVING THEIR CARS AND ASKED IF SOMEONE COULD HELP US.

THANKS TO A NICE MAN, WE WERE ABLE TO GET HOME WITHOUT ANY TROUBLE. THEY TRANSFERRED THE GAS WITH A HOSE.

YOU HAD TO INHALE A LITTLE, LIKE DRINKING THROUGH A STRAW, AND THEN IT RAN INTO OUR TANK. MY MOM DIDN'T SAY ANYTHING BUT IT WAS OBVIOUS THAT SOONER OR LATER SHE WAS GOING TO EXPLODE AT HER ABSENTMINDED HUSBAND.

BUT EVEN WITH RATION CARDS, YOU HAVE TO PLAN IN ADVANCE IF YOU WANT TO FILL UP...

WE'RE LUCKY BECAUSE MY MOM WORKS NEXT DOOR TO THE STATION. SHE'S ONE OF THE FIRST TO SEE A DELIVERY FROM HER OFFICE WINDOW.

AND EVEN IF THERE'S NO DELIVERY YET, A LINE OF CARS WILL ALREADY HAVE FORMED. THEY'RE SOME- TIMES THERE THE WHOLE NIGHT, OR EVEN FOR SEVERAL DAYS. ANYWAY, THEY AREN'T MUCH USE WITHOUT GAS.

MY DAD SOMETIMES LEAVES OUR FIAT THERE AND WHEN MY MOM SEES THAT THE GAS HAS ARRIVED, SHE ENTRUSTS THE CAR KEYS TO ONE OF HER COLLEAGUES (SHE DOESN'T KNOW HOW TO DRIVE) AND HE MOVES OUR CAR UP TO THE PUMP.

BEEP BEEP
TOOT

SOMETIMES THIS IS HOW HE SPENDS HIS WHOLE WORKDAY, BECAUSE OTHER COLLEAGUES HAVE ASKED HIM TO DO THE SAME THING.

THE SECOND THE NEWS GETS OUT, EVERYONE HURRIES OVER AND WHOLE STREETS GET BLOCKED OFF. VERY OFTEN, IT'S DIFFICULT TO FIND THE END OF THE LINE.

IT LOOKS LIKE ALL THE CARS IN THE CITY ARE WAITING HERE!

SOME ARE ALREADY OUT OF GAS AND ARE PUSHING THEIR CARS, QUITE A FEW HAVE PLENTY BUT ARE FILLING UP ALL KINDS OF CONTAINERS TO USE UP THEIR RATION CARDS ANYWAY...YOU NEVER KNOW.

KGH 5362

GAS ISN'T EGGS AFTER ALL, IT DOESN'T GO BAD. THEY STORE IT IN THEIR APARTMENTS OR IN THE CELLAR LIKE MY DAD DOES BECAUSE HE SAYS IT SMELLS TOO STRONG IN THE HOUSE. BUT SOMETIMES HE PUTS IT ON THE BALCONY BECAUSE HE'S SCARED IT'LL BE STOLEN.

I REALLY LIKE THE SMELL OF GAS, BUT OUT IN THE OPEN ON THE BALCONY, YOU CAN'T SMELL ANYTHING. THOUGH AS SOON AS YOU GO DOWN TO THE CELLAR, IT'S ALL YOU CAN SMELL!! DAD SAYS YOU'D THINK THERE WERE HIDDEN GAS DEPOSITS UNDER OUR BUILDING.

WE LIVE OVER A MINE- FIELD!

ONE DAY IT'S GOING TO GO OFF UNDER OUR FEET, YOU'LL SEE!!

THE ONES WHO WORRY ABOUT IT ARE THE ONES WHO DON'T HAVE CARS...MAYBE THEY'RE JEALOUS...

DESPITE ALL THIS, MY CITY IS ANIMATED BY A FLEET OF BICYCLISTS IN THE MORNINGS. THEY'RE ON THEIR WAY TO WORK, TO SCHOOL... ULTIMATELY, PEOPLE DON'T USE THEIR CARS MUCH...

GAS IS A LUXURY. PEOPLE HOARD IT FOR THE DAY THEY'LL REALLY NEED IT. TO FLEE COMMUNISM FOR EXAMPLE...

EVERY SUNDAY (AFTER MASS!), MY PARENTS AND I PLANT OURSELVES IN FRONT OF THE TELEVISION TO WATCH "CONCERT OF WISHES".

TWO PRESENTERS, A MAN AND A WOMAN, READ OUT POSTCARDS FROM VIEWERS WITH WISHES FOR THEIR LOVED ONES, FRIENDS, FAMILY...

FOR MR. AND MRS. GRODZKI, FROM THEIR GRANDCHILDREN, ON THE OCCASION OF THEIR WEDDING ANNIVERSARY...

WISHING YOU GOOD HEALTH, LOTS OF WEALTH, AND JOY! AND HERE IS ANNA JANTAR TO SING FOR THEM!!

IT'D BE SO COOL TO GET A CARD THROUGH THE TELEVISION, TO SEE THIS ELEGANT WOMAN READ A MESSAGE JUST FOR US...

WE'RE NOT IN TOUCH WITH OUR FAMILY FAR AWAY VERY OFTEN. WE JUST EXCHANGE CARDS AT CHRISTMAS, EASTER, AND ON BIRTHDAYS. WE DON'T HAVE A TELEPHONE AND NO ONE ELSE IN OUR FAMILY HAS ONE EITHER.

TYLE SŁOŃCA W CAŁYM MIEŚCIE, NIE WIDZIAŁEŚ TEGO JESZCZE, POPATRZ OH POPATRZ

SZEROKIMI ULICAMI NIOSA SZCZEŚCIE ZAKOCHANI, POPATRZ, OH POPATRZ!

WE'VE BEEN ON THE WAITING LIST FOR A PHONE FOR EIGHT YEARS...APPARENTLY IT'S VERY COMPLICATED TO INSTALL. TO GET NEWS MORE OFTEN, MY MOM CALLS A FAMILY MEMBER'S OFFICE FROM HER OFFICE.

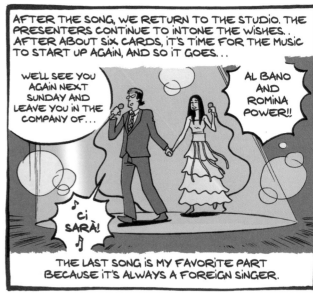

AFTER THE SONG, WE RETURN TO THE STUDIO. THE PRESENTERS CONTINUE TO INTONE THE WISHES... AFTER ABOUT SIX CARDS, IT'S TIME FOR THE MUSIC TO START UP AGAIN, AND SO IT GOES...

WE'LL SEE YOU AGAIN NEXT SUNDAY AND LEAVE YOU IN THE COMPANY OF...

AL BANO AND ROMINA POWER!!

CI SARÀ!

THE LAST SONG IS MY FAVORITE PART BECAUSE IT'S ALWAYS A FOREIGN SINGER.

UNA STORIA D'AMORE E UN MONDO MIGLIORE! CI SARÀ! UN AZZURRO PIÙ INTENSO ED UN CIELO PIÙ IMMENSO!

THEY SING SO BEAUTIFULLY...

CI SARÀ

THEY'RE SINGING IN ITALIAN.

DO YOU KNOW ITALIAN?

NO, BUT YOU CAN TELL.

I CAN'T TELL...HOW DO YOU KNOW THESE THINGS?

MY DAD KNOWS EVERYTHING.

AND ONE SUNDAY, I SAW HER. SHE WAS RESPLENDENT ON THE STAGE. SHE WAS SOO, SO BEAUTIFUL AND SHE WAS SINGING IN FRENCH...

PLEIN DE PLUiiiiE SUR NOS PLAAiNEUS

SANTA MARiiiA!

PLEIN DE BLÉÉÉ SUR NOS TERREUUS DANS NOS MAiSOONS PLEEEiNES DE FLEUUURS, PROTÉGEZ CEUX QUE J'AiMEUU

MiREiLLE MATHiEU!

DAD, CAN YOU CUT MY HAiR? i WANT HER HAiRSTYLE!

LISTEN, YOU'RE TOO YOUNG, IT WON'T SUIT YOU. WHEN YOU GET TO BE HER AGE...

SANTA MARiiiA!

BUT i REALLY WANT iT NOW. PLEASE...

AFTER MUCH INSISTENCE, HE FINALLY DID IT...

i LOOK BEAUTIFUL LIKE MiR...

AH!

iT TAKES SUGAR WATER TO GET iT TO STAY iN PLACE.

BUT ONLY ONCE!! i DON'T BUY SUGAR TO PUT iT IN HAIR!!

EVEN AMONG MY FAMILY, MY NEW HAIRCUT GETS A REACTION.

OH MY GOD!

YOU LOOK LiKE THAT SiNGER WHO BELTS IT OUT ON KONCERT ŻYCZEŃ!!

i'M IN SEVENTH HEAVEN.

AT SCHOOL, HOWEVER, i PUT MY HAiR UP WiTH BARRETTES...

SO NO ONE WILL BE JEALOUS.

THE FRUITS OF OUR LOINS

i DON'T LIKE GOING TO THE BATHROOM. WHY SHOULD i?

WHAT WE DO IN THERE ISN'T VERY INTERESTING. IT SMELLS BAD AND IT'S ALSO KIND OF SAD, TOO.

WE EAT SO MANY GOOD THINGS AND THEN THIS IS WHAT HAPPENS TO THEM... i THINK IT'S SAD.

MY DAD EXPLAINS IT TO ME: EATING MAKES YOU GO TO THE BATHROOM, GOING TO THE BATHROOM KEEPS YOU ALIVE. I'D RATHER SKIP THE MIDDLE STEP.

IN OUR SMALL APARTMENT, EVERYONE KNOWS WHAT EVERYONE ELSE IS DOING. NOTHING GOES UNNOTICED.

WHERE'S MARZI?

IN THE BATHROOM, SHE'S BEEN IN THERE FOR A WHILE IN FACT...

i WON'T GO IN THERE WHEN ANYONE'S EATING. i DON'T WANT TO DISGUST THEM.

THE WORST IS WHEN OTHERS GET UPDATED TOO.

NO, MARZI CAN'T COME PLAY RIGHT AWAY...

NO, NO, SHE'S HERE, BUT SHE'S IN THE BATHROOM.

i CAN HEAR MY DAD SHOUTING IN THE STAIRWELL, HIS VOICE MUST BE ECHOING THROUGHOUT THE ENTIRE BUILDING.

MARZI BATHROOM

ONCE, THE NEIGHBORS ALL SHOWED UP AND STOOD TALKING IN THE FRONT HALL JUST AS i SAT DOWN... I GET ALL WORKED UP BEHIND MY DOOR!

BESIDES, MY MOM KNOWS MY STOMACH IS A LITTLE UPSET. SHE SHOULD HAVE TOLD THEM TO GO INTO THE LIVING ROOM.

I TELL MYSELF, COME ON, GO AHEAD, THEY DO IT TOO. EVERYONE HAS TO. YOU WON'T BE SPARED.

I FORCE MYSELF. I MOAN, BUT I CAN'T DO IT!!

I TRY TO CONCENTRATE, BUT ALL OF A SUDDEN, I HEAR:

AND WHERE'S MARZI?

SHE'S IN THE BATHROOM, SHE HAS AN UPSET STOMACH...

NOOO

SHE ATE TOO MANY CHERRIES, I THINK SHE HAS DIARRHEA.

THANKS, MOM! NOW ALL I HAVE TO DO IS COME OUT AND PRETEND TO BE INVISIBLE.

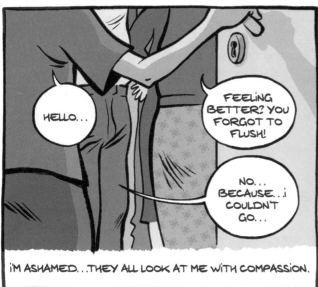

HELLO...

FEELING BETTER? YOU FORGOT TO FLUSH!

NO... BECAUSE...I COULDN'T GO...

I'M ASHAMED...THEY ALL LOOK AT ME WITH COMPASSION.

NO BIG DEAL, IT'LL HAPPEN NEXT TIME!!

OH, THAT'S TOO BAD, YOU COULDN'T GO!

HAVING REACHED THIS CONCLUSION, THEY GO BACK TO THEIR ADULT CONVERSATION. I FEEL HUMILIATED. MAYBE ALL MY FRIENDS WILL HEAR I HAVE DIARRHEA.

ONCE IN AWHILE, AUNT STASIA ASKS ME TO TAKE CARE OF BABY MAGDA BECAUSE SHE HAS TO TAKE THE GIRLS OUT SHOPPING. I REALLY LIKE MAGDA, SO I DON'T MIND.

BLBLBL

EEEH AH AH

I PLAY WITH HER, OR RATHER, I PLAY ON MY OWN WITH HER TOYS BECAUSE SHE'S PRETTY QUIET AND JUST LOOKING AT HER OWN HANDS CAN MAKE HER EUPHORIC.

SHE HAS RUSSIAN DOLLS SHE INHERITED FROM HER TWO OLDER SISTERS. THEY'RE VERY WELL-LOVED.

MONIKA AND ANIA ALREADY DROOLED ALL OVER THEM, BUT YOU CAN MAKE OUT THEIR COLORS AND THEY'RE STILL SHAPED LIKE DOLLS.

ALL OF A SUDDEN, MAGDA STARTS TO CRY. HER FINGERS DON'T MAKE HER HAPPY ANYMORE. I TRY TO MAKE FACES. I STICK MY TONGUE OUT AT HER AND THEN I LOOK MEAN BUT IT DOESN'T WORK.

WAAH!!

OOHH! WHAT SMELLS SO BAD?

MAGDA...

THEY HAD EXPLAINED WHAT TO DO. I OPEN THE WINDOW, I UNDRESS THE BABY, I'VE ALREADY IDENTIFIED THE SCENE OF THE CRIME...

ARGH

I CAN'T DO IT! WHY IS THIS HAPPENING TO ME?

I LOOK AT HER QUESTIONINGLY, SHE'S STILL WAILING. I GET TO IT, I CAN'T JUST LEAVE THE BABY IN THIS STATE!

I TAKE OFF HER DIAPER, I TRY NOT TO BREATHE. I PUT IT IN A BAG BECAUSE IT'S REUSABLE, I WASH HER BOTTOM...IT'S INCREDIBLE, SHE HAS IT EVERYWHERE!!

I FEEL PROUD OF MYSELF NOW. MAGDA IS SPEAKING A LANGUAGE I DON'T UNDERSTAND BUT SHE SEEMS HAPPY. I TELL MYSELF THAT IT REALLY ISN'T THAT HARD. IF YOU WANT TO GO TO THE BATHROOM, YOU GO. YOU DO WHAT YOU NEED TO DO AND THAT'S IT!

GAGAGOO
BLABT

BAGUBU

MAGDA WASN'T EVEN EMBARRASSED IN FRONT OF ME. IT'S A SIGN. WHAT WERE THE CHANCES OF THIS HAPPENING WHILE I WAS TAKING CARE OF HER?

WHEN AUNT STASIA COMES BACK, SHE LAUGHS. SHE EXPLAINS THAT ALL BABIES POOP A LOT. THAT IT'S ALL THEY DO IN FACT. THAT NIGHT, I INTERROGATE MY PARENTS:

WHAT WAS I LIKE WHEN I WAS LITTLE? WHAT DID I DO?...

WHAT DO YOU MEAN WHAT DID YOU DO? YOU DID WHAT ALL BABIES DO! YOU SLEPT, YOU DRANK MILK, YOU CRIED, YOU DIDN'T WANT TO EAT...

AND...WELL...IN TERMS OF POOPING...I WANTED TO KNOW...HMM...DID I DO IT A LOT?

OH THAT, YES!

OH! I'M LIKE EVERYONE ELSE. IT BRINGS ME DOWN...AND THEN MY DAD ADDS:

ONE TIME EVEN, DO YOU REMEMBER, MARIA? WE LEFT HER AT ELA AND BRONEK'S TO GO TO OUR COUSIN'S WEDDING...

THEY NEVER FORGOT THE POOP YOU TOOK THERE!

IN FACT I'M SURPRISED THEY'VE NEVER MENTIONED IT TO YOU!

SUPER! I'LL NEVER GO SEE THEM AGAIN.

WE CHANGED SCHOOLS THIS YEAR. THE OLD ONE WAS VERY CLOSE BUT THE AUTHORITIES DECIDED THAT ALL THE CHILDREN IN OUR BUILDING SHOULD GO TO ONE FARTHER AWAY...

BECAUSE IT'S UNFAIR TO HAVE A SCHOOL SO NEARBY.

OUR SCHOOL IS NUMBER SEVEN.

MONIKA IS IN THE SAME CLASS AS ME AND WE'RE ALWAYS TOGETHER, BUT GRADUALLY ANOTHER GIRL HAS JOINED US. HER NAME IS GOSIA.

IT'S STRANGE BECAUSE SHE LIVES IN THE SAME BUILD- ING, JUST THREE FLOORS ABOVE US, RIGHT ON TOP OF ME BUT WE'D NEVER NOTICED HER BEFORE.

ACTUALLY, I HAD SEEN HER. I'D RUN INTO HER IN FRONT OF THE ELEVATOR.

SHE WAS ALWAYS WITH HER FATHER OR MOTHER. SHE WAS VERY SMALL AND LOOKED AT ME LIKE I WAS FROM OUTER SPACE.

AT FIRST, SHE DIDN'T WALK HOME FROM SCHOOL WITH US. HER MOM WOULD COME GET HER, SHE'D CARRY HER BAG AND HOLD GOSIA'S HAND. MY MOM NEVER DID THAT.

BUT I'D RATHER HAVE IT THIS WAY...MONIKA'S COMPANY IS MORE ENJOYABLE THAN MY MOM'S. WE DO WHATEVER WE WANT, WITHOUT ADULTS, IT'S GREAT!

THOUGH I'VE NOTICED GOSIA'S MOM WATCHING US EVERY SO OFTEN. MAYBE LATER SHE REPORTS ON US TO OUR PARENTS. OR WE SIMPLY SERVE AS EXAMPLES FOR GOSIA OF HOW NOT TO BEHAVE.

DO YOU SEE THOSE TWO? NEVER DO ANYTHING LIKE THAT!

THEY ACT LIKE MONKEYS!!

THAT'S WHY WE DECIDED TO WALK BEHIND THEM, OR EVEN CHANGE OUR ROUTE ENTIRELY.

NOT LONG AFTER, GOSIA STARTED COMING HOME FROM SCHOOL ALONE AND THAT'S HOW SHE JOINED US.

WE BECAME FRIENDS QUICKLY, IT'S REMARKABLY PRACTICAL TO LIVE IN THE SAME BUILDING!

ALSO, SHE'S SOMEONE WHO WORKS VERY HARD AT SCHOOL, AND THAT IMPRESSES ME!

IT'S SOMETIMES HARD TO ALL GET ALONG WHEN YOU'RE THREE... THREE IS UNEVEN, IT'S LIKE HAVING FIVE WHEELS ON A CARRIAGE. THREE IS TOO MANY OR NOT ENOUGH.

AT SCHOOL, I SIT NEXT TO GOSIA. SHE'S VERY FOCUSED AND WELL-BEHAVED. SHE HAS PRETTY NOTEBOOKS THAT SHE WRITES EVERYTHING IN WITH BEAUTIFUL COLORED PENCILS.

I PLAY AT HOME OR IN THE STAIRWELL WITH MONIKA. GOSIA NEVER COMES. HER PARENTS WON'T LET HER BECAUSE THEY KNOW WE RUN WILD AND GOSIA MUST ABSOLUTELY NOT BEHAVE LIKE THAT!

I'M SURE THEY DON'T APPRECIATE OUR GAMES, ESPECIALLY THE ONE WHERE WE TAKE THE ELEVATOR TO GO RING DOORBELLS. GOSIA IS A LITTLE JEALOUS, SHE'D LIKE TO PLAY WITH US.

BUT WHEN WE'RE ALL TOGETHER, IT DOESN'T ALWAYS WORK...

SO GIRLS, AREN'T WE GOING TO PLAY?

NO, WE HAVE TO FINISH OUR HOMEWORK FIRST...

COME ON, WE CAN DO IT LATER!!

HURRY UP! THE SOONER WE START, THE SOONER WE CAN GO PLAY!

HMPFF, I'M LEAVING NOW...

GOSIA PUSHES ME TOWARDS BEING GOOD. MONIKA CAN'T STAND IT...

FIVE MINUTES LATER, SHE'S BACK...

OH! YOU'RE NOT FINISHED YET!!

ANOTHER TIME, WE'RE PLAYING AT GOSIA'S...

MARZI, CAN YOU GO DOWN AND GET YOUR COLORED PENCILS? WE'RE GOING TO DRAW TOGETHER.

BUT WHEN I GET BACK, THE DOOR IS LOCKED!

I KNOCK, I RING, NOTHING WORKS, I EVEN SHOUT...

IT'S ME! OPEN UP!! I HAVE THE PENCILS!

I KNOCK AGAIN, I KNOW THEY'RE IN THERE. THEY'RE GIGGLING SOFTLY BEHIND THE DOOR. THEY'RE PROUD OF THEMSELVES.

I GET REALLY ANGRY. I'M SURE MONIKA TURNED GOSIA AGAINST ME. SHE'S MORE DECEITFUL, IT DOESN'T SURPRISE ME, BUT GOSIA... I THOUGHT SHE REALLY LIKED ME. I WAS WRONG...

WHAT ARE YOU DOING?

I KNOW YOU'RE IN THERE, I HEAR YOU!

I'M GOING TO BREAK THE DOOR DOWN!!

LOOK, I'M GOING TO DRAW ON IT!

IT'S EASY TO ERASE...

MONIKA!! I KNEW SHE WAS BEHIND THIS!

WHY ARE YOU DOING THIS?!?

BECAUSE, HEE HEE HEE!

MONIKA, I'LL NEVER LEND YOU MY PENCILS AGAIN, FORGET IT!!

I DON'T CARE, GOSIA'S ARE PRETTIER AND THEY'RE EVEN SCENTED, UNLIKE YOURS!

AT HOME, I CRY, IT'S NOT FAIR. I PICTURE THE TWO OF THEM HAVING FUN TOGETHER.

IN THE MORNING, THEY DON'T COME GET ME FOR SCHOOL. I KNOCK AT MONIKA'S AND HER MOM TELLS ME THAT GOSIA ALREADY CAME AND THEY'VE LEFT! I RUN AND CATCH UP TO THEM...

WHY DIDN'T YOU COME GET ME?!?

BECAUSE. YOU'RE NOT WITH US. WALK ON YOUR OWN!

THEY HOLD HANDS AND MOVE AWAY... I DON'T LIKE GOSIA ANYMORE, THAT CHUBBY LITTLE GOOSE. "THAT ONE'S GOOD FOR DINNER!" AS MY AUNT NIUSIA WOULD SAY. THAT THOUGHT MAKES ME LAUGH.

GOSIA IS NEW, WE'RE FIGHTING OVER HER, FOR HER ATTENTION. AND SHE HAS MORE MONEY THAN WE DO. SHE HAS NICE CLOTHES. THINGS WE'RE NOT USED TO.

OOF!

AAH!

SHE REPRESENTS ANOTHER WORLD WE'RE BOTH CURIOUS ABOUT AND NEITHER OF US WANTS TO SHARE. I'M THE LOSER TODAY.

I DON'T LIKE MONIKA ANYMORE EITHER. SHE'S DROPPED ME. I KNOW SHE'LL BE BACK ONE DAY... BUT IT'LL BE TOO LATE! I'LL HAVE A NEW FRIEND AND I'LL NEVER PLAY WITH MONIKA AGAIN!

SHE BETTER NOT THINK I HAVE NOTHING TO DO BUT WAIT FOR HER! I HAVE A LOT TO KEEP ME BUSY!

IN THE EVENINGS, GOSIA DOESN'T COME PLAY IN THE STAIRWELL AND MONIKA CAN'T RESIST... THAT MUST BE HER KNOCKING ON THE DOOR...

HI, IS MARZI HERE?

YES, SHE'S IN HER ROOM, COME IN.

HOW DARE SHE COME OVER AS IF NOTHING HAS HAPPENED.

MARZI, ARE YOU COMING TO PLAY?

YES,

BUT ON ONE CONDITION: I CHOOSE THE GAME.

OK.

YOU KNOW WHAT?! NEXT TIME, I'LL BE MORE ADAMANT!

EVERYONE GETS A TURN TO BE LEFT OUT...

THE 1ST OF MAY, LABOR DAY, IS A VERY IMPORTANT HOLIDAY IN POLAND. ALL THE CITIES IN MY COUNTRY ORGANIZE A BIG PARADE THAT LASTS SEVERAL HOURS AND WHICH ALL THE SURROUNDING RESIDENTS PARTICIPATE IN.

EVERYONE HAS TO BE THERE. NO ONE SAYS SO OPENLY, BUT IF YOU DON'T GO, YOU COULD SUFFER CONSEQUENCES AT YOUR JOB.

THE AUTHORITIES ACTIVELY SCRUTINIZE EVERYONE'S BEHAVIOR, EVEN THE CHILDREN'S. THE WINDOWS ON ALL THE BUILDINGS SPORT FLAGS OR PORTRAITS OF GOVERNMENT OFFICIALS.

I GO IN THE MORNING WITH MY PARENTS. THE STREETS ARE FULL OF PEOPLE, EVERY COMPANY SETS UP A MEETING PLACE FOR ITS EMPLOYEES. I STAY WITH MY MOM, WHILE MY DAD GOES TO ANOTHER MEETING PLACE.

IT BEGINS IN FRONT OF THE CULTURAL CENTER. THERE ARE LOUDSPEAKERS EVERYWHERE PROCLAIMING THE BENEFITS OF SOCIALISM, I DON'T UNDERSTAND ANYTHING BUT IT SEEMS TO PLEASE EVERYONE BECAUSE THEY SMILE AND APPLAUD WHENEVER THE VOICE STOPS.

ALL EUROPE IS WATCHING US TODAY. THEY THINK WE'RE NOT HAPPY IN POLAND. SHOW THEM HOW WRONG THEY ARE!

SHOW THEM HOW WELL WE ARE DOING! LONG LIVE MAY 1ST, LONG LIVE LABOR DAY!

THE PEOPLE ARE REQUIRED TO BEHAVE THIS WAY SO NO ONE CAN ACCUSE THEM OF HAVING A BAD ATTITUDE AND SO THEY'LL BE LEFT ALONE.

MY MOM'S BOSS IS ALREADY THERE, HE NOTES HER ARRIVAL AND MY PRESENCE ON HIS PAD. SHE HAS TO SIGN HER NAME. LATER, PEOPLE WILL CHECK AND COMPARE ALL THE NOTEBOOKS.

THEY'LL SEE THAT MY FATHER CAME ALONE BUT THAT I WAS WITH MY MOTHER AND THEY'LL KNOW THAT I TOO WAS INSTILLED WITH A LOVE OF WORK FROM MY EARLIEST DAYS. THE WHOLE FAMILY WAS PRESENT AT THE MAY 1ST PARADE. CHECKMARK!

ONLY OLD PEOPLE ARE EXCUSED. THEY WATCH US FROM THE WINDOWS DECORATED WITH POSTERS, FLAGS AND PORTRAITS.

EACH BUSINESS WALKS SEPARATELY TO MAKE ITSELF CLEARLY VISIBLE. THEIR REPRESENTATIVES CARRY BIG LOGOS. FOR EXAMPLE, MY DAD FOLLOWS AN ENORMOUS SIGN: HSW, DEPARTMENT OF TOOLS.

WE TRAVERSE THE CITY THIS WAY FOR SEVERAL HOURS, SINGING AND SHOUTING LOUDLY HOW MUCH WE LOVE SOCIALISM AND OUR WORK. ON THIS DAY, WE HAVE TO BE HAPPY.

THEN WE FINALLY SPREAD OUT, WE FIND MY DAD AND WALK WITH HIM, BUT WHEN WE PASS OUR APARTMENT COMPLEX, WE SLIP AWAY DISCREETLY. YOU HAVE TO BE VERY VIGILANT BECAUSE EYES ARE ALWAYS WATCHING AND SOMETIMES THEY CAN DENOUNCE YOU...

MY DAD THINKS I'M STRANGE BECAUSE I SCREAM WHENEVER I SEE A SPIDER...

PAJĄK!

PAJĄK!

HELP!!

HE SAYS IT REALLY SURPRISES HIM BECAUSE I'M NOT SCARED OF HORSES BUT I RUN AT THE SIGHT OF SUCH A TINY CREATURE.

YOU THINK IT'LL CHASE YOU DOWN AND BITE OR KILL YOU MAYBE?

WELL... YES!

I CAN'T EXPLAIN WHY I'M SO FRIGHTENED AND WHAT FRIGHTENS ME THE MOST.

I CAN'T EXPLAIN BECAUSE HE DOESN'T LISTEN, HE MAKES FUN OF MY FEAR.

TAKA DUŻA DZIEWCZYNA, A PAJĄKÓW SIĘ BOI!

"A BIG GIRL LIKE YOU BEING SCARED OF SPIDERS!"

IT MOSTLY BOTHERS ME WHEN THEY MOVE. THEY'RE VERY AGILE AND MAKE WEBS...WHICH IS EVEN CREEPIER A SPIDER IMMOBILE ON A WALL CAN EASILY LAUNCH ITSELF OFF AND BE ALMOST ANYWHERE IN A FLASH!

I ALSO DON'T LIKE THAT THEY HAVE EIGHT LEGS AND THAT THEY ALL MOVE AT THE SAME TIME. EEK...

I CAN'T KILL THEM, I FREEZE UP. ALSO BECAUSE KILLING'S NO FUN. SO I LEAVE THAT TO OTHERS. I SCREAM, CRY AND WAIT FOR SOMEONE TO COME HELP ME.

AND NO MATTER WHO SHOWS UP, THEY LAUGH AT ME. NO ONE EMPATHIZES.

EVEN MY MOM DOESN'T UNDERSTAND MY ARACHNOPHOBIA, ALTHOUGH SHE HATES FROGS AND FROGS AREN'T EVEN SCARY. NOT AS SCARY AS SPIDERS ANYWAY!

THE WORST IS THE FOREST. IT'S CRAWLING WITH SPIDERS BUT I STILL LOVE GOING THERE...

EVERY FALL, I GO MUSHROOM PICKING IN THE FOREST WITH MY DAD AND OUR ACROSS-THE-HALL NEIGHBORS.

WE USUALLY MAKE THESE EXCURSIONS ON FRIDAYS AFTER SCHOOL AND WORK. WE GO BY BICYCLE.

IF WE MAKE A PLAN AHEAD OF TIME FOR THE WEEKEND, WE GO BY CAR AND LEAVE VERY EARLY IN THE MORNING. ON SATURDAYS AND SUNDAYS WE SET THE ALARM FOR 5 AM, MUSHROOM TIME...

IT'S 5 AM, MARZI AND MUSHROOMS WAKE UP...

I MUCH PREFER GOING BY BICYCLE ON FRIDAY AFTERNOONS...

WHEN I RIDE ON MY DAD'S, I HAVE TO KEEP MY FEET SPREAD WIDE APART SO THEY DON'T TOUCH THE WHEELS BECAUSE THAT COULD BE REALLY DANGEROUS.

I LOVE TRAVELING THIS WAY. WE LEAVE THE CITY AND FIND OURSELVES ON A TREE-LINED ROAD.

HERE WE ARE ALREADY. IT'S RELAXING, AND BOY DOES THE FOREST SMELL GOOD!

SOMETIMES WE RACE. MY DAD IS THE TALLEST, WITH THE LONGEST LEGS, SO WE ALWAYS WIN!

BUT WHEN IT COMES TO THE PICKING COMPETITION, WE'RE NOT THE CHAMPIONS. WE SPLIT UP INTO THREE TEAMS. ME AND MY DAD, ANIA AND HERS, AND ANDRZEJ AND HIS MOM.

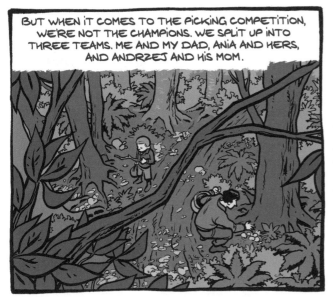

MY DAD GETS MAD AT ME... I AM A LITTLE SCARED IN FACT.

DID YOU COME FOR THE MUSHROOMS OR THE SPIDERS?!?

I ALWAYS WALK WITH A STICK IN MY HAND SO I WON'T ACCIDENTALLY WANDER INTO A SPIDER WEB BETWEEN TWO TREES. FOR JUST THIS REASON, I OFTEN FOLLOW SOMEBODY ELSE... WHICH ISN'T A GREAT STRATEGY FOR FINDING MUSHROOMS.

BUT i USUALLY TRY TO COPE WITH MY FEAR ALONE. i ALREADY FEEL MORE BRAVE WITH MY STICK. AND iF i REALLY CONCENTRATE ON LOOKING FOR MUSHROOMS...

i CAN FORGET ABOUT THOSE LiTTLE CREATURES HiDiNG EVERYWHERE.

WE'RE ALL VERY CLOSE TO EACH OTHER. SO WE TALK, WE JOKE AROUND, AND AS SOON AS WE FiND AN UNUSUAL MUSHROOM, WE RUN OVER TO SHOW iT.

THiS ONE'S POiSONOUS!!

BUT iT'S SO BEAUTi- FUL...

REMEMBER THAT THE MOST BEAUTiFUL ONES ARE THE MOST DANGEROUS!

CAN i AT LEAST KEEP iT AS A SOUVENiR?

THAT'S NOT A GOOD iDEA, ONCE iT'S BEEN PiCKED iT'LL DECOMPOSE, AND EVEN TOUCHiNG iT iS TOXiC...

i REALLY LiKE LOOKiNG FOR MUSHROOMS. THEY'RE BEAUTiFUL AND FRAGiLE AND FEEL SO SOFT. i'D BE ALMOST HAPPY TO COME HERE JUST TO STROKE THEM.

TOO BAD THEY DON'T HAVE MOUTHS TO SMiLE OR TALK TO US WiTH. THESE MUSHROOMS ARE ACTUALLY TiNY MEN WHO HiDE THEiR HEADS UNDER A HAT BECAUSE THEY'RE SHY.

THEY TAKE iT OFF WHEN WE'RE NOT LOOKiNG... SO i STAY CROUCHED DOWN iN SiLENCE, BREATHiNG GENTLY, WAiTiNG FOR A MUSHROOM TO iNADVER- TENTLY TAKE OFF HiS HAT, SO i CAN SEE HiS HEAD.

WHAT ARE YOU DOiNG THERE? ARE YOU COUNTiNG ANTS? YOU'RE REORDERiNG THEiR LiVES HERE TOO?!

i'M OBSERViNG THE MUSHROOMS.

ARE YOU WAiTiNG FOR THEM TO GROW?

DAD! YOU'RE ANNOYiNG ME!!

SHH! WE DON'T SHOUT iN THE FOREST. iT'S NOT OUR HOUSE, iT BELONGS TO THE BiRDS AND OTHER ANiMALS...

LiKE SPiDERS ...

THEM TOO, YES...

AND WE SCARE THEM WHEN WE SHOUT. WOULD YOU LiKE iT iF SOMEONE CAME TO YOUR HOUSE UNiNViTED AND STARTED TO YELL?

WELL, NO...

SO YOU UNDERSTAND, WE NEED TO RESPECT THE iNHABiTANTS OF THE FOREST.

SOMETIMES WE SPREAD OUT SO MUCH THAT i CAN'T SEE ANYONE BESIDES MY DAD. THE FOREST ITSELF IS QUITE VARIED. SOME OF THE TREES GROW VERY CLOSE TOGETHER. i FIND IT HARD TO SLIP BETWEEN THEM.

THERE AREN'T AS MANY WEBS HERE, WHICH MEANS i FEEL MORE COMFORTABLE AND FOR ONCE, i REALLY AM MORE INTERESTED IN THE MUSHROOM PICKING.

AFTERWARDS, ALL SIX OF US MEET AT THE PLACE WHERE WE LEFT OUR BICYCLES AND COMPARE BASKETS...

DAD!!

YOU HAVE AN ENORMOUS SPIDER ON YOUR SHOULDER!! KILL IT, PLEASE! i'M SCARED!!

i'M NOT GOING TO KILL IT, WHY SHOULD i? IT'S NOT HURTING ME, THE POOR THING IS MORE SCARED THAN YOU ARE!

NO, THAT'S NOT TRUUEE! DO YOU SEE HOW IT'S CLIMBING UP YOUR JACKET!!

IT WANTS ONLY ONE THING, THAT'S TO SAVE ITSELF...WOULD YOU LIKE TO TAKE IT HOME? IT'S CUTE.

i'M PUTTING IT DOWN HERE, LOOK, IT'S RUNNING AWAY...

AS LONG AS IT'S NOT HEADING MY WAY...

WE DRINK THE TEA WE BROUGHT IN A THERMOS. IT'S ALREADY LATE, EVENING IS SLOWLY STARTING TO FALL.

ONCE, WE COVERED SO MUCH GROUND WE ALMOST COULDN'T FIND THE BICYCLES AGAIN. THE FOREST IS HUGE AND WHEN DUSK FALLS, ALL THE TREES LOOK MONSTROUSLY BIG AND FRIGHTENING.

HELLO?!

EVER SINCE THEN, WE'VE TRIED TO REMEMBER TO BRING A COMPASS.

WE HEAD HOME, LEAVING BEHIND A PEACEFUL FOREST WHOSE CREATURES CAN NOW RETURN TO THEIR NORMAL LIVES...

ALL THE MUSHROOM MEN CAN FINALLY TAKE OFF THEIR HATS!

AT HOME, I SHOW MY MOM THE THINGS IN MY BAG: BEAUTIFUL LEAVES, FEATHERS, ACORNS, A PIECE OF SNAKE SKIN, PINE CONES...HERE'S MY COLLECTION!

AND WHAT'S THAT?

I'M NOT REALLY SURE. I THOUGHT IT WAS PRETTY SO I PICKED IT UP.

I THINK IT'S A DRIED ANIMAL DROPPING...

NOO!!

YES, I'M ALMOST POSITIVE, GO LOOK IN YOUR ENCYCLOPEDIA...

YOU COLLECTED A WILD BOAR DROPPING.

IT HAD SEEMED SO EXOTIC I WANTED TO KEEP IT.

LATER THAT NIGHT, MY DAD AND I MADE LITTLE MEN OUT OF ACORNS AND MATCHES WHILE MY MOM PREPARED THE MUSHROOMS...WE DIDN'T PICK THAT MANY BUT SHE SAYS WE ALREADY HAVE MORE THAN ENOUGH.

ENOUGH TO CONTAMINATE US!!

SHE DOESN'T PARTICULARLY LIKE OUR GOING MUSHROOM PICKING. SHE SAYS IT'S DANGEROUS.

WE SHOULDN'T EAT MUSHROOMS... THE GROUND IS STILL RADIOACTIVE!

BUT THEY SAID WE COULD PICK THEM. THAT THE DANGER WAS OVER...

HMMPF... THEY SAY A LOT OF THINGS...

ACCORDING TO HER, THEY'RE STILL TOXIC. THE CONTAMINATION FROM CHERNOBYL IS NOT OVER.

SHE HANGS THEM UP, GRUMBLING THE WHOLE TIME..

LOOK! THEY'RE BIGGER THAN EVER NOW!

THEY'RE GROWING TOO FAST.

WHY IS IT HARMFUL FOR MUSHROOMS BUT NOT FOR ME?

I FEEL LIKE I'M GROWING AS UNRESTRAINEDLY AS THEY ARE. I DON'T GROW IN THE EARTH BUT I WALK ON IT. THAT'S ALMOST THE SAME THING. SO AM I TOXIC TOO? RADIOACTIVE? DANGEROUS?

AND TO WHOM? TO OTHERS? OR TO MYSELF?

MY MOM THINKS IF YOU EAT MUSHROOMS YOU SHOULD DRINK SEVERAL GLASSES OF VODKA TO NEUTRALIZE THEIR HARMFUL EFFECTS...BUT CHILDREN CAN'T DRINK IT.

CHOMP CHOMP

I EAT A FEW ANYWAY. AFTER ALL, THE BEETS AND POTATOES THEY FORCE ME TO SWALLOW GROW IN THE EARTH TOO...SO?

FUR AND FEATHERS

WINTER VACATION BEGINS AND AS ALWAYS, I SPEND IT AT MY GRANDMOTHER JADZIA'S IN SKOWIERZYN.

LET'S GO MARZI, COME HELP US!!

THIS YEAR IT'S VERY COLD AND THE ENTIRE CITY IS COVERED IN SNOW. OUR LITTLE CAR REFUSES TO START ANYWHERE BELOW NEGATIVE TWENTY.

WE HAVE TO PUSH IT, WHICH MAKES FOR QUITE A SIGHT.

BUT ONCE A FEW PASSERSBY GET INTO THE ACTION, PUSHING OUR FIAT 126 OVER THE ICE BECOMES A PIECE OF CAKE.

BRATAKLATAKLATAKLATA

THE ENGINE STARTS UP, WITH A SOUND A LITTLE LIKE COOKING POTS IN A WASHING MACHINE.

BECAUSE THERE'S LESS TRAFFIC IN THE COUNTRY THAN IN THE CITY, YOU CAN USUALLY DRIVE FASTER... BUT NOT WHEN IT SNOWS.

SLOW DOWN, WILL YOU! WE'LL END UP IN A DITCH...

MY MOM CAN NEVER REFRAIN FROM COMMENTING ON MY DAD'S DRIVING, EVEN AT TEN KILOMETERS AN HOUR.

THANKS TO THE DANGEROUS CONDITIONS, THE TRIP TOOK THREE TIMES AS LONG...

BE GOOD, DON'T BOTHER GRANDMA, OKAY?!

MY PARENTS RETURN THAT SAME DAY, LESS WORRIED ABOUT THE ROADS BECAUSE THE SUN HAS MELTED THE SNOW A LITTLE.

MY GRANDMOTHER AND AUNT'S HOUSE IS LIKE THE VILLAGE RUMOR MILL (I FIND IT VERY EDUCATIONAL BECAUSE I HEAR THEM DISCUSS THINGS I HAD NO IDEA ABOUT).

SINCE NIUSIA IS A SEAMSTRESS, THERE ARE ALWAYS LOTS OF PEOPLE COMING BY TO HAVE AN OUTFIT STITCHED OR TO GET THE HOLES IN THEIR SWEATERS FIXED, ETC...THEY'LL STAY AND CHAT, DRINK TEA. IT'S NEVER BORING, AND YOU GET TO KNOW EVERYTHING ABOUT EVERYONE...

YOU KNOW WHO GOT A PACKAGE FROM THEIR FAMILY IN THE UNITED STATES AND WHAT WAS IN IT. YOU KNOW WHO GOT DRUNK ON SPIRITS (99% UNDISTILLED ALCOHOL) AND TURNED PURPLE...

BUT SINCE IT WAS SO COLD OUTSIDE, HIS WIFE THOUGHT IT WAS HIS NORMAL SKIN COLOR...HE JUST SMELLED STRANGE...LUCKILY, HE'S FINE.

YOU KNOW WHO FATHERED THE CHILD WHO LIVES OVER BY THE DAIRY, WHO'S BEING RAISED BY HIS MOTHER AND GRANDPARENTS.

YOU KNOW THIS MAN ALREADY HAS THREE CHILDREN AND A WIFE WHO'LL BE THE LAST TO FIND OUT.

YOU KNOW WHY WIESIEK D. HAS A SCREW LOOSE (APPARENTLY, A WOMAN'S SEVENTH CHILD IS ALWAYS SOMETHING OF AN IDIOT!). YOU KNOW WHO'S SLEEPING WITH WHOM, WHO GETS SICK BECAUSE OF IT AND WHY...

MEEOW!

IF MY PARENTS ONLY KNEW WHAT I WAS HEARING! THEY DON'T EVEN LET ME WATCH PEOPLE KISSING ON TV!!

HERE, I CAN SIT AND LISTEN TO EVERYTHING AND ANYTHING.

OLD WIDOW BRONISŁAWA IS HIDING A BIG PACKET OF DOLLARS UNDER HER PILLOW!

IT'S BECAUSE HER SON IS SECRETLY IN THE UNITED STATES...

IN SHORT, NOTHING ESCAPES THE VILLAGE OF SKOWIERZYN!

THERE'S ANOTHER PLACE WHERE EVERYTHING GETS TALKED ABOUT: IN FRONT OF THE GROCERY STORE, BUT IT'S NOT THE WOMEN WHO GET TOGETHER TO GOSSIP THERE.

THE MEN ARE GOOD BLABBERMOUTHS TOO, THEY DRINK AND TELL TALES OUTSIDE. IT'S ROUGH IN WINTER, ESPECIALLY WHEN IT'S HORRIBLY COLD, BUT THEY DO IT ANYWAY.

THEN THEY COME HOME AND TELL THEIR WIVES WHO, OBVIOUSLY, MAKE SURE THE NEWS TRAVELS.

EVERY SO OFTEN, I BICYCLE TO THE STORE WITH MY AUNT TO SEE IF ANYTHING NEW HAS COME IN.

ONCE IN A WHILE WE HAPPEN UPON A WOMAN WHO'S COME LOOKING FOR HER HUSBAND.

YOU DON'T HAVE ANY BETTER USE FOR YOUR MONEY!?

DO YOU UNDERSTAND WHAT I'M SAYING OR HAS THE VODKA TURNED YOU INTO A COMPLETE IDIOT?!?

YOU'RE GOING TO FREEZE TO DEATH OUT HERE ONE DAY! THERE'LL BE NO ONE TO HELP! YOUR FRIENDS WILL BE TOO DRUNK TO NOTICE!

GET UP, NOW! LOOK AT YOURSELF, YOU CAN HARDLY STAND! I'M NOT GOING TO CARRY YOU AGAIN!!

YOUR OWN CHILDREN ARE ASHAMED OF YOU, THE OTHER KIDS POINT AND SHOUT THAT THEIR FATHER IS A DRUNK, THAT HE COMES CRAWLING HOME...

THESE SPEECHES ARE COMMON BUT THEY DON'T MAKE ANY DIFFERENCE BECAUSE EVERY VILLAGER HAS BEEN THERE, DRINKING 'TIL HE'S PASSED OUT, AT LEAST ONCE IN HIS LIFE. I DON'T KNOW HOW THEY DO IT, BUT THERE'S ALWAYS THE SAME NUMBER OUT FRONT!

SOME OF THE THINGS THE ADULTS TALK ABOUT AT MY AUNT'S ESCAPE ME. I NOTE THE WORDS I DON'T KNOW AND AS SOON AS THE HOUSE CLEARS OUT, I TRY TO FIND OUT MORE.

WHAT DOES CAESARIAN MEAN??

DID IT COME UP AT SCHOOL? HOW DO WE EXPLAIN IT, MOM?

OH DEAR!

MY AUNT RISES TO THE CHALLENGE, HOWEVER...

IT HAS TO DO WITH BIOLOGY, YOU SEE...WHEN A MOTHER IS EXPECTING A BIG, BIG BABY.....HOW SHOULD I PUT IT?...

THEY HAVE TO OPERATE ON THE MOTHER TO GET IT OUT!

SO THEY MAKE A BIG HOLE IN HER STOMACH!!!

MAYBE BETTER TO WAIT FOR BIOLOGY CLASS...

IT'S TERRIBLE...

ONE NIGHT, I ACCOMPANY MY GRANDMOTHER TO ONE OF HER FRIEND'S HOUSES WHERE A BUNCH OF WOMEN HAVE GATHERED TO CLEAN GOOSE FEATHERS FOR STUFFING CUSHIONS AND QUILTS...

IN THE SUMMER, WHEN THE GEESE HAVE A GOOD DOWNY COAT, THEY'RE CAUGHT AND DE-FEATHERED. THEIR FEATHERS ARE COLLECTED IN BAGS AND WHEN THERE'S NO MORE WORK IN THE FIELDS, THAT IS TO SAY IN THE WINTER, THE OLD LADIES SORT THE BAGS AND WORK TOGETHER IN ONE BIG ROOM.

ONE DAY HERE, THE NEXT THERE, ALWAYS THE SAME CIRCLE OF FRIENDS. IT'S FUNNY AND I HELP GRANDMA A LITTLE.

YOU PICK OUT A FEATHER FROM THE BAG AND YOU PULL OFF JUST THE DOWN, THROWING OUT THE QUILL, UNDERSTAND?

HERE, PUT IT IN THIS LITTLE BAG, YOU CAN MAKE YOURSELF A SMALL PILLOW, WHAT DO YOU THINK?

WHAT A FUNNY THING TO DO!

I PULL OUT A QUILL AND PUT IT ASIDE. I'LL TRY TO WRITE WITH IT THE WAY THEY USED TO. THE DOWN IS VERY SOFT AND LIGHT...

LITTLE BITS FLOAT IN THE AIR AND FILL THE WHOLE ROOM WITH SNOW THAT, INSTEAD OF FALLING, FLIES TOWARDS THE CEILING. IT FEELS LIKE A FAIRY UNIVERSE.

THE OLD WOMEN SING PSALMS. YOU CAN SING OTHER THINGS TOO, BUT THEY PREFER RELIGIOUS SONGS.

IT ALMOST FEELS LIKE A WITCHES' COVEN HUMMING WITH INCANTATIONS!

I SEE TRACES OF GOOSE BLOOD ON A FEW QUILLS (SOMEONE MUST HAVE BEEN TOO FORCEFUL WHEN THEY DE-FEATHERED THE GOOSE LAST SUMMER) AND IT MAKES ME FEEL SICK.

KIDS TODAY ARE SCARED OF EVERYTHING!

A DROP OF BLOOD AND THEY FALL ON THE GROUND IN A FAINT! HA HA!

OOOH...

THE LADIES NEVER FAIL TO MAKE A COMMENT.

I REMEMBER WHEN WE WERE KIDS, WE DIDN'T GIVE IT A SECOND THOUGHT. WE'D LIVED THROUGH THE WAR, WE WERE USED TO BLOOD!

AH, THE YOUTH OF TODAY...

NATURALLY, IT WAS BETTER BEFORE, EVERYONE GLORIFIES THE PAST. AND THEY ALL AGREE, THEY NOD THEIR HEADS AS THEY WORK AND THROW COMPASSIONATE LOOKS MY WAY EVERY SO OFTEN.

SINCE I'M TIRED OF WORKING, I GO SEE MY UNCLE WŁODEK (MY DAD'S OLDER BROTHER) AND HIS WIFE HELA WHO LIVE JUST NEXT DOOR.

THEY ALWAYS HAVE PIERNIK AT THEIR HOUSE. IT'S A HONEY AND SPICE CAKE I REALLY LOVE.

WŁODEK ONLY HAS ONE LEG. WHEN HE WAS YOUNG, HE CAUGHT GANGRENE. HE HAD HURT HIS CALF AND WENT IN THE RIVER WITH HIS CUT...

IT GOT INFECTED AND THE DOCTORS HAD TO AMPUTATE HIS LEG ABOVE THE KNEE. NOW HE GETS AROUND WITH CRUTCHES.

I LIKE HIM A LOT. HIS TEMPERAMENT IS A LOT LIKE MY DAD'S. HE'S NICE TO EVERYONE AND ALWAYS IN A GOOD MOOD.

IN SPITE OF HIS HANDICAP, HE WORKS A BIT IN THE FIELDS, BUT MOSTLY HE SEWS WORK GLOVES. HE MAKES DOZENS EVERY DAY.

HE HAS MANY ANIMALS: TWO HORSES, SEVERAL COWS, RABBITS, FERRETS, CHINCHILLAS, SABLES, GEESE, CHICKENS, TURKEYS, PIGS, CATS AND DOGS.

RRRR
RRRR
RRRR
RRRR

AND AMONG THE LATTER IS A LITTLE DOG: ŁATKA (LITTLE SPOT). SHE LOVES MY UNCLE AND IS VERY PROTECTIVE OF HIM. WHEN HE SHOWS ME HOW HE MAKES HIS GLOVES, SHE STICKS TO HIS SIDE. SHE'S USUALLY ON HIS KNEE.

BUT THIS TIME, SHE'S ON A LITTLE WOODEN BENCH, ROYALLY SEATED ON TOP OF A COLLECTION OF RAGS.

SHE BIRTHED A LITTER A FEW DAYS AGO. DO YOU WANT TO SEE HER PUPPIES?

YES!

ŁATKA BARES HER TEETH, SHE DOESN'T WANT ANYONE TO TOUCH HER OFFSPRING. SHE STARTS TO BARK. ONLY WŁODEK CAN APPROACH HER.

HE PULLS A LITTLE SLEEPING PUPPY FROM OUT OF THE BUNDLE.

HE'S SO BEAUTIFUL!! CAN I HOLD HIM?

HE'S ALL WARM AND SOFT. HE PRESSES AGAINST ME AS IF I WERE HIS MOM... ŁATKA KEEPS A CLOSE WATCH ON WHAT WE'RE DOING WITH HER CHILD.

WE GIVE HIM BACK.

DO YOU HAVE A LOT?

FIVE, THREE MALES AND TWO FEMALES.

BUT I'LL FIND SOMEONE TO TAKE THEM...

SMACK

FOR NOW THOUGH, ALL FIVE ARE FREE?!

SHE'LL BE SAD WHEN YOU TAKE THEM FROM HER!

IT WON'T BE THE FIRST TIME IT'S HAPPENED TO HER.

DO YOU THINK YOU COULD GIVE ME ONE?

WE'LL HAVE TO SEE WHAT YOUR DAD SAYS. A DOG IN AN APARTMENT, HE MIGHT NOT LIKE THE IDEA.

DAD LOVES ANIMALS, I'LL CONVINCE HIM, WHEN CAN I COME GET IT?

I RUN BACK TO MY GRANDMOTHER'S FRIEND'S HOUSE. THE OLD WOMEN ARE FINISHED. I RUSH OVER TO TELL GRANDMA THE GOOD NEWS.

OH LOOK AT YOU, YOU ATE PIERNIK! COME HERE, YOU'VE GOT IT ALL OVER YOUR FACE!

HER PILLOW IS GOING TO BE VERY FLAT NO DOUBT!!

SHE WETS HER FINGER WITH SALIVA AND RUBS MY CHIN. I HATE THAT BUT I'M TOO PREOCCUPIED TO PROTEST.

GRANDMA, ŁATKA HAD HER LITTER! DO YOU WANT TO SEE THE PUPPIES?

AND UNCLE WŁODEK GAVE ME ONE!

DO YOU WANT TO SEE HIM?

AH, JÓZEK IS GOING TO BE THRILLED ...

I MANAGE TO DRAG HER OVER TO MY UNCLE'S ...

IT'S FOR THE CHILD, OTHERWISE HE JUST HAS TO MAKE HER A BROTHER. SHE'S ALONE, SHE'S BORED...

HAVE YOU LOST YOUR MIND?!

YOU'LL AT LEAST TAKE IT BACK, IF HE DOESN'T WANT IT?

BACK AT GRANDMA'S FRIEND'S HOUSE, I CAN'T CONCENTRATE ON ANYTHING ELSE. THE OLD WOMEN ARE BAKING A CAKE, IT'S THE CUSTOM AFTER FEATHER CLEANING. WE ALSO DRINK TEA AND SING SOME MORE.

SOMETIMES THEY ALL PRAY TOGETHER WITH A ROSARY, MY DAD CALLS THEM THE DEVOTEES. I SING ALONG AND EAT CAKE. OVERJOYED BY THE IDEA THAT VERY SOON I'LL HAVE A LITTLE DOG...

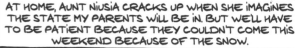

TY POJDZIEJZ GÓ A JA DOLINĄ

AT HOME, AUNT NIUSIA CRACKS UP WHEN SHE IMAGINES THE STATE MY PARENTS WILL BE IN. BUT WE'LL HAVE TO BE PATIENT BECAUSE THEY COULDN'T COME THIS WEEKEND BECAUSE OF THE SNOW.

IN THE MEANTIME, I GO BACK TO MY UNCLE'S OFTEN.

SHE'S AFTER ME, ALL THE TIME! WHEN ARE WE GOING TO SEE UNCLE WŁODEK?

I REALLY AM TAKING HIM. YOU WON'T GIVE HIM TO ANYONE ELSE, PROMISE?

DON'T WORRY, HE'S YOURS.

REGARDLESS OF HOW MY PARENTS REACT, I'VE DECIDED I'M TAKING THIS DOG. THEY SHOULD HAVE COME SOONER, I'VE WAITED LONG ENOUGH.

ON SUNDAYS, BEFORE GOING TO MASS, WE HAVE A BIG BREAKFAST "TO FORTIFY US AGAINST THE COLD" AS MY UNCLE ADAM SAYS. I EAT THE SOUP BUT I HIDE THE MEAT IN SECRET... IT'LL BE FOR MY DOG.

USUALLY, I PRAY FOR MASS TO BE OVER AS QUICKLY AS POSSIBLE, BUT THIS SUNDAY, I PRAY ABOVE ALL THAT NOBODY ELSE TAKES MY DOG AND THAT MY PARENTS WILL AGREE TO IT.

MY DAD COMES TO GET ME ALONE, ON THE BUS. HE WAS SCARED TO BRING THE CAR BECAUSE OF THE ICE AND SNOW.

DAD!! CAN I HAVE A DOG? HE'S SO BEAUTIFUL, SO TINY! IT'S ŁATKA'S PUPPY. UNCLE WŁODEK ALREADY GAVE HIM TO ME!! PLEASE... I HAVEN'T PICKED HIM UP YET SO THAT HE'D HAVE MORE TIME WITH HIS MOM.

WHAT? BUT... HUH?!!

CAN WE GO GET HIM TO-GETHER?

MY GRANDMOTHER IS SMILING IN A CORNER OF THE KITCHEN.

MOM?! WHY DIDN'T YOU SAY NO?!

AND WŁODEK? DO YOU EXPECT US TO TURN THE APARTMENT INTO A ZOO?

LISTEN, HE'S GOING TO BE VERY SMALL LIKE ŁATKA... AND IF YOU SAW THE WAY YOUR DAUGHTER LOOKED AT HIM...

IN ANY CASE, IF YOU DON'T WANT THE DOG, TELL HER YOURSELF!

SHE EXPLAINS HOW I'VE ALREADY THOUGHT OF EVERYTHING ABOUT HIS ARRIVAL, HOW I EVEN MADE HIM A LITTLE PILLOW IN GOOSE DOWN AND HOW I COLLECT ANYTHING I CAN FOR HIM...LIKE THE LITTLE BITS OF MEAT HIDDEN IN THE BOTTOM OF MY BAG.

ALL THREE OF US GO TO UNCLE WŁODEK'S. HE LAUGHS AT MY DAD'S EXPRESSION.

LISTEN, IF YOU DON'T WANT HIM, IT'S NO BIG DEAL, SOMEONE ELSE WILL TAKE HIM.

NOOO! I WANT HIM, DAAAAD...

I CAME ON THE BUS, THERE'S NO WAY TO TAKE HIM BACK. DOGS AREN'T ALLOWED!

HE'S SO LITTLE, I COULD HIDE HIM UNDER MY COAT!!

HAVE YOU THOUGHT ABOUT WHAT YOUR MOM'S GOING TO SAY?

MOM LOVED MY GUINEA PIG, SO HOW COULD SHE NOT LOVE A CUTE LITTLE DOG!

YOU HAVE AN ANSWER FOR EVERY THING...

HE FINALLY AGREES AND WE CHOOSE A LITTLE PUPPY TOGETHER. ŁATKA ISN'T HAPPY, BUT SHE DOESN'T BARK. SHE'S MOSTLY SAD, SITTING IN A CORNER, WATCHING THE MEN HANDLE HER CHILDREN.

I'LL BRING YOUR SON BACK TO VISIT SOME-TIMES SO YOU CAN SPEND TIME WITH HIM, I PROMISE...

AT GRANDMA'S, WE FIX UP A PLACE FOR HIM TO SPEND THE NIGHT. I LOOK AT HIM FOR A LONG TIME BEFORE GOING TO SLEEP.

THE NEXT DAY, ON THE BUS, THE CONDUCTOR DOESN'T NOTICE ANYTHING. THE DOG SLEEPS THE WHOLE WAY.

AT ONE POINT, HE STARTS SHAKING AND I FEEL A WARMTH SPREAD OVER MY SWEATER. HE PEED! BUT I DON'T SAY ANYTHING TO MY DAD.

MY MOM IS VERY SURPRISED, BUT TO MY GREAT JOY, SHE ADOPTS HIM RIGHT AWAY. WE CALL HIM DŻEKI LIKE THE CHARACTER IN THE CARTOON "MALI MIESZ-KANCY WIELKICH GÓR" BECAUSE HE LOOKS LIKE HIM. HE'S MISCHIEVOUS AND PLAYFUL!

WIF WIF

WIF

I'M NOT ALONE ANYMORE. I HAVE A LITTLE COMPANION WHO I WALK WITH PRIDE!

NIGHT STRIKE

MY PARENTS LEAVE FOR WORK AT 7 IN THE MORNING. I GET UP A LITTLE LATER BECAUSE MY FIRST CLASS ISN'T UNTIL 7:30 AND MY SCHOOL'S MUCH CLOSER THAN MY MOM'S OFFICE OR MY DAD'S FACTORY.

THEY BOTH GET HOME AROUND 3:30. I'VE ALREADY BEEN HOME FOR ABOUT 2 HOURS. THOSE ARE THE DAYS WE EAT TOGETHER.

BUT EVERY OTHER WEEK, MY DAD WORKS THE SECOND SHIFT FROM 3:00 TO 11:00. SO WE THEN HAVE LUNCH TOGETHER.

I LIKE IT BETTER WHEN HE'S ON THE MORNING SHIFT. I GET TO SPEND MORE TIME WITH HIM IN THE AFTERNOONS.

IN FACT, I DON'T LIKE IT AT ALL WHEN HE WORKS AT NIGHT. I ALWAYS HAVE A HARD TIME GETTING TO SLEEP WHEN I KNOW HE'S NOT HOME YET, ESPECIALLY SINCE LATELY, HE HASN'T BEEN COMING HOME AT HIS NORMAL TIME.

SOMETHING STRANGE IS GOING ON IN OUR CITY, PEOPLE ARE TENSE AND ENTHUSIASTIC ALL AT THE SAME TIME.

WHERE'S DAD?

WHAT ARE YOU DOING UP AT THIS HOUR?

WHERE IS HE?

GO BACK TO BED, IT'S LATE!

BUT WHERE IS HE?

WHAT DO YOU MEAN WHERE?? AT WORK! WHERE DO YOU THINK HE IS??

IT'S ONE IN THE MORNING, HE NEVER WORKS THIS LATE.

YES, YES, OF COURSE HE DOES! YOU DON'T KNOW ANYTHING ABOUT IT, YOU'RE USUALLY ALREADY ASLEEP.

THAT'S NOT TRUE! YOU KNOW THAT...

GO TO BED, I'M SURE HE WON'T BE LONG. LISTEN, DZEKI CAN SLEEP WITH YOU TONIGHT.

WHAT ABOUT YOU? ARE YOU WAITING UP FOR HIM?

OH, YOU KNOW, I'M NOT TIRED YET. I HAVE TWO OR THREE LITTLE THINGS TO DO, AND THEN I'LL REHEAT THE SOUP... OTHERWISE HE'LL GO TO BED WITHOUT DINNER.

SHE'S TRYING TO MOLLIFY ME SO I WON'T WORRY, BUT I SENSE SHE'S TERRIFIED BY MY DAD'S ABSENCE.

THWOCK
THWOCK

MOCK THWOCK

THWOCK
THWOCK
THWOCK
THWOCK

MY MOM LEAVES, SHE'S GOING TO KNOCK AT THE UPSTAIRS NEIGHBOR'S. HER HUSBAND WORKS IN MY DAD'S FACTORY.

I HOLD MY BREATH AND LISTEN SO I WON'T MISS ANYTHING.

YES, HE'S HERE. HE'S ON THE MORNING SHIFT THIS WEEK. BUT DON'T WORRY, YOURS ISN'T ALONE!

IF WE DON'T REBEL, WE WON'T HAVE ANYTHING! HE'S UNDERSTOOD THAT...

THWO
THW
TH
THWO

I WON'T BE ABLE TO SLEEP. I HAVE TO WAIT FOR HIM. AND IF HE DOESN'T COME BACK? NOT EVER? WHAT IF HE WAS KILLED AND I NEVER SAW HIM AGAIN?...

HE'S REBELLING...THAT MEANS THERE'S SOMETHING HE'S NOT HAPPY ABOUT AND WANTS TO CHANGE... IS IT DANGEROUS?

BUT HE'S NOT ALONE, "THEY" CAN'T DO SOMETHING BAD TO ALL THOSE PEOPLE, CAN THEY? WHOEVER "THEY" ARE?

MY DOG WAKES UP, HE MUST HEAR SOMETHING.

ALMOST ALL THE LIGHTS ARE OUT IN THE BUILDING ACROSS FROM US. THERE ARE FIVE LIT WINDOWS. MAYBE SOMEONE THERE IS WAITING FOR A LOVED ONE, MAYBE MY DAD IS WITH HIM?...

IN THE KITCHEN, MY MOM IS PRAYING. I HEAR HER MURMURING THE ROSARY. NORMALLY, HER WHISPER-ING PUTS ME TO SLEEP, BUT RIGHT NOW IT WORRIES ME. WHY IS SHE SAYING THE ROSARY NOW? IT'S LONG AND SHE NEVER SAYS IT AT HOME!

WHAT'S GOING ON? WHERE'S MY DAD? ARE WE AT WAR? THE CITY IS SO SILENT AND BLACK IT SEEMS HOSTILE AND SCARILY EVIL.

AND, OUTSIDE, SOMEWHERE IN THE NIGHT, IS MY DAD WITH HIS BICYCLE. HE SHOULDN'T BE AT WORK ANYMORE AND HE'S NOT HOME YET... BUT THERE ARE OTHER DADS WITH HIM, WITH THEIR BICYCLES.

IT'S COMFORTING TO THINK HE'S NOT ALONE. ALL OF A SUDDEN I HEAR THE SQUEAKING OF AN OLD BICYCLE THAT STOPS DOWNSTAIRS. IS IT HIM? SOMEBODY ENTERS OUR BUILDING BUT IT'S SO DARK I CAN'T MAKE OUT ANYTHING ... IS IT MY DAD?

AT LEAST ONE PERSON ON EVERY FLOOR WORKS AT HIS FACTORY. THAT LEAVES MORE OR LESS A ONE IN TEN CHANCE OF IT BEING HIM.

THE TIME IT TAKES HIM TO DROP OFF HIS BICYCLE IN THE CELLAR FEELS LIKE AN ETERNITY. THE SILENCE IS DEAFENING. UNBEARABLE. MY HEART BEATS VERY LOUDLY. SO LOUDLY I'M SCARED IT'LL WAKE UP THE WHOLE FLOOR.

THE ELEVATOR! HE MUST HAVE CALLED THE ELEVATOR THAT'S GOING DOWN TO PICK HIM UP. THEN I HEAR IT RISING. IT'S VERY NOISY, IT'S AN OLD MACHINE. IS IT GOING TO STOP AT OUR FLOOR?

IT'S STILL GOING UP... DID IT PASS THE 5TH FLOOR? I CAN'T HEAR ANYTHING OVER MY HEART! SHH, THERE! THE ELEVATOR STOPPED! SO IT IS HIM! MY DAD IS BACK!!

I CAN GO TO SLEEP NOW... GOOD NIGHT, DAD...

ENTRECHATS AND LITTLE MICE

RECENTLY, I'VE BEEN TAKING CLASSICAL DANCE CLASSES AT THE LOCAL CULTURAL CENTER. I GO WITH GOSIA. MONIKA CAN'T COME.

RAZ DWA TRZY ...

THE TEACHER WOULDN'T LET HER INTO THE CLASS BECAUSE YOU HAVE TO BE VERY THIN. SHE WASN'T EVEN SURE ABOUT ME. SHE SAID I SEEMED AWKWARD.

TWENTY GIRLS SHOWED UP FOR THE FIRST CLASS. WE ALL HAD TO DANCE FOR HER. I WAS VERY INTIMIDATED.

PERFORMING IN FRONT OF ALL THESE PEOPLE I DIDN'T KNOW EMBARRASSED ME A LITTLE. I THINK THE OTHER GIRLS FELT THE SAME WAY. IT MADE US ALL CLUMSY.

AFTER THAT, SHE SHARED HER IMPRESSIONS.

LOOK AT YOU MOVE! LIKE COWS AT A COUNTRY FAIR... GRACEFULNESS, GIRLS!

BUT I'LL HELP YOU, YOU'LL SEE...

YOU'LL ALL BECOME REAL BALLERINAS!!

OKAY, YOU'RE TOO FAT, SORRY. YOU'RE TOO HEAVY FOR BALLET... PRIMO, LIGHTNESS, SECONDO, GRACE.

WELL... IF YOU WANT TO TAKE THIS CLASS, YOU COULD ALWAYS GO ON A DIET.

WE WENT HOME TOGETHER. MONIKA WAS CRYING BUT NEITHER GOSIA NOR I COULD CONSOLE HER BECAUSE WE WERE BURSTING WITH JOY THAT WE GOT IN. SO WE WALKED IN SILENCE.

POOR MONIKA, SHE ISN'T FAT AT ALL! ACCORDING TO HER, SHE HAS BIG BONES. SHE'S MUSCULAR AND NOT AS ANEMIC AS GOSIA AND ME.

AND THEN, THERE'S A PART OF ME THAT'S HAPPY SHE DIDN'T GET IN. I'LL HAVE GOSIA ALL TO MYSELF. THE TWO OF US WILL SHARE SOMETHING MONIKA CAN'T DISRUPT.

THOUGH EVERY TIME GOSIA COMES TO GET ME FOR BALLET CLASSES, MONIKA TRIES TO COME UP WITH A REASON TO STOP ME!

YOUR MOM MIGHT HAVE FORGOTTEN HER KEYS. YOU CAN'T JUST GO!!

WHAT'LL SHE DO IF THE DOOR'S LOCKED WHEN SHE GETS BACK?

OKAY, I'LL LEAVE YOU MY KEYS SINCE YOU'RE NOT COMING, YOU CAN GIVE THEM TO HER...

OUR TEACHER IS VERY WIRY, IT'S ALMOST LIKE SHE DOESN'T HAVE CHEEKS, BUT HOLES UNDERNEATH HER EYES INSTEAD. HER NAME IS BOŻENA.

I SEE YOU!

SHE'S KNOWN THROUGHOUT THE WHOLE CULTURAL CENTER FOR HER BAD TEMPER. EVERYONE LAUGHS ABOUT IT EXCEPT US, BECAUSE WE'RE THE ONES HER ANGER IS USUALLY DIRECTED AT...

APPARENTLY SHE'S BITTER BECAUSE SHE WASN'T ACCEPTED INTO THE RUSSIAN BALLET...

SHE MIGHT NOT BE VERY NICE, BUT SHE DANCES VERY WELL. WE STAND OPEN MOUTHED WHEN SHE STARTS TO TWIRL.

SHE DOESN'T LIKE ME. SHE KEEPS WATCH ON ME. IT'S BECAUSE ONCE, IN THE DRESSING ROOM BEFORE CLASS, I WAS GOOFING AROUND WITH THE OTHERS AND I IMITATED MS. BOŻENA...

LOOK AT YOURSELF! HOW ARE YOU MOVING YOUR FOOT? TENSE YOUR GLUTEAL MUSCLES, LIKE ME...

AND DON'T FORGET, PRIMO LIGHTNESS, SECONDO, GRACE-FULNESS...

CLAP CLAP CLAP

BRAVA, BRAVA! WE'RE GOING TO VERIFY RIGHT AWAY WHETHER YOU CAN CONTROL YOUR GLUTES...

EVER SINCE THAT INCIDENT, NOT A SINGLE CLASS GOES BY WHERE I ESCAPE HER ATTENTION, I'VE BECOME HER SCAPEGOAT.

SHE TELLS ME I'M TOO THIN, WHICH IS PERFECT FOR BALLET, BUT I DON'T HAVE WHAT IT TAKES TO BECOME A BALLERINA.

HEE HEE

I'VE NEVER SEEN SOMEONE WITH SO LITTLE BALANCE!

THERE'S NO POINT DISCUSSING IT WITH HER, SHE NEVER LISTENS TO US.

EVERY TIME SOMEONE TRIES TO SPEAK, SHE LOOKS AT THE WALL AND MOVES HER HANDS AS THOUGH SHE WAS SHOOING AWAY A SWARM OF FLIES (EVEN THOUGH THERE ARE NO FLIES).

CHILDREN, LIKE FISH, HAVE NO VOICES! SO SHUT UP AND MOVE TO THE BARRE!!

PFFFT
PFFFT
PFFFT

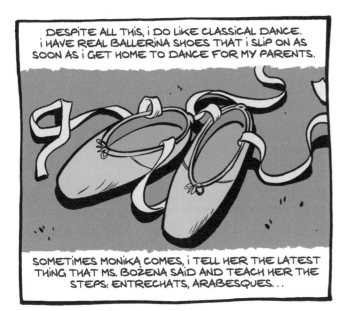

DESPITE ALL THIS, I DO LIKE CLASSICAL DANCE. I HAVE REAL BALLERINA SHOES THAT I SLIP ON AS SOON AS I GET HOME TO DANCE FOR MY PARENTS.

SOMETIMES MONIKA COMES, I TELL HER THE LATEST THING THAT MS. BOŻENA SAID AND TEACH HER THE STEPS: ENTRECHATS, ARABESQUES. . .

BUT MONIKA HASN'T BEEN COMING OVER FOR THE PAST FEW DAYS. SHE'S SICK WITH A STOMACH ACHE AND HASN'T EVEN BEEN GOING TO SCHOOL. WHEN I BRING OVER HER CLASS NOTEBOOKS, SHE'S ASLEEP. AUNT STASIA IS WAITING FOR ME.

AH, MARZI! TELL ME, WHAT EXACTLY DID THE DANCE TEACHER TELL YOU ALL?

WHAT DO YOU MEAN?!?

GA GA

AT THE NEXT CLASS, MS. BOŻENA RECEIVES A VISIT FROM AUNT STASIA. SHE LOOKS VERY SMALL NEXT TO HER.

WHAT DID YOU SAY TO MY DAUGHTER? THAT SHE'S FAT?! WHAT'S WRONG WITH YOU? SHE'S A YOUNG GIRL. . .

SHE'S REFUSING TO EAT BECAUSE OF YOU!!!

BUT YOU DON'T UNDER-STAND. . .

NO! YOU'RE THE ONE WHO DOESN'T UNDER-STAND! YOU SHOULD NOT BE WORKING WITH CHILDREN. I'M GOING TO LET IT BE KNOWN, DON'T YOU WORRY. YOU'RE COMPLETELY IRRESPONSIBLE!!

SHE COULD COME BACK, YOU KNOW, AND JOIN US. . .

COME BACK?? TO BE HUMILIATED!?! ONE OF YOUR STUDENTS TOLD ME ABOUT YOUR METHODS!!

MONIKA ISN'T THE ONLY ONE WHO WON'T BE BACK, YOU'RE OUT OF HERE! TRUST ME!

THE WHOLE BUILDING COULD HEAR AUNT STASIA. SHE WAS VERY WORKED UP.

RHAAAA !

DOM KULTURY

WE DIDN'T HAVE CLASS FOR SEVERAL WEEKS AFTER THAT. UNTIL A NEW TEACHER COULD BE FOUND.

BUT IT'S TOO LATE FOR MONIKA. SHE'S LEAVING OUR BUILDING... SHE'S MOVING.

MONIKA'S DAD CAME HOME FROM CZECHOSLOVAKIA. AND WITH THE MONEY HE MADE THERE, HE BOUGHT LAND TO BUILD A BRAND NEW HOUSE...

EVEN MY DAD HELPED.

THEY'VE BEEN LIVING IN THEIR NEW HOUSE ABOUT TEN KILOMETERS FROM US FOR SOME TIME NOW. SO MONIKA CHANGED SCHOOLS...

I STAYED WITH GOSIA. NOW THAT IT'S JUST THE TWO OF US, THERE ARE FEWER FIGHTS. WE'RE TRUE FRIENDS.

BUT EVERYTHING GOSIA SAYS AND DOES IS SO PRACTICAL AND LOGICAL THAT SOMETIMES I MISS MONIKA. OUR IDIOTIC GAMES, AS MY MOM WOULD SAY, HAVE NO BEARING ON THE GAMES I PLAY WITH GOSIA.

MONIKA AND I NEVER QUESTIONED ANYTHING. GOSIA IS ALWAYS ASKING ME THINGS AND I DON'T KNOW HOW TO ANSWER.

TO PLAY DOLLS, SHE NEEDS DOLLS. SHE CAN'T PRETEND THAT BUTTONS ARE DOLLS. HER GAMES ARE VERY STATIC. WE BARELY MOVE. WE STAY SITTING ALMOST THE WHOLE TIME.

ACTUALLY, I DON'T REALLY LIKE PLAYING DOLLS WITH GOSIA BECAUSE HERS IS VERY BEAUTIFUL. SHE'S NEW WITH LONG HAIR AND KNEES AND ELBOWS THAT BEND. AND SHE EVEN WEARS MODERN CLOTHES.

MINE IS A CLOTH DOLL. SHE'S SOFT AND DOESN'T EVEN SIT UP. AUNT NIUSIA MADE ALL HER CLOTHES FROM PIECES OF FABRIC LEFT OVER FROM THE CLOTHES SHE STITCHED FOR ME.

WHICH MEANS THAT CECYLIA, MY DOLL, WEARS A DRESS WITH TRACTORS ON IT, LIKE ME. GOSIA'S IS NAMED BARBIE, SHE'S SMALLER THAN MINE BUT SHE HAS A PRETTY SMILING FACE AND WHITE TEETH. CECYLIA'S MOUTH IS STARTING TO PEEL OFF.

A DISTANT COUSIN OF MY MOM'S GAVE HER TO ME. SHE'S AN ADOPTED DOLL. SHE USED TO HAVE ANOTHER NAME. WHEN I SAW HER FOR THE FIRST TIME SHE WAS A LITTLE DIRTY AND SMELLED LIKE OLD PICKLES.

IT'S BECAUSE SHE'D BEEN STORED IN A DAMP CELLAR. MY DAD WASHED HER. SHE DID END UP ALL CLEAN, BUT SHE LOST HER ORIGINAL SHAPE.

SHE HAS A LEG THAT DANGLES AND VERY STRAIGHT BANGS. BUT SHE'S MY DOLL AND I LOVE HER ANYWAY.

NONE OF WHICH STOPS ME FROM BEING A LITTLE EMBARRASSED TO BRING HER OUT IN FRONT OF GOSIA. WHEN SHE FIRST SAW HER, SHE ASKED ME: "IS THAT THE ONLY ONE YOU'VE GOT?" POOR CECYLIA...SHE MEANS SO MUCH TO ME, WHILE IN GOSIA'S EYES, SHE'S WORTHLESS.

THAT'S THE REASON I DON'T LIKE PLAYING DOLLS WITH GOSIA VERY MUCH. I'D LIKE TO SPARE CECYLIA THAT. SHE EVEN THINKS PLAYING WITH THE CARS MY COUSIN GAVE ME IS STRANGE...

CARS?!

...

I DON'T KNOW HOW TO RESPOND. ALL I CAN SAY IS, I LIKE CARS. SO MOST OF THE TIME, I PLAY HER DOLL'S TAXI.

EVERY SO OFTEN, I GO TO PEWEX WITH MY PARENTS. WE USUALLY GO BEFORE THE BIG HOLIDAYS. IT'S THE ONLY PLACE YOU CAN BE SURE TO FIND WHAT YOU'RE LOOKING FOR.

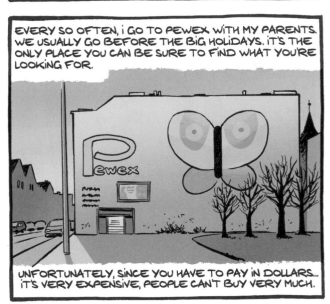

UNFORTUNATELY, SINCE YOU HAVE TO PAY IN DOLLARS... IT'S VERY EXPENSIVE, PEOPLE CAN'T BUY VERY MUCH.

BUT THERE'S NOTHING IN THE REGULAR STORES, AND ALL THE SALES CLERKS DO ALL DAY IS SAY "NIE MA!"

SUGAR?

NIE MA!

FLOUR?

NIE MA!

SOAP?

NIE MA!

TOILET PAPER?

NIE MA!

SO WE GO TO PEWEX!

WALKING IN THERE IS LIKE ENTERING INTO A FINER WORLD. EVERYTHING SMELLS GOOD AND EVERYTHING SPARKLES. THERE ARE RUGS UNLIKE ANY I'VE NEVER SEEN AT PEOPLE'S HOUSES, AND ALSO SOME VERY SLEEK FURNITURE, IN BLOND WOOD.

IT'S NOT LIKE OUR REGULAR STORES WHERE WE SEE MORE CUSTOMERS THAN ITEMS FOR SALE.

JUST THEN, I SEE HER. SHE'S ON A SHELF AND SMILES AT EVERYONE... A BARBIE!

AND SHE'S NOT ALONE. THERE ARE A LOT OF BARBIES, ALL BEAUTIFUL AND FULL OF JOY, ARRAYED ON A SHELF AT EXACTLY MY EYE-LEVEL.

THEY LOOK LIKE ADULTS—BUT PERFECT. THEY'RE THIN, TALL, PRETTY, WELL-DRESSED, AND HAVE LONG HAIR.

I'D LIKE MY MOM TO LOOK LIKE THEM. THEY SEEM SO NICE. MY DAD WOULD BE HAPPY TOO.

AT LEAST HERE, THE SALES CLERKS DON'T ASK FOR RATION CARDS. THEY EVEN GREET US WITH BIG SMILES!

HELLO, LITTLE LADY...

WHAT WOULD YOU LIKE?

WHICH IS VERY DIFFERENT FROM: "WHAT'S SHE WAITING FOR AGAIN?", "WE'RE OUT!" ETC. THE SALES CLERKS AT PEWEX AREN'T AS PRETTY AS THE DOLLS THEY SELL, BUT THEY SEEM JUST AS NICE.

I ASK MY MOM IF SHE'LL BUY ME ONE OF THOSE DOLLS, BUT SHE DOESN'T HEAR BECAUSE SHE'S BUSY DELIBERATING OVER THE PRICE OF PORK WITH MY DAD.

WHEN SHE FINALLY PAYS ATTENTION TO ME, BECAUSE I'VE BEEN TUGGING ON HER SLEEVE, HER RESPONSE IS INSTANTANEOUS: "NO, WE DON'T HAVE MONEY FOR THAT!"

MY PARENTS COME HERE TO BUY SAUSAGES AND ALCOHOL. THERE ARE PRIORITIES IN LIFE.

I HAVE TEARS IN MY EYES, BUT I DON'T SAY ANYTHING. I KNOW WE DON'T HAVE ANY MONEY, WE NEVER HAVE ANY MONEY. THEY'RE ALWAYS REPEATING IT.

MY DAD USED TO BUY ME CHEWING GUM HERE: "DONALD" AND "TURBO", HE'D GIVE THEM TO ME IN SECRET BECAUSE MY MOM SAYS IT RUINS YOUR APPETITE...I HAD TO BLOW BUBBLES VERY DISCREETLY...

"DONALD" LASTS A VERY LONG TIME, ALMOST A WHOLE DAY. THERE'S A FUNNY STORY ABOUT THE DUCK ON THE WRAPPER. "TURBO" HAS A PICTURE OF A CAR AND ITS MAXIMUM SPEED. I COLLECT ALL OF THEM.

BUT LATELY MY MOM'S BEEN CLAIMING THAT ACCORDING TO THE AUTHORITIES CHEWING GUM IS CARCINOGENIC...

THEY JUST DON'T LIKE THAT IT'S PRODUCED ABROAD!

THEY SAY IT'S NOT GOOD FOR YOU, SO IT'S NOT GOOD FOR YOU!

NOW WHEN WE GO TO PEWEX I DON'T EVEN GET CHEWING GUM...BUT THIS TIME, TO CONSOLE ME, THEY BOUGHT ME A BOX OF 24 COLORED PENCILS. THEY'RE BEAUTIFUL AND SMELL GOOD.

BACK AT HOME, I TELL MY MOM NOT TO BUY ANY MEAT OR FOOD FOR ME SO WE CAN SAVE UP THE MONEY FOR THE DOLL.

HA, HA! AREN'T YOU SILLY!

GOSIA HAS A BARBIE...

HER PARENTS EVEN BOUGHT HER A MR. BARBIE!!

MY MOM GETS ANNOYED AND TELLS ME THAT WE DON'T LIVE LIKE THEY DO, THAT WE'RE POOR AND THAT GOSIA'S PARENTS HAVE GOOD JOBS, THEY HAVE MEANS..

GOSIA HAS A COLOR TELEVISION. THE SANDWICHES HER MOM MAKES HER FOR SCHOOL COME WRAPPED IN SHINY PAPER WHILE MINE ARE WRAPPED IN A GREY CRACKLY PAPER WITH TRACES OF BUTTER ON IT.

LOTS OF KIDS HAVE SHINY PAPER. I TOLD MY MOM THIS ONCE. SHE ANSWERED THAT I SHOULD BE HAPPY TO HAVE SANDWICHES EVERY DAY, THE PAPER DOESN'T MATTER!

GOSIA HAS A JEAN SKIRT, I'D LIKE TO HAVE ONE TOO, IT'S REALLY PRETTY. IN FACT, EVERYONE THINKS GOSIA'S VERY CUTE.

EVEN IWONA'S MOM WHO'S A TEACHER AT SCHOOL.

WHEN SHE COMES TO SEE HER DAUGHTER DURING BREAK, SHE GOES UP TO GOSIA AND GENTLY PINCHES HER CHEEKS...

HOW PRETTY YOU ARE, GOSIA!

EVEN IWONA ISN'T AS PRETTY!

WHAT A CUTE FACE!!

I DON'T KNOW HOW MUCH IWONA LIKES HEARING THIS, OR IF IT'S WHY GOSIA'S CHEEKS ARE SO CHUBBY.

WILL YOU TELL YOUR MOM I'M COMING BY THE STORE TO SEE IF THERE'S ANYTHING FRESH TO BUY?

"FRESH" MEANS MEAT! GOSIA'S DAD WORKS IN A FACTORY WHERE THEY KILL ANIMALS AND CUT THEM INTO PIECES TO SELL. EEEK... AND HER MOM IS ONE OF THE SALES CLERKS!

THEY ALWAYS HAVE PLENTY OF MEAT. MY MOM SAYS THEY DO WELL BY THE SYSTEM AND DON'T WANT IT TO CHANGE.

YOU JUST HAVE TO LOOK AT THEIR CAR...

THEY DON'T DRIVE A BEAT-UP FIAT 126, THEY HAVE A SKODA!!

BUT MY PARENTS WORK A LOT TOO. SO WHY DON'T WE HAVE ENOUGH MONEY? WHY DON'T I HAVE A JEANS SKIRT OR A BARBIE OR SHINY PAPER ON MY SANDWICHES?

WHEN I ASK MY MOM WHY WE DON'T HAVE MORE MONEY, SHE TELLS ME THE DIFFERENCE IS MEAT. THEY CAN TAKE AS MUCH AS THEY WANT AND RESELL IT UNDER THE COUNTER... BUT I DON'T UNDERSTAND!

WHY DO PEOPLE LOVE MEAT SO MUCH?

OF COURSE MY PARENTS COULD NEVER HAVE AS MUCH MONEY. MY DAD WORKS WITH IRON, AND MY MOM ON A TYPEWRITER. NO ONE GOES CRAZY FOR THOSE THINGS.

SO MUCH FOR BARBIE, I WON'T DIE IF I DON'T HAVE ONE. BUT I FEEL LIKE WE'RE NOT HAPPY AND THAT BOTHERS ME EVEN MORE.

GOSIA HAS A TELEPHONE, NOT A TOY ONE, A REAL TELEPHONE THAT CALLS PEOPLE.

MY PARENTS HAVE BEEN WAITING FOR ONE SINCE WE MOVED TO THIS BUILDING... WHEN I WAS A BABY. GOSIA'S PARENTS MOVED HERE MUCH LATER. IT'S JUST A MATTER OF GREASING THE HAND, SAYS MY MOM (?!?)

GOSIA HAS A CAMERA, IT'S VERY BEAUTIFUL. WE CAN'T TOUCH IT, JUST LOOK AT IT. IT SITS ON A BOOKSHELF IN HER ROOM WHERE EVERYONE WHO COMES OVER CAN SEE IT.

I'D LIKE TO HAVE ONE TOO. BUT MY MOM SAYS THERE ARE MORE PRESSING AND IMPORTANT THINGS TO BUY THAN A CAMERA OR A DOLL.

I HAVE TEARS IN MY EYES EVERY TIME I ASK HER FOR SOMETHING AND SHE SAYS NO.

SHE TRIES TO EXPLAIN TO ME CALMLY THAT WE AREN'T THE SAME, THAT WE'RE SOMEWHAT WORSE OFF, BUT IT DOESN'T REALLY MATTER BECAUSE JUSTICE WILL BE DONE IN HEAVEN... BECAUSE THE GOOD GOD EXISTS AND WATCHES OVER US AND HAS MERCY UPON US.

I'D LIKE GOD TO EXACT HIS JUSTICE NOW! BESIDES HOW CAN HE BE GOOD WHEN I CRY AND ALL HE DOES IS WATCH?

I'M PITIFUL, AREN'T I?

FOR CHRISTMAS, I GOT SOCKS AND UNDERWEAR, PAJAMAS AND THREE SKEINS OF WOOL FOR A SWEATER...

THE PAJAMAS SMELL BRAND NEW. I'M GOING TO SLEEP IN THEM TONIGHT. THEY'RE WHITE AND HAVE A LITTLE YELLOW BUTTERFLY EMBROIDERED ON THE SHIRT POCKET.

AT SCHOOL, EVERYONE IS TALKING ABOUT THEIR CHRISTMAS PRESENTS. A FEW DON'T SAY ANYTHING, AND I'M ONE OF THEM.

GOSIA KNOWS WHAT I GOT, SHE ASKED ME ON THE WAY TO SCHOOL. I THINK SHE'S SORRY FOR ME.

I DON'T HAVE THE COURAGE TO ASK HER WHAT SHE GOT, IT WOULD PROBABLY MAKE ME CRY.

SO WE DON'T SAY ANYTHING, WE WALK IN SILENCE.

SHE GIVES ME SOME CANDY, A KRÓWKA, WHICH IS DELICIOUS BUT ALSO VERY CHEWY.

WE CAN BARELY OPEN OUR JAWS, FUNNY SOUNDS ARE COMING OUT OF OUR MOUTHS! IT CRACKS US UP!

IN THE END, HAPPINESS DEPENDS ON SO FEW THINGS. NOT NECESSARILY A ROW OF DOLLS, A JEANS SKIRT, OR A FRIDGE FULL OF MEAT...

MONIKA WAS LIKE ME, THAT'S WHY I NEVER REALIZED I WAS FROM A POOR FAMILY.

I MISS HER A LOT.

REZYSTOR

THE STATE OF WAR IN POLAND LASTED 586 DAYS.

FIVE HUNDRED-EIGHTYSIX DAYS OF FEAR AND SUFFERING.

DURING THIS PERIOD, NUMEROUS FACTORIES WENT ON STRIKE. EACH TIME, THE ZOMO (THE RIOT POLICE) INTERVENED AND "PACIFIED" THE STRIKERS. SOMETIMES, THEY WERE EVEN BACKED UP BY THE ARMY.

LOTS OF PEOPLE WERE ARRESTED AND JAILED. LOTS OF OTHERS DIED...

THIS WAS WHY EVERYONE WAS SCARED OF PROTESTING OPENLY. IT COULD MEAN ENDANGERING THEMSELVES OR THEIR LOVED ONES.

SO PEOPLE CAME UP WITH DIFFERENT WAYS TO DEMONSTRATE THEIR OPPOSITION...

OFFICIALLY, WE ARE NO LONGER IN A STATE OF WAR, BUT PEOPLE ARE STILL ON EDGE. THEY NEVER KNOW WHAT SURPRISE THEIR GOVERNMENT MIGHT HAVE IN STORE FOR THEM.

DZIENNIK

IT USED TO BE THAT EVERY NIGHT, WHEN THE EVENING NEWS CAME ON, ALL THE GROWN-UPS WOULD HURRY TO WATCH IT, TO NOT MISS A SINGLE NEWS STORY. BUT LATELY THE OPPOSITE HAS BEEN HAPPENING.

QUITE SIMPLY, WE'VE BEEN KEEPING OUR TELEVISIONS DARK, NOT TURNING THEM ON. NOT ONLY THE TV, BUT ALL THE LIGHTS IN THE HOUSE.

SUDDENLY, IT'S COMPLETELY DARK, EVERYWHERE, IN ALL THE NEIGHBORING BUILDINGS...THE WHOLE CITY GOES DARK FOR A MOMENT, AS IF THERE WERE NO ONE LEFT.

WHEN I ASK WHY WE'RE DOING THIS, MY DAD ANSWERS THAT PEOPLE ARE REFUSING TO WATCH TELEVISION BECAUSE THEY'RE NOT SAYING ANYTHING REAL ON IT. IT'S A SILENT PROTEST.

THEY MAKE US DO A LOT OF THINGS, BUT THEY CAN'T MAKE US DO THAT!!

WE HAVE A CHOICE, AND WE'RE CHOOSING NOT TO WATCH ANYMORE.

PEOPLE SHUT OFF THEIR SETS. ONE LESS OBLIGATION!

AFTER TURNING OFF THE TVS AND THE LIGHTS, WE BEGAN TO LIGHT CANDLES AND PLACE THEM IN THE WINDOWS. A PRIEST TOLD US TO DO THIS.

IN FACT, CHURCHES ARE THE ONLY PLACES WHERE PEOPLE CAN GATHER. WE STAY AFTER MASS TO TALK, TO LISTEN TO THE PRIESTS AND EXCHANGE POINTS OF VIEW. PEOPLE FEEL SAFE THERE.

SO AT NIGHT, WHEN IT'S DARK OUT, WE LIGHT CANDLES. EVERYONE DOES THE SAME THING. IT'S VERY BEAUTIFUL TO SEE SO MANY WINDOWS LIT UP BY THESE TINY LITTLE LIGHTS.

MY DAD SAYS WE'RE PREPARED TO LIVE LIKE CAVEMEN BECAUSE THAT'S HOW THEY TREAT US.

SOMETIMES, INSTEAD OF STAYING IN THE DARK APARTMENT, WE GO WALK AROUND FOR HALF AN HOUR, THE LENGTH OF THE NEWS BROADCAST. LOTS OF PEOPLE DO THE SAME THING. THEY'RE CALLED "DEMONSTRATION WALKS."

THE ADULTS OPENLY DISCUSS THE SITUATION IN A WAY THEY NEVER WOULD HAVE DARED BEFORE.

WHEN POPE JOHN-PAUL II COMES TO POLAND HE'S ALWAYS SURROUNDED BY A HUGE RETINUE. YOU COULD ALSO SAY HE'S UNDER SURVEILLANCE.

HE HAS TO BE CAREFUL WHAT HE SAYS...

DURING HIS LAST VISIT, ON A LIVE TV AND RADIO BROADCAST, JUST BEFORE BOARDING THE AIRPLANE HE SAID:

MY COUNTRYMEN, CONTINUE, I AM PROUD OF YOU. I AM WITH YOU.

NO ONE COULD DO ANYTHING ABOUT IT. HE SAID IT AND WE ALL HEARD HIM. OUR HEARTS FILLED WITH JOY AND HOPE...WE ARE NOT ALONE. SOMEONE OUTSIDE POLAND IS THINKING ABOUT WHAT'S HAPPENING HERE, WE HAVEN'T BEEN FORGOTTEN.

THERE'S ALSO THIS MUSTACHED MAN WHO ISN'T SCARED OF ANYTHING. WE TALK ABOUT HIM AT HOME A LOT. HIS NAME IS LECH WAŁESA AND HE'S THE HEAD OF AN ORGANIZATION THAT'S REBELLING AGAINST THE AUTHORITIES.

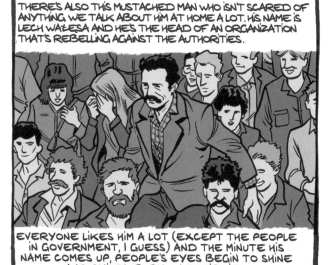

EVERYONE LIKES HIM A LOT (EXCEPT THE PEOPLE IN GOVERNMENT, I GUESS) AND THE MINUTE HIS NAME COMES UP, PEOPLE'S EYES BEGIN TO SHINE AND SMILES FORM ON THEIR LIPS.

THERE'S ANOTHER FORM OF PROTEST AGAINST THE AUTHORITIES ALSO TAKING PLACE. IT'S MOSTLY MEN WHO DO IT.

THEY ATTACH AN ELECTRIC RESISTOR TO THEIR JACKET LAPELS SO THAT IT STICKS UP AND IS VISIBLE.

SINCE IT'S DIFFICULT TO PROCLAIM RESISTANCE LOUD AND CLEAR TO THE PEOPLE IN POWER, THEY DO IT THIS WAY.

WE'RE ALL LIKE THESE RESISTORS, SILENT BUT PRESENT AND MOST IMPORTANT, CONSCIOUS, CHILDREN TOO, THAT NOTHING IS WORKING IN OUR COUNTRY.

PEOPLE BEGIN TO DECLARE THEIR DISCONTENT RIGHT UNDER THE AUTHORITIES' NOSES. THEY BRING THEIR INNERMOST THOUGHTS, SO LONG HIDDEN, INTO THE LIGHT OF DAY.

GŁODNI WSZYSTKICH KRAJÓW ŁĄCZCIE SIĘ!

THEY REVEAL THEMSELVES WITHOUT TAKING ACTION, BUT EVEN THOUGH THEY'RE SCARED, THEY'RE NOT GOING TO GIVE IN TO IT THIS TIME. THEY'RE NOT GOING TO STAND IN THE SHADOWS FEELING OPPRESSED AND AFRAID ANYMORE.

THEY'RE READY TO CHANGE THAT.

GDAŃSK

WE ARE OPPOSED TO THE ENDLESS LINES, TO THE LACK OF GOODS, TO OUR EMPTY FRIDGES...

TO THE AUTHORITIES WHO DEMAND SO MUCH AND OFFER SO LITTLE IN RETURN...

WE ARE OPPOSED TO OUR LACK OF FREEDOM!

WE ARE RECLAIMING THE LIVES OUR GOVERNMENT FORBIDS US FROM LIVING. WE DON'T WANT TO BE SCARED ANYMORE, WE FEEL TRAPPED AND SPIED ON CONTINUALLY...

JESTEŚMY GŁODNI

GŁÓD

"WE WANT NORMALITY AND DIGNITY..."

"IS IT TOO MUCH TO HOPE FOR?"

BIG BROTHER

BEING AN ONLY CHILD IS A DRAG...

THERE'S NO ONE TO TALK TO ABOUT ANYTHING SERIOUS.

MY PARENTS CLAIM THEY WANT TO BE THERE FOR ME WHENEVER I FEEL PLAGUED BY DOUBTS. BUT TO TELL YOU THE TRUTH, THEY RUN AWAY THE MINUTE I TELL THEM WHAT THE PROBLEM IS.

THEY SAY I'M TOO YOUNG, THAT THE WORLD IS MUCH TOO COMPLICATED AND THAT MY MIND CAN'T GRAPPLE WITH ALL THIS COMPLEXITY.

PERHAPS...

STILL, I'D LIKE THEM TO STOP GIVING ME THOSE NAUSE-ATING SMILES.

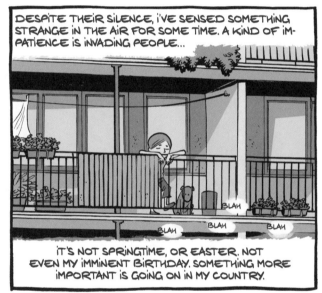

DESPITE THEIR SILENCE, I'VE SENSED SOMETHING STRANGE IN THE AIR FOR SOME TIME. A KIND OF IM-PATIENCE IS INVADING PEOPLE...

IT'S NOT SPRINGTIME, OR EASTER. NOT EVEN MY IMMINENT BIRTHDAY. SOMETHING MORE IMPORTANT IS GOING ON IN MY COUNTRY.

TO FIND OUT WHAT'S HAPPENING, I EAVESDROP ON THE ADULTS' CONVERSATIONS.

BUT THEIR LANGUAGE'S VERY CODED AND HARD TO DECIPHER.

UNDERSTANDING WHAT THEY MEAN REQUIRES A LOT OF EFFORT.

YOU'D NEED A SPECIAL DICTIONARY THAT'D TRANSLATE THEIR WORRIES, JOYS, AND HYSTERICS...

WHY? WHY DO THEY TALK LIKE THAT? IT'S THE REASON EVERYTHING IS SO COMPLICATED...

BLAH BLAH BLAH SOCIAL MOBILIZATION BLAH BLAH BLAH BLAH PROTEST BLAH BLAH IDEOLOGY BLAH BLAH

IT'S THE REASON THEY CAN'T FIND SIMPLE WORDS TO EXPLAIN THESE SERIOUS THINGS. EVEN THOUGH WE'RE LIVING IN THE SAME WORLD.

CHILDREN HAVE NO CHOICE, THEY HAVE TO TRY TO UNDERSTAND ADULTS. THEY KNOW ONE DAY THEY'LL BELONG TO THAT WORLD.

ADULTS MUST HAVE FORGOTTEN THAT THEY WERE CHILDREN ONCE TOO AND DIDN'T UNDERSTAND ANYTHING EITHER. ONLY THE TEACHERS AT SCHOOL KNOW HOW TO TALK TO US.

THEY HELP US BRIDGE THE GAP. THEY MUST HAVE BEEN DESIGNED FOR IT.

SZEŚĆ KONTYNENTÓW

EUROPA
AMERYKA
AFRYKA
AZJA
AUSTRALIA
ANTARKTYDA

APA ŚWIAT

IT WAS ONLY AT SCHOOL I REALIZED I WASN'T THE ONLY ONE WITH QUESTIONS.

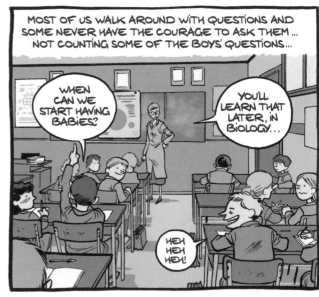

MOST OF US WALK AROUND WITH QUESTIONS AND SOME NEVER HAVE THE COURAGE TO ASK THEM ... NOT COUNTING SOME OF THE BOYS' QUESTIONS...

WHEN CAN WE START HAVING BABIES?

YOU'LL LEARN THAT LATER, IN BIOLOGY...

HEH HEH HEH!

OTHER STUDENTS' QUESTIONS ARE MORE ABOUT SOCIAL ISSUES.

WHAT'S THE DIFFERENCE BETWEEN THE ZOMO AND THE MILITIA?!

WHAT'S SOLIDARNOŚĆ ALL ABOUT?

I THOUGHT THAT THE MILITIA PROTECTED AND DEFENDED PEOPLE BUT ON TV I SAW THEM CLUBBING WORKERS LIKE MY DAD...

MY MOM SAYS THEY CAN PUT ANYONE IN PRISON!

YEAH, IT'S TRUE! ME TOO!!

OUR TEACHERS FINALLY PROVIDE THE NECESSARY EXPLANATIONS...

MY COUNTRY IS INDIRECTLY GOVERNED BY THE USSR, WHO SOME CALL "BIG BROTHER"...

AND I THINK EVERYONE'S HAD IT WITH THIS DEPENDENCE BECAUSE SOMETIMES OUR BIG BROTHER HAS BEHAVED VERY MEANLY TO HIS LITTLE SISTER, POLAND...

AS A RESULT, SHE WANTS TO LEAVE THE FAMILY, WHICH IS WHERE SOLIDARNOŚĆ COMES IN.

EACH FACTORY HAS ITS OWN SOLIDARNOŚĆ. IT'S AN ORGANIZATION THAT PROTECTS THE WORKERS OF THAT FACTORY.

AND ALL THE LITTLE SOLIDARNOŚĆ ANSWER TO THE MAIN SOLIDARNOŚĆ WHICH IS LOCATED ON THE DOCKS AT GDAŃSK, A CITY ON THE BALTIC COAST, IN THE NORTH OF THE COUNTRY.

THAT'S WHERE IT WAS BORN.

IT'S LED BY LECH WAŁĘSA, AND ALTHOUGH THIS ORGANIZATION IS POWERFUL, IT'S ILLEGAL. SO, WHEN IT CALLS FOR SOMETHING, THE GOVERNMENT DOESN'T EVEN BOTHER TO RESPOND.

IT'S DISAPPOINTING...

BUT SINCE SOLIDARNOŚĆ IS BECOMING MORE AND MORE POWERFUL, THE PEOPLE ARE FEELING MORE EMPOWERED.

AS A RESULT, THEY'RE NOT AS SCARED TO PROTEST AND, FRANKLY, TO ASK FOR WHAT THEY DESERVE.

THEY'RE NOT ASKING FOR THE MOON, JUST FOOD IN THE STORES AND, AS THE ADULTS LIKE TO SAY, OUR DIGNITY.

AND NICER SALES CLERKS, I WOULD ADD...

AND CHEWING GUM!

AND THE FREEDOM TO TRAVEL ABROAD!

I'D GO TO FRANCE!

AND WOULDN'T IT BE GREAT TO HAVE A TELEPHONE AT HOME!

WHY DO YOU WANT ONE SO MUCH? I HAVE ONE BUT NO ONE TO CALL...

THAT'S TRUE, BUT THINK ABOUT IT! IF I HAD ONE, WE COULD BE ON THE PHONE TO EACH OTHER FOR HOURS...

YEAH, BUT I LIVE JUST UPSTAIRS FROM YOU!

THESE DEMANDS MAKE BIG BROTHER MAD, BUT SOLIDARNOŚĆ ISN'T TRYING TO ANGER HIM.

IN FACT, IT WANTS THE OPPOSITE. ITS GOAL IS TO FIND NON-VIOLENT SOLUTIONS.

BUT BIG BROTHER CONTINUES AND THE POLISH PEOPLE ARE BEGINNING TO UNDERSTAND THAT HE ONLY SPEAKS ONE LANGUAGE.

IN ANY CASE, HE DOESN'T WANT TO GIVE US UP, OR TO LEAVE US ALONE.

BUT FROM WHAT I UNDERSTAND, SOLIDARNOŚĆ WON'T GIVE UP EITHER...THERE WILL HAVE TO BE A WINNER AND A LOSER...

MAYBE IT'S EASIER TO BE AN ONLY CHILD AFTER ALL, THAN TO HAVE A BIG BROTHER WHO'S SO BOSSY AND STUBBORN ...

142

i WAS BORN ON APRIL 8TH. PLANNING MY BIRTHDAY IS ALWAYS COMPLICATED BECAUSE THIS DATE INEVITABLY FALLS IN THE MIDDLE OF LENT.

MY MOM REFUSES TO HAVE A PARTY WHEN THE ATMOSPHERE ISN'T RIGHT. LENT EXCLUDES ALL JOY... SO WE POSTPONE IT A LITTLE.

GENERALLY THE GUESTS ARE INVITED FOR THE END OF APRIL WHICH I DON'T MIND... AS LONG AS I'M NOT FORGOTTEN.

IT'S NOT A BIG PARTY. JUST THE USUAL PEOPLE COME. I SEE THEM OFTEN, BUT IT'S STILL NEAT TO HAVE THEM ALL TOGETHER.

AND IT GIVES THEM A CHANCE TO SIT DOWN AT A TABLE AND TALK.

BUT MY MOM'S FAMILY ALMOST NEVER TRAVELS. SOMETIMES ONLY MY MOM'S COUSIN TERESKA COMES. SHE'S THE REPRESENTATIVE.

EVEN IF THEY DON'T COME, I ALWAYS GET SOMETHING FROM THEM. MY AUNT GIVES ME A JAR OF PRESERVED MEAT (!). MY COUSIN, A BOOK OR A SWEATER SHE KNIT FOR ME...

MY MATERNAL GRANDMOTHER IS THE MOST ORIGINAL...

SHE GIVES ME HER GIFT IN MARCH. OR EVEN FEBRUARY.

A COMPLETELY CRUMPLED BILL IN A BALL. SHE DOESN'T SAY HAPPY BIRTHDAY (IN FACT, I WONDER IF SHE'S EVER SPOKEN TO ME?), BUT SHE NEVER FORGETS ME

THIS YEAR, AS USUAL, MY MOM HAS PLANNED MY BIRTH-DAY FOR THE LAST WEEKEND IN APRIL. SPRING IS APPROACHING, IT'S GETTING WARM...AND NOT ONLY IN THE LITERAL SENSE OF THE WORD...

THIS ENTHUSIASM IS TIED TO THE STRIKES THAT ARE BREAKING OUT IN VARIOUS CITIES' FACTORIES.

MY MOM COMES HOME FROM WORK WITH NEWS OF OUR FAMILY IN KRAKÓW.

MIETEK IS STRIKING IN NOWA HUTA!

I SPOKE TO DZIDZIA ON THE PHONE. SHE WAS IN TEARS...

WHY IN TEARS? I THOUGHT THEY WERE STRIKING TO MAKE OUR LIVES BETTER?!

IF HE'S THERE, I WANT TO BE A PART OF IT TOO!

JOZEK, NO!!

IF WE'RE LUCKY, THEY'LL ONLY FIRE YOU. AND THEN WHAT'LL WE DO?

AS YOU KNOW, IT'S THE LOWEST IN RANK WHO PAY THE HIGHEST PRICE. YOU'RE ONLY A UNION MEMBER, NOT AN ACTIVIST...

YOU'RE AT THE BOTTOM OF THE LADDER. WHEN THEY WANT TO PUNISH SOMEONE, YOU'RE NOT THE ONE THEY'LL SPARE.

ON THE CONTRARY, THEY'LL START WITH THE PEOPLE LIKE YOU!

I'M NOT A MEMBER JUST SO THEY CAN PROTECT ME, BUT TO LEND THEM MY SUPPORT AS WELL.

IF I DON'T GO, THERE'S NO POINT BEING IN THE UNION.

TWO DAYS LATER, MY DAD DOESN'T COME HOME FROM THE FACTORY.

I'M ALREADY FAMILIAR WITH THIS FEELING. I'VE EXPERIENCED IT SEVERAL TIMES. PRETTY OFTEN, TO BE HONEST, BUT I WASN'T ALWAYS SO CONSCIOUS OF WHAT IT MEANT.

NOW I FEEL LIKE I KNOW THAT EVEN GIVEN THE WORKERS' DETERMINATION, THE STRIKES ARE STILL DANGEROUS.

I'M STILL A STUDENT. UNFORTUNATELY, THE TEACHERS AREN'T STRIKING. I GO TO SCHOOL, NOTHING CHANGES.

ROBOTNICY !!! PRZYŁĄCZCIE SIĘ DO STRAJKU W IMIĘ WOLNOŚCI

EXCEPT MY DAD DOESN'T COME HOME. HE STAYS THERE WITH THE OTHER WORKERS. THEY'RE BLOCK-ING THE MACHINES AND REFUSING TO WORK ON THEM.

THE DAY IT HAPPENS, THERE'S NO ONE HOME WHEN I GET BACK FROM SCHOOL...

THE STRIKE'S OVER. THE ZOMO INTERVENED AND THREATENED TO CALL IN THE ARMY...

WHERE WERE YOU?

YOU'RE STILL WEARING YOUR SCHOOL CLOTHES.

WHERE'S DAD?

TAKE THEM OFF BEFORE THEY GET DIRTY.

WHAT'S GOING ON?

I HAVE TO GO OUT AGAIN, I'M JUST MAKING YOU SOME DINNER.

GO OUT WHERE?!

TO TAKE CARE OF SOMETHING.

WHAT IS IT?

IT'S NOTHING.

TO UNDERSTAND THE WORLD OF ADULTS, YOU HAVE TO DO EVERYTHING JUST LIKE THEY DO. I CAN'T JUST PUT ON DRESSES AND MY MOM'S HIGH HEELS.

I HAVE TO LOOK AT WHAT THEY LOOK AT, LISTEN TO WHAT THEY LISTEN TO, AND READ WHAT THEY READ.

WE DON'T HAVE MANY BOOKS AT HOME, BUT THEY ARE MOSTLY FAT BOOKS ABOUT POLISH HISTORY...I PRETTY MUCH KNOW THEM ALL.

BUT I FIND ONE I'D MISSED. IT'S NOT VERY PRETTY. IT'S PRINTED IN A VERY SMALL FONT AND SOMETIMES THE TEXT LOOKS BLURRY. IT'S CALLED "THE CRIME OF KATYŃ".

THE BOOK IS CHOCK-FULL OF WORDS THAT CHILL MY BLOOD: HOMICIDE, MASSACRE, MASS EXECUTIONS...THERE ARE PHOTOS OF PEOPLE WHO HAVE DISAPPEARED.

AND THEN OF BODIES THAT WERE FOUND, OR RATHER, THEIR REMAINS.

IT DESCRIBES HOW THE RUSSIANS EXECUTED 15,000 POLISH SOLDIERS, 8,000 OF WHOM WERE OFFICERS, DURING THE SECOND WORLD WAR.

THESE SOLDIERS WERE SUPPOSED TO BE PART OF A POLISH ARMY FIGHTING ALONGSIDE THE RUSSIANS, WHO DECLARED THEM "FRIENDS", BUT THEY WERE SECRETLY KILLED!

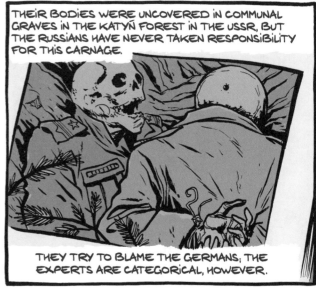

THEIR BODIES WERE UNCOVERED IN COMMUNAL GRAVES IN THE KATYŃ FOREST IN THE USSR, BUT THE RUSSIANS HAVE NEVER TAKEN RESPONSIBILITY FOR THIS CARNAGE.

THEY TRY TO BLAME THE GERMANS; THE EXPERTS ARE CATEGORICAL, HOWEVER.

"AS LONG AS THE SYSTEM OF SOVIET TYRANNY LASTS, A MORTAL DANGER THREATENS CIVILIZATION, AND PEACE WILL NEVER BE ACHIEVED."

I DON'T UNDERSTAND ALL OF IT. FRIGHTENED, I PUT IT BACK ON THE SHELF, BUT ITS SPINE POINTS AT ME TO REMIND ME WHAT I'VE SEEN.

THE MURDERERS WERE NEVER PUNISHED...

ACCORDING TO THIS BOOK, THE USSR REPRESENTS A MORTAL DANGER. I REALIZE MY COUNTRY STILL DEPENDS ON IT, AND IT'S BEHIND ALL THESE PACIFICATIONS. INCLUDING THE ONE IN MY DAD'S FACTORY.

AND MY DAD ISN'T HOME. I DON'T KNOW WHERE HE IS AND I'M AFRAID MY MOM DOESN'T KNOW EITHER.

I'M IMAGINING THE WORST POSSIBLE SCENARIOS IN MY HEAD. I'M THINKING OF HIM. A LOT.

ONLY HE KNOWS HOW I GET CARRIED AWAY BY MY IMAGINATION, HE'S ALWAYS THE ONE WHO REASONS WITH ME. I TRY TO HEAR HIS VOICE...

THAT'S ENOUGH OF YOUR "WHAT-IFS..."

THINK WITH YOUR HEAD, LOVE WITH YOUR HEART, NOT THE OTHER WAY AROUND!

AND SO WHAT IF MUSHROOMS GREW IN THE OVEN?

WE WOULDN'T GO PICK THEM IN THE FOREST, THAT'S IT!

SOMETIMES ON SUNDAYS, I DON'T GO TO CHURCH WITH MY DAD. HE GOES ALONE. WITH THE WALK THERE AND BACK, HE'S GONE ABOUT TWO HOURS.

EVEN THOUGH I KNOW WHERE HE'S GOING, I OFTEN IMAGINE DIFFERENT SCENARIOS...

I TELL MYSELF HE'S NOT GOING TO CHURCH AT ALL, BUT REJOINING HIS OTHER FAMILY...

THAT HIS OTHER WIFE LIVES ACROSS THE STREET AND HE HAS CHILDREN WITH HER TOO.

WHEN HE COMES BACK, I WATCH HIM CLOSELY. DOES HE SEEM DIFFERENT? IS HE SAD TO HAVE HAD TO LEAVE THEM TO COME BACK TO OUR HOUSE? I'D LIKE TO GO WITH HIM, TO GET TO KNOW MY BROTHERS AND SISTERS...

WE'D EAT BEIGNETS WITH ROSE JELLY AND WE'D ACT OUT THE MIKADO...I'D LIKE THAT SO MUCH!

MAYBE WHEN HE LEAVES FOR WORK, HE DOESN'T GO THERE EITHER. HE GOES TO HIS OTHER HOME. AND MAYBE HE'S THERE NOW, AND HERE I AM WORRYING ABOUT HIM!

IS HE HAPPIER THERE WITH THEM THAN HERE WITH US? IF HE DOESN'T COME BACK, THE ANSWER WILL BE CLEAR.

MY MOM COMES HOME VERY LATE. ALONE. SHE SEEMS TIRED AND ISN'T HUNGRY. IT'S STRANGE, THAT NEVER HAPPENS.

DO YOU KNOW HOW LATE IT IS?!?

WHAT DO YOU MEAN, WHERE? YOU KNOW VERY WELL HE'S ON STRIKE!

i WAS WAITING FOR YOU...WHERE'S DAD?

BUT ZDZICH TOLD ME THAT THE ZOMO WAS...

LISTEN, GO TO BED! IT WILL BE OVER TOMORROW AND YOU'LL SEE HIM!

TOMORROW COMES, BUT NOT MY DAD.

i DON'T HAVE SCHOOL, IT'S SATURDAY. i WAS SUPPOSED TO HELP MY MOM PREPARE THE SUNDAY DINNER FOR MY BIRTHDAY, BUT WHEN i WAKE UP, SHE'S NOT THERE...

SHE LEFT ME A LITTLE NOTE: "THE TEA IS IN THE THERMOS, YOU'RE GROWN, YOU CAN MAKE YOUR OWN TOAST."

AH, THAT'S IT! NOW, i'M GROWN BUT SHE DOESN'T TREAT ME LIKE THAT MOST OF THE TIME. IT JUST SUITS HER TODAY.

WHEN ZDZICH AND MY DAD TALK ABOUT POLITICS, THEY OFTEN RAISE THEIR VOICES WHEN IT COMES TO SOLIDARNOŚĆ.

IS IT BETTER TO JOIN IT OR NOT? MY DAD IS SURE WE SHOULD JOIN, ZDZICH FEELS THE OPPOSITE...

SINCE SOLIDARNOŚĆ IS ILLEGAL, EMPLOYERS TELL THEIR WORKERS THEY'LL LOSE THEIR JOBS IF THEY JOIN.

BUT SO MANY OF THEM RUN THAT RISK! THEY CAN'T FIRE ALMOST ALL THE FACTORY'S WORKERS...

MY DAD DOESN'T SAY THAT ZDZICH IS SELFISH, ONLY THAT WE HAVE TO THINK MORE BROADLY, THAT FEAR AND A LACK OF ENGAGEMENT WON'T CHANGE THE COUNTRY.

i'M PROUD OF MY DAD, BUT TODAY i WISH HE WAS MORE LIKE ZDZICH.

MY MOM DOESN'T COME HOME UNTIL LATE IN THE AFTERNOON, AND REMAINS JUST AS EVASIVE...

I KNOW WHAT SOLIDARNOŚĆ IS...

I KNOW WHAT THE ZOMO DO...

YOU CAN TALK TO ME, MOM...

SHE BURSTS INTO TEARS AND HOLDS ME AGAINST HER TIGHTLY.

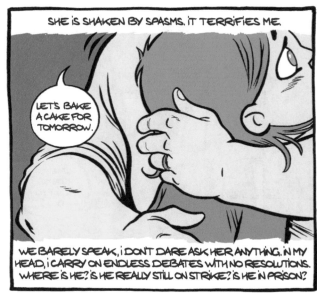

SHE IS SHAKEN BY SPASMS. IT TERRIFIES ME.

LET'S BAKE A CAKE FOR TOMORROW.

WE BARELY SPEAK. I DON'T DARE ASK HER ANYTHING. IN MY HEAD, I CARRY ON ENDLESS DEBATES WITH NO RESOLUTIONS. WHERE IS HE? IS HE REALLY STILL ON STRIKE? IS HE IN PRISON?

WHAT ARE THEY DOING TO HIM RIGHT NOW? I'VE ALREADY HEARD STORIES...SO MANY PEOPLE HAVE BEEN THERE...

THEY CLUB THEM, ROUND THEM UP, TAKE THEM TO THE STATION, STRIP THEM, HUMILIATE THEM...

IT APPALLS ME TO THINK ABOUT IT, BUT I CAN'T HELP MYSELF. I CAN'T DO ANYTHING, WHILE THEY'RE HURTING MY DAD WHO I LOVE.

I'D RATHER HE BE WITH HIS OTHER FAMILY, THAT HE BE PUTTING HIS OTHER KIDS TO BED WHILE HIS WIFE RUNS HIM A BATH...

I HATE THEM! HOW CAN THEY BE SO CRUEL?

I UNDERSTAND THE DIGNITY SOLIDARNOŚĆ IS ASKING FOR NOW.

HOW CAN THEY HURT SOMEONE FOR WANTING TO IMPROVE HIS LIFE AND THE LIVES OF HIS LOVED ONES?

ARE THEIR LIVES GOOD? DO THEIR CHILDREN SLEEP WELL AT NIGHT?

SUNDAY...

WOOF! WOOF!

AH! YOU'RE AWAKE ALREADY!!

CAN YOU TAKE DŽEKI OUT?

MY DAD ALWAYS TAKES THE DOG OUT IN THE MORNING. FROM MY BED, I CAN USUALLY HEAR HIM LOUDLY TALKING TO THE NEIGHBORS OUTSIDE... AND WE LIVE ON THE 5TH FLOOR!

IT MAKES ME LAUGH THAT HE TALKS SO LOUDLY. NOW, I MISS IT. I'D GIVE ANYTHING TO HEAR HIM FROM MY BED. WHAT A GREAT WAKE-UP SOUND!

SHH, YOUR DAD'S SLEEPING!

WOOF

HE'S HERE ?!?

WOOF WOOF!

YES.

SHE ACTS LIKE IT'S NO BIG DEAL...

WHAT HAPPENED? WHY DOES HE HAVE A CUT ON HIS FOREHEAD?

IT'S NOTHING. HE FELL.

WHAT DO YOU MEAN, FELL!?! THERE'S NO SNOW...

OFF HIS BICYCLE! YOU'VE FALLEN OFF YOUR BICYCLE BEFORE!!

THIS IS HOW I BECOME A CHILD AGAIN...

TODAY IS ALSO THE 1ST OF MAY. BUT THE AUTHORITIES IN MY CITY DID NOT ORGANIZE A PARADE THIS YEAR. NO POSTERS, NO FALSE SMILES. WE DON'T HAVE TO PRETEND WE'RE HAPPY TODAY.

THEY DON'T WANT TO EXACERBATE THE SITUATION, THEY SAY IT'D BE LIKE THROWING OIL ON THE FIRE.

AND I MUST ADMIT IT'S NICER LIKE THIS. IN THE AFTERNOON, WE GET TOGETHER WITH OUR NEIGHBORS.

THEY TREAT US LIKE A HERD OF COWS...

THEY MUST THINK WE'RE SOFT AND PASSIVE!

THAT'S IT!!

ONE THING'S FOR SURE, WE ARE TOO GENTLE, LIKE COWS!

BUT THEY'RE NOT HERE TO TALK ABOUT COWS, IT'S MY BIRTHDAY FINALLY...

STO LAT!

AND THIS YEAR, MY BEST PRESENT ISN'T AN OBJECT.

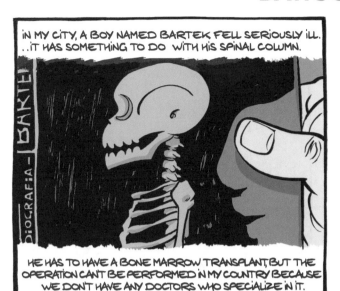

IN MY CITY, A BOY NAMED BARTEK FELL SERIOUSLY ILL. ...IT HAS SOMETHING TO DO WITH HIS SPINAL COLUMN.

HE HAS TO HAVE A BONE MARROW TRANSPLANT, BUT THE OPERATION CAN'T BE PERFORMED IN MY COUNTRY BECAUSE WE DON'T HAVE ANY DOCTORS WHO SPECIALIZE IN IT.

BARTEK HAS TO GO TO GERMANY TO SAVE HIS LIFE. BUT HIS PARENTS CAN'T AFFORD TO PAY FOR THE OPERATION AND HIS STAY ABROAD.

SO GERMANY PROPOSED THAT MY CITY START A DRIVE TO COLLECT BARCODES FROM PACKAGING. BUT NOT JUST ANY BARCODES, ONLY THOSE BEGINNING WITH THE NUMBER 4.

TO BE HONEST, WE HAD NO IDEA WHY... BUT IF WE COULD SAVE BARTEK THIS WAY, WE'D ALL PARTICIPATE...

IT ONLY APPEARS ON THE PACKAGING OF GERMAN PRODUCTS. THERE AREN'T ANY AT OUR HOUSE. I CHECK EACH BOX CAREFULLY, BUT I CAN'T FIND THIS FAMOUS 4.

I'VE COLLECTED CHOCOLATE WRAPPING PAPERS FOR A LONG TIME. I HAVE A LOT, AND ALL DIFFERENT KINDS, EVERYONE I KNOW SAVES THEM FOR ME.

SOMETIMES THE WRAPPING STILL SMELLS LIKE CHOCOLATE... TO MY GREAT JOY, I SEE THE NUMBER 4 ON SOME OF THEM. I CUT THE BARCODES OUT CAREFULLY. I FOUND 5. THAT'S NOT VERY MANY.

TO IMPROVE OUR HAUL, WHOLE SCHOOLS GO TO THE CITY DUMP. EVERYONE HAS SCISSORS. WE HAVE A LOT OF FUN!

AAAH

YOU JUST CAN'T FORGET TO WASH YOUR HANDS AFTERWARDS. THE TEACHER IS CONSTANTLY REMINDING US OF THIS AS SHE WATCHES US DIVE INTO THE PILES OF GARBAGE.

THE DRIVE REVEALS EACH FAMILY'S STATUS. THOSE WHO ARE WELL-OFF AND THOSE WHO AREN'T. WE SEE WHAT PEOPLE EAT, AND WHO HAS FAMILY ABROAD...

WOW! THIS LOOKS GOOD!!

BLECHH!!

SOME KIDS GET TIRED OF CUTTING THEM OUT AT HOME, SO THEY BRING IN WHOLE BOXES.

IT'S TO PROVE THEY DIDN'T FIND THEM AT THE DUMP!

MAYBE THEY WANTED TO MAKE A SHOW OF IT IN FRONT OF THE WHOLE SCHOOL...

THE CHILDREN SEEM IMPRESSED, BUT THE TEACHERS GET MAD.

ARRGH! YOU COULDN'T HAVE DONE THIS AT HOME?!

GET OUT YOUR SCISSORS AND CUT...

TOMEK IS ONE OF THEM. HE'S RICH, BUT MOST IMPORTANT, HE'S HANDSOME...HE'S IN A DIFFERENT CLASS, SO I DON'T SEE HIM VERY OFTEN.

DURING BREAK, I WATCH HIM PLAY WITH HIS FRIENDS IN THE HALL...AND I'M NOT THE ONLY ONE...

HE STARTS CUTTING NEXT TO ME.

MARZI, YOU COLLECT CHOCOLATE WRAPPERS, RIGHT? HERE'S ONE FOR YOU...

THANKS...

HE KNOWS I'M POOR, THAT WHAT I KNOW BEST ABOUT CHOCOLATE IS ITS PACKAGING...

BUT HE ALSO KNOWS MY NAME...

WE PUT OUR BARCODES TOGETHER. OUR SCHOOL COLLECTED ALMOST 3,000 IN THE END.

KRANKENHAUS

GERMANY WILL BUY THEM BACK FROM US. I HOPE BARTEK WILL BE ABLE TO HAVE HIS OPERATION AND GET BETTER.

MY PARENTS RARELY LET ME WATCH TELEVISION WITH THEM AT NIGHT. BUT THEY MAKE AN EXCEPTION FOR A SHOW THAT AIRS EVERY TUESDAY ON CHANNEL 2.

NIEWOLNICA, ISAURA!

escrava ISAURA

DO ROMANCE DE BERNARDO GUIMARÃES

IT'S CALLED "ISAURA THE SLAVE."

IT TELLS THE STORY OF A YOUNG WOMAN WHO BELONGS TO A RICH MERCHANT, A MAN WHO OWNS COTTON FIELDS IN BRAZIL.

EVEN THOUGH ISAURA IS A SLAVE, SHE'S WELL-EDUCATED AND DOESN'T WORK IN THE FIELDS LIKE THE OTHERS. SHE TAKES CARE OF THE HOUSE.

THIS IS THANKS TO THE OWNER'S WIFE, WHO TREATS HER LIKE HER OWN DAUGHTER.

BUT ONE DAY THE OWNER'S SON, LEONCIO, RETURNS FROM HIS STUDIES AND IT MARKS THE END OF ISAURA'S COMFORTABLE LIFE. SHE GOES BACK TO BEING A SLAVE.

SHE'S IN LOVE WITH TOBIAS, ANOTHER RICH PLANTER WHO LOVES HER TOO AND WANTS TO BUY HER. BUT LEONCIO WON'T ALLOW IT.

MIERDA!

EVEN THOUGH HE HAS JUST MARRIED MALVINA, HE CONTINUES TO HARASS THE BEAUTIFUL ISAURA...

OUR BEDS ARE TURNED DOWN AND OUR TEETH BRUSHED. WE STAY UP ONLY FOR ISAURA, AND WE GO TO BED IMMEDIATELY AFTERWARDS.

MY MOM IS VERY MOVED BY EACH EPISODE. YOU HAVE TO ADMIT SHE DOESN'T HAVE AN EASY LIFE, THAT POOR GIRL!

EVERY WEDNESDAY MORNING AT SCHOOL, SHE'S ALL WE CAN TALK ABOUT. EVEN THE TEACHERS...

I WATCHED IT AT THE NEIGHBORS. MY TV SET BROKE AT THE LAST MINUTE!

OHH!

SOME STUDENTS DO THEIR HAIR A LITTLE LIKE THE HEROINE. MY HAIR ISN'T LONG ENOUGH, UNFORTUNATELY.

BUT IT'S NOT JUST HER HAIR THAT INTERESTS US. IT'S ALSO SURPRISING. ISAURA COULD BE TAKEN INTO HER OWNERS' HOME BECAUSE SHE WAS LOVED...

BUT ABOVE ALL BECAUSE SHE IS THE ONLY SLAVE WHO ISN'T BLACK LIKE THE OTHERS. IT'S THE FIRST TIME I'VE EVER SEEN PEOPLE THIS COLOR!

IN PRESCHOOL, WE LEARNED A POEM ABOUT BAMBO, A LITTLE BLACK BOY.

MURZYNEK BAMBO W AFRYCE MIESKA, CZARNĄ MA SKÓRĘ TEN NASZ KOLEZKA

HIS LIFE WAS JUST LIKE OURS, HE WENT TO SCHOOL, PLAYED PRANKS...JUST LIKE US, BUT IN AFRICA.

I DIDN'T UNDERSTAND WHAT IT MEANT "TO BE BLACK"?! NOW, THANKS TO THIS TV SHOW, I DO. IT'S LIKE BEING THE COLOR OF CHOCOLATE...

HMMM... HERE, THIS IS FOR YOU...

IT'S GOOD BECAUSE WHEN YOU'RE SHY AND EMBARRASSED AND YOU BLUSH, IT'S A LOT LESS OBVIOUS!

BUT WHAT MAKES THE BIGGEST IMPRESSION ON ME IS THAT ALL THE BLACK PEOPLE ARE SLAVES IN THIS SHOW...IN THE POEM, BAMBO WASN'T ONE.

THEY'RE BLACK, THAT'S WHY THEY'RE SLAVES.

BUT THEN WHY IS ISAURA A SLAVE?

SHE'S NOT REALLY WHITE, SHE'S MIXED!

YEAH, AND THAT'S WHY SHE CAN WORK IN THE HOUSE.

BUT WHY ARE THE BLACKS SLAVES?!?

AND THE WHITES LOOK DOWN ON THEM BECAUSE THEY'RE SLAVES!

I DON'T KNOW!..

NO IDEA...

THEY'RE UNLUCKY.

WHICH IS CERTAINLY BECAUSE THEY'RE BLACK. THEY BEAT THEM, I'VE SEEN IT!

IT'S ONLY A SHOW, AFTER ALL...

ANYWAY, THE SERIES REVOLVES AROUND ISAURA'S HEARTBREAKS.

WHEN MY DAD'S ON THE AFTERNOON SHIFT, HE DOESN'T FINISH UNTIL 11 PM, SO HE MISSES THE SHOW. I CAN'T WAIT UP FOR HIM BECAUSE IT'S TOO LATE, BUT THE NEXT MORNING I TELL HIM EVERYTHING THAT HAPPENED.

¡SAURA DIDN'T THINK ANYONE WAS HOME... SHE WENT IN AND STARTED PLAYING THE PIANO IN TEARS.

SHE PLAYED SO BEAUTIFULLY...

BUT LEONCIO WAS HIDING BEHIND THE DOOR AND HEARD EVERYTHING! HE WAS MOVED TOO... BUT HE SMILED EVILLY THE WAY ONLY HE CAN!

MOST SURPRISINGLY, THE TWO LEAD ACTORS CAME AND VISITED POLAND.

THE WHOLE COUNTRY WAS VERY MOVED. UNFORTU-NATELY, THEY DIDN'T COME TO MY CITY, THEY ONLY WENT TO THE BIG METROPOLISES LIKE WARSZAWA, KRAKÓW, AND KATOWICE.

THEY HAVE CONQUERED OUR HEARTS!

WE SAW THEM GETTING OFF THE PLANE LIVE ON THE TV NEWS. THERE WAS A CROWD TO WELCOME THEM.

THEY VISITED SCHOOLS, HOSPITALS, FACTORIES...

EVER SINCE THE FOURTH EPISODE, 84% OF POLES, REGARDLESS OF AGE OR CLASS, CAN BE FOUND IN FRONT OF THEIR TELEVI-SIONS ON TUESDAY NIGHTS!!

POLAND LOVES LUCIELA SANTOS AND RUBEN DE FALCO, AND THEY LOVE US BACK. THEIR ARRIVAL IN OUR COUNTRY HAS INSPIRED ENORMOUS ENTHUSIASM, A FEW OF OUR MORE SENSITIVE CITIZENS HAVE EVEN FAINTED AT THE SIGHT OF OUR HEROES!

THEY WERE EVEN WELCOMED IN CHINA, WHICH APPARENTLY ADORES THE COUPLE AS MUCH AS WE DO. THE ACTORS ACCOM-PANIED THE BRAZILIAN PRESIDENT THERE ON AN OFFICIAL VISIT.

I WAS A LITTLE DISAPPOINTED. THESE TWO PEOPLE HAD NOTHING TO DO WITH ¡SAURA AND LEONCIO. THEY HAD DIFFERENT NAMES AND DIDN'T ACT THE SAME.

IT'S A SHOW, YOU KNOW...

THEY'RE ONLY ACTING, LIKE YOU WHEN YOU PRETEND TO BE SOMEONE ELSE!

I ONLY DO THAT ALONE IN MY ROOM. BUT EVERYONE IS WATCHING THEM...

PERHAPS I'M BEING WATCHED TOO, AND I JUST DON'T KNOW IT... ONE DAY A WEEK, PEOPLE ARE GATHERING IN FRONT OF THEIR TELEVISIONS TO LOOK AT ME.

I DECIDE TO PAY MORE ATTENTION TO MY BEHAVIOR, TO TRY TO SOUND SMART, BUT IT'S SOON VERY CLEAR THAT I HAVEN'T ACHIEVED THEIR LEVEL OF SUCCESS BECAUSE NOBODY'S TALKING ABOUT ME...

MY DAD IS RIGHT. ISAURA AND LEONCIO AREN'T REAL. THE ACTORS ARE LYING AND I DON'T LIKE IT. EVEN SO, EVER SINCE THE DEBUT OF THIS SERIES, A LOT OF ISAURAS AND LEONCIOS HAVE BEEN BORN!

FLICK

EVEN GOSIA IS CRAZY ABOUT THIS SHOW. SO MUCH SO THAT EVERY TIME WE PLAY TOGETHER, SHE WANTS TO BE ISAURA.

WE PLACE TWO CHAIRS IN FRONT OF THE TV AND POSITION OURSELVES SO THAT WE'RE REFLECTED IN THE SCREEN. WE'RE NOW IN A TV STUDIO, QUESTIONING ISAURA ABOUT HER VISIT TO POLAND.

DEAR VIEWERS, I HAVE THE PLEASURE OF WELCOMING TO OUR STUDIOS...

ISAURA!

HELLO!!

I HOLD ONTO THE MICROPHONE THAT GOES WITH MY DAD'S TAPE RECORDER, IT FEELS MORE AUTHENTIC THAT WAY.

WE SMOKE COLORED PENCILS FOR CIGARETTES. GOSIA IS REALLY TRANSFORMED. SHE HAS PUT A PART IN THE MIDDLE OF HER HAIR FOR THE INTERVIEW.

WHY DON'T YOU TRY TO ESCAPE FROM LEONCIO'S HOUSE?

IT'S NOT THAT EASY, YOU KNOW. LEONCIO'S MEN ARE EVERYWHERE, HE'D FIND ME VERY QUICKLY...

SOMETIMES, I'M THE STUDIO GUEST... OFTEN I'M MIREILLE MATHIEU...

HELLO MIREILLE. WE SEE YOU ON KONCERT ŻYCZEŃ BUT WE DON'T KNOW MUCH ABOUT YOU. TELL US ABOUT YOURSELF.

I WAS BORN IN PARIS. MY PARENTS WERE HUMBLE WORKERS, BUT I SANG FROM A VERY YOUNG AGE.

I STILL LIVE THERE, IT'S A WONDERFUL CITY. IT HAS ABSOLUTELY...

EVERYTHING!

AT THE END OF THE SHOW, I MAKE UP MY OWN WORDS AND SING FOR THE POLISH VIEWERS.

AKROPOLIS ADIÉ

ADIÉÉÉ

L'AMOURRR !!!

TV IS PRETTY GREAT...

THE HALF-COW FEAST

SCARCITY BREEDS SOLIDARITY. IN ONE OF MY CLASSMATES' BUILDINGS, THE NEIGHBORS WENT IN TOGETHER ON AN ENORMOUS FREEZER.

THEY KEPT IT IN THE BASEMENT.

THEN, THEY WENT TO THE COUNTRY AND BOUGHT A HALF-COW!

WITHOUT RATION CARDS, OF COURSE...

THEY DIVVY IT UP IN THE FREEZER. EACH PERSON KEEPS HIS MEAT IN HIS DESIGNATED SPACE.

THAT WAY THEY'LL BE ABLE TO HAVE A PIECE OF COW WITHOUT WAITING FOR HOURS OUTSIDE A STORE.

BUT SOMETIMES THE ELECTRICITY GOES OUT AND EVERYTHING THAWS!

SO IT ALL HAS TO BE EATEN IMMEDIATELY. IT WOULD BREAK THEIR HEARTS TO HAVE TO THROW EVEN A BIT OF IT AWAY!

SO THE WHOLE BUILDING HAS A PARTY AND SOMETIMES THEY EVEN INVITE PEOPLE FROM OTHER BUILDINGS. A HALF-COW IS A LOT OF FOOD.

IT'S A JOYOUS EVENT DESPITE THE MISADVENTURE.

USUALLY, PEOPLE PRAY THAT THERE WON'T BE A BLACKOUT...

GRGLLRGL

I'M SURE AT LEAST A FEW PRAY FOR THE OPPOSITE!

SCRAMBLED

I DON'T LIKE EATING MUCH, BUT MY MOM MAKES ME SWALLOW EVERYTHING ON MY PLATE.

TONIGHT, IT'S SCRAMBLED EGGS...

FIRST OF ALL, I'M NOT HUNGRY, AND SECONDLY, I DON'T LIKE SCRAMBLED EGGS. SHE KNOWS THIS, BUT SHE STILL INSISTS, SAYING THEY'RE FULL OF GOOD THINGS MY GROWING BODY NEEDS.

I'M GOING TO MAKE MYSELF A LITTLE SANDWICH, BUT NOT A WHOLE MEAL, PLEASE...

THERE'S NO DISCUSSION! YOU'RE GROWING FAST, YOU NEED TO EAT! LOOK AT THIS DELICIOUS DINNER I MADE YOU...

IT DOESN'T LOOK LIKE ANYTHING. IT DOESN'T MAKE YOU WANT TO EAT IT, QUITE THE OPPOSITE. IT MAKES ME WANT TO THROW UP. THIS DISH LOOKS LIKE A MEAL THAT'S ALREADY BEEN CHEWED.

I DON'T WANT TO! I'M NOT HUNGRY!

EAT!!

BUT IT'S NOT EVEN GOOD...

YOU'RE GOING TO EAT, OK? IT'S NOT GOOD, SHE SAYS!!

I'LL HAVE YOU KNOW THERE ARE CHILDREN WHO HAVE NOTHING TO EAT WHO WOULD DREAM ABOUT WHAT YOU HAVE ON YOUR PLATE!

STOP BEING SO DIFFICULT AND EAT!

I START TO CRY INTO MY PLATE. I'M REALLY NOT HUNGRY, BUT SHE DOESN'T SEEM TO CARE AT ALL.

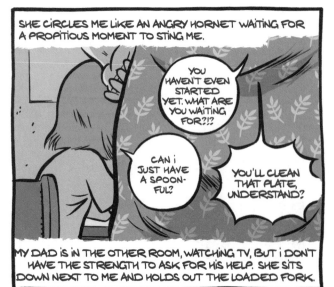

SHE CIRCLES ME LIKE AN ANGRY HORNET WAITING FOR A PROPITIOUS MOMENT TO STING ME.

YOU HAVEN'T EVEN STARTED YET. WHAT ARE YOU WAITING FOR?!?

CAN I JUST HAVE A SPOON-FUL?

YOU'LL CLEAN THAT PLATE, UNDERSTAND?

MY DAD IS IN THE OTHER ROOM, WATCHING TV, BUT I DON'T HAVE THE STRENGTH TO ASK FOR HIS HELP. SHE SITS DOWN NEXT TO ME AND HOLDS OUT THE LOADED FORK.

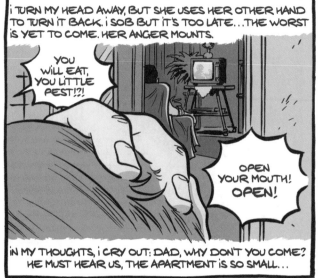

I TURN MY HEAD AWAY, BUT SHE USES HER OTHER HAND TO TURN IT BACK. I SOB BUT IT'S TOO LATE...THE WORST IS YET TO COME. HER ANGER MOUNTS.

YOU WILL EAT, YOU LITTLE PEST!?!

OPEN YOUR MOUTH! OPEN!

IN MY THOUGHTS, I CRY OUT: DAD, WHY DON'T YOU COME? HE MUST HEAR US, THE APARTMENT IS SO SMALL...

SHE STUFFS THE LOADED FORK IN MY MOUTH, WHILE I TRY TO CLOSE IT. SHE FORCES IT IN AND HURTS ME. SHE HITS ME ON THE HEAD TO MAKE ME OPEN WIDER...

EAT! DIRTY LITTLE GUTTERSNIPE!!

THIS TIME I OBEY, BUT I WON'T EAT ANY MORE. I CAN'T. MY STOMACH IS ALREADY FULL WITH STRESS, FEAR, AND POWERLESSNESS.

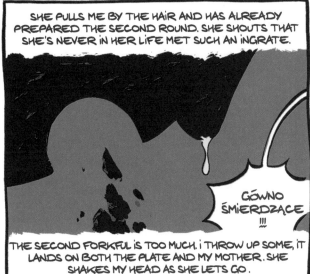

SHE PULLS ME BY THE HAIR AND HAS ALREADY PREPARED THE SECOND ROUND. SHE SHOUTS THAT SHE'S NEVER IN HER LIFE MET SUCH AN INGRATE.

GÓWNO ŚMIERDZĄCE !!!

THE SECOND FORKFUL IS TOO MUCH. I THROW UP SOME, IT LANDS ON BOTH THE PLATE AND MY MOTHER. SHE SHAKES MY HEAD AS SHE LETS GO.

I TRY TO WIPE MY MOUTH, BUT SHE SLAPS ME, SCREAMING THAT I WASTE FOOD, THAT I'M EVIL BECAUSE NOT ONLY DID I NOT EAT, BUT I VOMITED ONTO MY PLATE, SO THAT NO ONE ELSE CAN FINISH IT.

LOOK! THIS IS HOW SHE THANKS US! AFTER WE WORK SO HARD SO THE LITTLE MISS CAN EAT!

GO WASH YOUR FACE!!!

I RUN AND LOCK MYSELF IN THE BATHROOM.

I TRY TO CALM DOWN A LITTLE, WHILE MY MOM GETS ANGRY AT MY DAD.

YOU JUST SIT THERE AND SAY NOTHING! YOU DON'T REACT WHEN YOUR DARLING DAUGHTER MAKES A MESS!!

ALL YOU DO IS SMOKE!

GO ON, SMOKE! CHOKE YOURSELF WITH YOUR CIGARETTES!! LEAVE ME ALL ALONE WITH HER...

I DON'T UNDER-STAND...OUR NEIGHBOR REACTS WHEN HIS CHILDREN MISBEHAVE!

THAT'S WHY EVERYTHING WORKS LIKE CLOCKWORK OVER THERE!

YOU DO NOTHING! YOU JUST SIT THERE...

MY DAD DOESN'T RESPOND. HIS SILENCE MAKES HER EVEN MORE ANGRY.

SHE'S CRYING HARD. SHE COMPLAINS ABOUT ME TO I DON'T KNOW WHO. SHE TALKS LOUDLY, HER VOICE FILLS UP THE WHOLE APARTMENT.

WHY AM I BEING PUNISHED LIKE THIS?! TO HAVE SUCH A PEST UNDER MY ROOF?

WE'RE GOOD PEOPLE! WHERE DOES THIS INSOLENCE COME FROM?

HER EXPLANATION IS THAT GOD MUST BE PUNISHING HER FOR THE SINS OF OUR ANCESTORS. IT'S ALWAYS THE SAME, AS SOON AS WE START TO FIGHT...

I DON'T REALLY UNDERSTAND WHAT GOES ON IN MY MOM'S HEAD, WHICH IS WHY I USUALLY DON'T RESPOND, ESPECIALLY WHEN MY DAD ISN'T THERE.

BUT WHEN I DON'T SAY ANYTHING, IT'S JUST AS BIG A DEAL TO MY MOM. SHE THINKS I'M REFUSING TO TALK TO HER BECAUSE I FEEL SUPERIOR. I DON'T FEEL SUPERIOR OR INFERIOR. I JUST SIMPLY DON'T UNDERSTAND WHY SHE'S SCREAMING.

IF I FROWN, I'M NOT TRYING TO PROVOKE YOU MORE, MOM. IF I BITE MY LIPS, I'M NOT MAKING FUN OF YOU.

I'M JUST AFRAID OF YOUR ANGER.

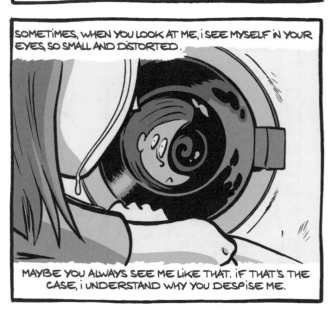

SOMETIMES, WHEN YOU LOOK AT ME, I SEE MYSELF IN YOUR EYES, SO SMALL AND DISTORTED.

MAYBE YOU ALWAYS SEE ME LIKE THAT. IF THAT'S THE CASE, I UNDERSTAND WHY YOU DESPISE ME.

IN YOUR EYES I'M NOT BEAUTIFUL. I'M NOT EVEN HUMAN. I'M LIKE A RAG DOLL.

I DON'T HAVE CLOTH DOLLS ANYMORE, BUT I KNOW LIKE WITH ANY TOY, WE ENJOY PLAYING WITH THEM, BUT ALSO TUGGING TO SEE IF THEY'LL TEAR. WE MISTREAT THEM.

THE DIFFERENCE IS I'M ALIVE, AND THEY'RE ONLY OBJECTS.

Proszek Do Prania

I'D LIKE TO EXPLAIN THIS TO YOU, MOM, BUT I THINK IT WOULD ONLY MAKE YOU MORE MAD...I'D RATHER NOT TRY ANYTHING AT ALL.

I'M STAYING IN THE BATHROOM A FEW MORE MINUTES...

MY HAIR IS PLASTERED WITH VOMIT. I'M TOO SHORT TO SEE MY REFLECTION IN THE MIRROR. I'D NEED THE STOOL FROM THE HALL, BUT I DON'T DARE GO OUT.

I TRY TO SEE MYSELF IN THE FAUCET.

MY EYES ARE RED AND SO'S MY FACE.

IT'S FUNNY. I DISCOVER MY HUGE NOSE. I LOOK LIKE ST. NICK. MY NOSE IS EVEN BIGGER THAN MY EYES. IT MAKES ME LAUGH.

I PLAY AROUND FOR ANOTHER MINUTE, BRINGING MY FACE CLOSE AND MOVING IT AWAY FROM THE TAP.

IT'S LIKE WHEN YOU LOOK AT YOURSELF IN THE CHRISTMAS TREE BALLS.

AND MY TEETH! THEY'RE HUGE! I'M LIKE A HORSE CONTEMPLATING HIS TOOTHY SMILE IN A MIRROR.

MY EAR TO THE DOOR, I WAIT FOR EVERYTHING TO CALM DOWN.

I HEAR MY MOM SOBBING IN THE KITCHEN. I THINK IT'S OVER. I CAN COME OUT AND HIDE IN MY BEDROOM.

I'LL GO TO BED ALONE, NO ONE WILL COME SAY GOODNIGHT.

AND TOMORROW, IT'LL BE AS IF NOTHING HAD HAPPENED.

EVERY SO OFTEN AT SCHOOL, THE NURSES DESCEND ON OUR CLASSROOMS.

THEY USUALLY APPEAR SUDDENLY AND IT'S VERY BAD NEWS BECAUSE IT MEANS ONE THING: VACCINES!

WE DON'T LIKE CATCHING SIGHT OF THEM, EITHER IN CLASS OR IN THE HALLS.

NURSES!!! I SAW NURSES!

IT WOULD BE MUCH BETTER IF THEY KEPT TO THE INFIRMARY AND WE COULD JUST CALL THEM IF WE NEEDED THEM. UNFORTUNATELY, THAT'S NOT HOW IT WORKS.

THEY ALSO COME TO CHECK OUR TEETH. THEY BRING TOOTHBRUSHES AND A SPECIAL PRODUCT. THEN WE ALL GO BRUSH OUR TEETH TOGETHER IN THE BATHROOM.

WE HAVE TO SPIT, BUT WE'RE NOT SUPPOSED TO RINSE OUR MOUTHS OUT FOR AT LEAST AN HOUR. IT'S HORRIBLE AND YUCKY. WHEN WE GO BACK TO CLASS, OUR MOUTHS STILL TASTE LIKE MEDICINE.

SOMETIMES THEY JUST CHECK FOR LICE...

YOU HAVE LICE!

NOT YOU, YOU'RE CLEAN

YOU'RE OKAY

YOU TOO!

LICE!!

LICE!!

OCCASIONALLY THEY COME AND CHOOSE A FEW OF US AT RANDOM...

YOU!

YOU!

YOU!

YOU!

ARGH

...THE VICTIMS. OFTEN, I'M ONE OF THEM.

THEY'LL CHOOSE THE WEIRDEST, TALLEST, FATTEST, OR THINNEST...THEY MEASURE OUR BLOOD PRESSURE, OBSERVE US LIKE MONKEYS IN A ZOO...

DO YOU GET LIGHT-HEADED?

DO YOU RUN OUT OF BREATH QUICKLY?

DO YOU FREQUENTLY FEEL NAUSEATED?

ONCE, A NURSE CAME IN AND ASKED THE TEACHER IF SHE COULD BORROW ONE STUDENT. SHE LOOKED US OVER FOR A MINUTE AND THEN:

YOU! COME WITH ME!

AGAIN!! IT'S ALWAYS ME. I DON'T KNOW WHY...WHAT IF I DON'T WANT TO BE BORROWED?

YOU'RE TALL, YOU CAN HELP ME...

WATER THE PLANTS.

UHH...

WILL THERE BE VACCINES AGAIN THIS YEAR?

MANY!

WHEN THEY COME GIVE THE VACCINES, THEY DON'T TELL US RIGHT AWAY.

THE CLASSROOM GROWS QUIET AND WAITS. TENSION MOUNTS...

WHEN THEY COME CHECK FOR LICE, THEY FLING THEMSELVES AT OUR HEADS...

THEY DON'T HAVE TOOTH-BRUSHES...

AND THEY LOOK VERY SERIOUS!

THEY'LL TALK TO THE TEACHER WHO'LL MAKE THE ANNOUNCEMENT:

YOU'LL LEAVE THE ROOM TEN BY TEN AND FOLLOW THESE LADIES...

WE ALREADY KNOW WHAT TO DO...

BUT WE CAN'T BE VACCINATED IF WE HAVE A LITTLE COLD. I NEVER FEEL WELL BEFORE A VACCINE, SO I'M NEVER IN THE FIRST ROUND. I DON'T HAVE TO FAKE IT, THE IDEA OF THE SHOT MAKES ME SICK...

IT'LL BE THE 22ND THEN, IN ONE WEEK.

TRY NOT TO GET SICK AGAIN!

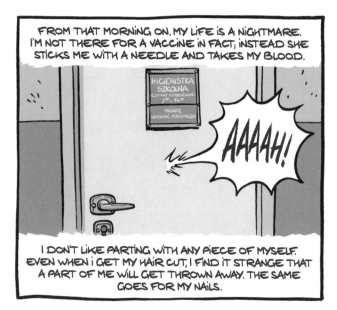

FROM THAT MORNING ON, MY LIFE IS A NIGHTMARE. I'M NOT THERE FOR A VACCINE IN FACT; INSTEAD SHE STICKS ME WITH A NEEDLE AND TAKES MY BLOOD.

AAAAH!

I DON'T LIKE PARTING WITH ANY PIECE OF MYSELF. EVEN WHEN I GET MY HAIR CUT, I FIND IT STRANGE THAT A PART OF ME WILL GET THROWN AWAY. THE SAME GOES FOR MY NAILS.

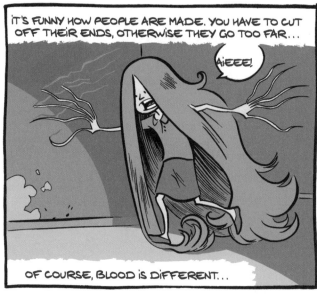

IT'S FUNNY HOW PEOPLE ARE MADE. YOU HAVE TO CUT OFF THEIR ENDS, OTHERWISE THEY GO TOO FAR...

AIEEE!

OF COURSE, BLOOD IS DIFFERENT...

LUCKILY TEETH DON'T GROW. I ALREADY DON'T LIKE THE DENTIST, BUT IF HE HAD TO SAW DOWN MY TEETH...

RRRRRR, STOP MOVING, OKAY?!

I'D RATHER GET DENTURES, LIKE MY GRANDMOTHER, RIGHT AWAY.

IT'S THE SCHOOL NURSES WHO DISCOVER THAT MY SPINAL COLUMN IS DEFORMED...

APPARENTLY I HAVE SCOLIOSIS!

OH REALLY?

GOSIA HAS IT TOO. IT'S CONVENIENT, SHE'S MY BEST FRIEND SINCE MONIKA MOVED AWAY. WE'RE THE ONLY TWO IN OUR CLASS WHO HAVE IT.

WE HAVE TO DO SPECIAL EXERCISES AT THE HOSPITAL IN A REHABILITATION ROOM IN THE BASEMENT.

SZPITAL

WE GO TOGETHER, SOMETIMES HER DAD TAKES US IN HIS BEAUTIFUL RED SKODA. IT'S NICE BECAUSE WE CAN TALK WITHOUT HAVING TO SHOUT OVER THE SOUND OF THE ENGINE...UNLIKE IN MY DAD'S FIAT 126.

IN THE ROOM, A MAN DRESSED LIKE A DOCTOR EXPLAINS WHAT WE HAVE TO DO. HE HAS A BIRD-SHAPED HEAD AND IT MAKES US LAUGH.

SEE HOW HE WALKS, HE LOOKS LIKE A PECKING STORK!

WE LIFT UP A VERY, VERY HEAVY BALL AND MY ARMS REALLY, REALLY HURT. IT WEIGHS SO MUCH THAT IF I DROPPED IT MY FACE WOULD BE DEFORMED JUST LIKE MY SPINE!

2...

AAAH...

EACH EXERCISE HAS TO BE REPEATED 15 TIMES...

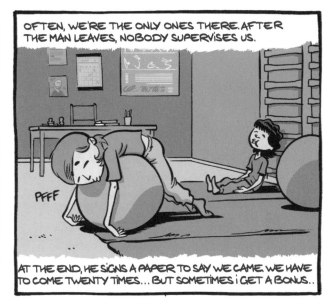

OFTEN, WE'RE THE ONLY ONES THERE. AFTER THE MAN LEAVES, NOBODY SUPERVISES US.

PFFF

AT THE END, HE SIGNS A PAPER TO SAY WE CAME. WE HAVE TO COME TWENTY TIMES... BUT SOMETIMES I GET A BONUS...

HE SITS ME ON A CHAIR IN FRONT OF A BIG MIRROR. THE WHOLE ROOM IS REFLECTED IN IT. I'M NOT ALLOWED TO MOVE.

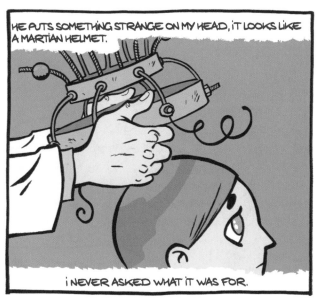

HE PUTS SOMETHING STRANGE ON MY HEAD, IT LOOKS LIKE A MARTIAN HELMET.

I NEVER ASKED WHAT IT WAS FOR.

THEN HE LEAVES, AND I STAY LIKE THAT, IN FRONT OF ALL THESE MIRRORS. AND ALL I CAN DO IS GIGGLE.

I SEE MYSELF STUCK THERE, WEARING A MIND-READING MACHINE OR A BRAIN SNATCHER (I DON'T KNOW). IT HAS ANTENNAS AND SOME PLUGS, AND ALSO STEEL WIRES.

I TOLD MY PARENTS ABOUT IT, BUT MY MOM SAID THE DOCTOR KNOWS WHAT HE'S DOING AND IT MUST BE FOR MY OWN GOOD.

ONE DAY, GOSIA CAME TO FIND ME AFTER SHE CHANGED. AT THE SIGHT OF THIS MACHINE, SHE BUSTED OUT LAUGHING.

WE LAUGHED SO MUCH THE HELMET ALMOST FELL OFF MY HEAD, AND WHEN I REACHED UP TO STRAIGHTEN IT I NOTICED IT BUZZED A LITTLE.

AFTER AWHILE, STAYING ON MY STOOL, IMMOBILE, BECOMES UNBEARABLE. OTHER PEOPLE COME DO THEIR EXERCISES AND LOOK AT ME STRANGELY. APPARENTLY, I'M THE ONLY ONE WHO GETS THIS MACHINE.

SO WHEN THE SESSIONS WITH GOSIA ARE OVER, I TRY TO LEAVE THE ROOM QUICKLY SO THIS MARTIAN THING WON'T BE STUCK ON MY HEAD.

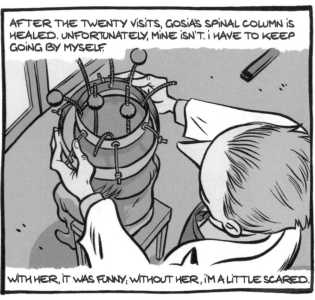

AFTER THE TWENTY VISITS, GOSIA'S SPINAL COLUMN IS HEALED. UNFORTUNATELY, MINE ISN'T. I HAVE TO KEEP GOING BY MYSELF.

WITH HER, IT WAS FUNNY; WITHOUT HER, I'M A LITTLE SCARED.

EVEN MORE SO BECAUSE THE FIRST THING SHE DOES WHEN WE MEET UP AFTERWARDS IS TRY TO FIGURE OUT WHAT THE HELMET IS FOR...

THEY'RE SENDING WAVES INTO YOUR HEAD AND YOU WON'T BE NORMAL ANYMORE!

GOSIA READS DETEKTYW MAGAZINE, SHE LEARNS ABOUT ALL KINDS OF WEIRD AND MEAN PEOPLE IN IT!

SOMETIMES SHE TELLS ME STORIES THAT SCARE ME SO MUCH I ALMOST START SUSPECTING MY NEIGHBORS OF HAVING COMMITTED HORRIBLE CRIMES.

YOU SHOULDN'T TRUST ANYONE!

AT THE BACK OF EACH ISSUE OF DETEKTYW THERE'S A MYSTERY CRIME TO SOLVE. GOSIA'S OBSESSED BY IT.

SHE METICULOUSLY DISSECTS ALL THE ELEMENTS OF THE CRIME AND, SURPRISINGLY, ALWAYS ENDS UP WITH THE RIGHT ANSWER.

SO? ACCORDING TO YOU, WHO KILLED HER?

WELL...

I THINK IT'S HER MOTHER...

HER MOTHER!!

YEAH! THERE WAS NO SIGN OF BREAKING AND ENTERING...

AND THE VICTIM DIDN'T DEFEND HERSELF. THAT MEANS SHE MUST HAVE KNOWN HER KILLER AND WASN'T AFRAID!

I SENT IN THE RESPONSE CARD.

THE SOLUTION WILL BE IN NEXT WEEK'S ISSUE.

I CAN'T WAIT! MAYBE I'LL WIN A SUBSCRIPTION?

BUT... HER MOTHER?!?

MARZI, WHAT WORLD DO YOU LIVE IN? I'M GOING TO LEND YOU SOME ISSUES...

YOU'LL LEARN.

NO! I'D RATHER YOU TELL ME...

OKAY...

YOU REMEMBER THE OTHER DAY. I WAS TELLING YOU ABOUT EDWARD K., NICKNAMED THE BUTCHER GNOME...

IT TERRIFIES ME AND I COULD PROBABLY TELL HER TO STOP, BUT AT THE SAME TIME, I WANT TO KNOW WHAT HAPPENS... AND, TRUTH BE TOLD, I LIKE BEING SCARED...

BUT WHEN I FIND MYSELF ALONE AT THE HOSPITAL WITH THIS MR. BIRD, I IMAGINE THE WORST...

WEEEE... EEEE

AAHAAHAAH

WEEEEEEEEEEEEEEE

RATUNKU!

RATUNKU!

AAHAAHAAHAA

HOW WILL THIS MACHINE HEAL MY SCOLIOSIS? IS IT GOING TO STRAIGHTEN OUT MY CROOKED SPINAL COLUMN?

MY FEAR ASIDE, WITHOUT GOSIA THERE I GET EASILY DISCOURAGED. TOO BAD, I MIGHT STAY TWISTED, BUT I'D PREFER TO SKIP DR. STORK'S STRANGE EXPERIMENTS ON MY BRAIN.

STRAWBERRY FIELDS FOREVER

VACATION ALWAYS STARTS THE SAME WAY. WORK BEFORE PLEASURE, AS MY DAD LIKES TO SAY...

FIRST, WE GO TO MY MOM'S FAMILY'S. THAT'S THE WORK.

THEY HAVE ACRES OF FIELDS AND WE HAVE TO HELP THEM. LUCKILY, THEY ARE STRAWBERRY FIELDS. SO I DON'T COMPLAIN. NOT AT FIRST ANYWAY.

I LOVE STRAWBERRIES! THE FIRST DAY, I'M CRAZY ABOUT THEM! THE SECOND DAY, A LITTLE LESS. THE THIRD DAY, I WISH IT WERE THE LAST...

BUT WE AREN'T EVEN HALFWAY THROUGH OUR VISIT... AND AFTER THE FIFTH DAY, I HATE THEM WITH ALL MY HEART!

WE SPEND ALL DAY IN THE FIELDS. I CAN'T LEAVE. FINE, I EAT TWO, THREE, TEN STRAWBERRIES...BUT THEN I CAN'T TAKE IT ANYMORE!

THEY CALL ME A FREELOADER...

IT MAKES ME MAD, BUT SINCE I DON'T HAVE A GOOD PLACE TO GO MOPE, I'M BACK BEFORE LONG AND THEY IMMEDIATELY PUT ME IN ANOTHER INTERMINABLE ROW OF STRAWBERRIES.

YOU ALWAYS WANT US TO TREAT YOU LIKE AN ADULT! LOOK, YOU HAVE A BEAUTIFUL ROW ALL TO YOURSELF, LIKE YOUR DAD AND MOM.

YES, BUT...

NO BUTS ABOUT IT! SQUAT DOWN AND GET TO WORK LIKE A GROWN-UP!

THE ADULTS ALWAYS FIND A WAY TO OUTSMART ME AND FOIL MY PLANS...I CAN PROTEST ALL I WANT, THEY DON'T HEAR...

A FISH IN A FIELD OF STRAWBERRIES, THAT'S ME!

I HAVE A LITTLE WILLOW BASKET TO FILL. AS SOON AS IT'S DONE, I LEAVE IT NEXT TO THE TRACK WHERE MY COUSIN PICKS IT UP. I GET ANOTHER AND GO BACK TO WHERE I LEFT OFF...AND SO IT GOES ALL DAY.

MY RECORD IS 12 BASKETS BRIMMING WITH STRAWBERRIES.

IN THE EVENING, WHEN I'VE REALLY HAD IT AND IT'S OBVIOUS I'M NOT PRETENDING, I CAN REST BY THE SIDE OF THE TRACK.

I PLAY WITH MY DOG, BUT I SENSE HE'S BORED TOO.

EVERY SO OFTEN, THEY STILL MAKE ME DO SOMETHING.

MY BASKET IS FULL! WOULD YOU BRING ME AN EMPTY ONE AND PICK UP THIS ONE?

I BECOME A PORTER.

BASKET!

I'M COMING!

BASKET!

RIGHT AWAY..

BASKET!

SIGH...

I DON'T LIKE THIS START OF VACATION. BUT FORTUNATELY, SOME NICE THINGS HAPPEN HERE TOO.

ONE OF THEM IS GETTING TO CRUSH STRAWBERRIES IN A CUP WITH SUGAR AND CRÈME FRAÎCHE!

ANOTHER IS THE WEIGHING. EVERY DAY, WE PICK ABOUT THREE HUNDRED BASKETS OF STRAWBERRIES. WE HAVE TO WEIGH THEM ALL AND TAKE THEM TO THE BUYER IN THE VILLAGE.

AND THEN THERE'S THE EVENING RITUAL. I OFTEN GO MILK THE COWS WITH MY AUNT. I REALLY LIKE WATCHING HER SQUIRT THE MILK INTO THE PAIL.

THE COW LOOKS PLEASED, IT'S LIKE THEY'RE GOOD FRIENDS.

MY AUNT TALKS TO HER AND STROKES HER WHILE THE COW NODS HER HEAD AS THOUGH SHE WERE SAYING OH, OH, THAT'S GOOD... OUT OF THE BLUE MY AUNT ASKS ME TO STAND STILL AND OPEN MY MOUTH WIDE...

IT'S HOT!! AND IT SMELLS STRONG...IT'S ALL OVER ME!

THEN SHE POURS THE MILK INTO A METAL JUG THAT SHE LOWERS INTO THE WELL SO IT WILL STAY COLD. SHE'LL SELL IT LATER.

BUT SHE POURS ME A SMALL BOWLFUL THAT I DRINK IN A FLASH. I LOVE MILK STRAIGHT FROM THE COW.

THE NEXT NIGHT I GET AN ALLERGIC REACTION, PROBABLY TO THE FRESH MILK. I SLEEP BADLY, GIANT STRAWBERRIES ARE CHASING ME...

THEN IT'S THE WEEKEND BUT IT'S JUST LIKE ANY OTHER DAY...WE PICK STRAWBERRIES!

SATURDAY NIGHT, MY AUNT FIXES THE SUNDAY DINNER. SHE LOOKS OVER HER CHICKENS, CATCHES THE ONE SHE'S CHOSEN AND CUTS ITS HEAD OFF ON A STUMP THAT'S ALREADY COATED IN BLOOD.

TCHOC!

FLOC

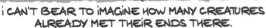

I CAN'T BEAR TO IMAGINE HOW MANY CREATURES ALREADY MET THEIR ENDS THERE.

HEADLESS, THE CHICKEN SHAKES A LITTLE AND THEN GOES STILL. MY AUNT STARTS PLUCKING IT OUTSIDE...

DO YOU WANT TO HELP?

NO!

I'M JUST GOING TO WATCH...

I OBSERVE HER. SHE'S SUCH A CALM, GENTLE PERSON, HOW CAN SHE KILL? WHEN I ASK HER IF IT'S EASY, SHE DOESN'T SEEM TO UNDERSTAND.

YOU KNOW, I DON'T KILL FOR THE FUN OF IT. I KILL TO EAT...

YOU CAN'T LIVE OFF ONLY STRAWBER-RIES AND POTATOES!

WHY NOT?

SHE EVISCERATES THE CHICKEN NEXT. SHE TAKES EVERYTHING OUT OF ITS STOMACH AND SHOWS ME... A MINI-COURSE IN ANIMAL BIOLOGY.

HERE'S THE STOMACH... LOOK, IT'S STILL FULL, SHE JUST ATE.

AND HERE'S THE LIVER.

YOU LIKE LIVER, RIGHT?

DEFINITELY NOT FROM THIS PERSPECTIVE...

MY DOG CIRCLES US. SHE GIVES HIM WHAT WE DON'T EAT, BUT HE WON'T TOUCH IT.

HE'S A REAL CITY DOG, SPOILED ROTTEN!!

IT'S NOT TRUE OF THEIRS, HE DEVOURS CHICKEN GUTS IN A SPLIT-SECOND...

THERE'S NO BATHROOM HERE, THERE ISN'T EVEN RUNNING WATER. WE CARRY IT FROM THE WELL TO USE IN THE KITCHEN AND TO BATHE.

WE HEAT IT IN HUGE POTS ON THE BIG KITCHEN STOVE.

WHEN IT'S TIME FOR A BATH, WE TAKE TURNS IN A ROOM WITH A BIG METAL TUB. IT'S EASY FOR ME, I CAN FIT MY WHOLE BODY INSIDE. BUT HOW DO THE ADULTS MANAGE?

SINCE IT'S WARM OUT, I BATHE OUTSIDE...

I COULD STAY HERE FOREVER, EVEN THOUGH THE WATER'S GROWING COLD. NIGHT IS BEGINNING TO FALL. LIFE IN THE COUNTRY IS WINDING DOWN.

THE BIRDS GO SILENT, THE SURVIVING CHICKENS GO TO SLEEP. I SMELL THE MARJORAM IN MY AUNT'S HERB GARDEN AND THE CLEAN LAUNDRY DRYING AROUND ME.

I SETTLE INTO THIS TUB AS THOUGH I WERE SETTLING INTO SOLITUDE.

AND I TELL MYSELF THAT IF SOLITUDE IS LIKE THIS TUB THAT FEELS AS THOUGH IT WERE MADE FOR ME, THEN I MUST BE MADE FOR SOLITUDE.

IT WILL BE MY REFUGE.

THE TUB IS MADE OF METAL, IT'S COLD AND UNCOMFORTABLE. BUT IT'S ALSO SOLID, MUCH MORE SOLID THAN I AM. IT PROTECTS ME LIKE A KNIGHT'S ARMOR. AND ONCE YOU ADD HOT WATER, IT BECOMES COMFY AND COZY.

MY MOM COMES OUT OF THE KITCHEN TO RINSE ME OFF WITH A BIG POT OF BOILING WATER WHICH SHE DILUTES IN A PAIL OF COLD WATER.

IT'S DIVINE!

WHEN I COME BACK INSIDE, THE MEN ARE IN THE TV ROOM, THEY'RE WATCHING A MATCH, TALKING AND PROBABLY DRINKING VODKA.

THE WOMEN ARE PREPARING FOR TOMORROW: OUTFITS FOR CHURCH, SUNDAY LUNCH WHICH IS ALWAYS A FEAST. WHAT AM I MEANT TO DO IN THE MIDST OF ALL THIS?

THEY SEND ME ON A MISSION. I HAVE TO FIND OUT WHETHER THE MEN ARE DRINKING IN SECRET. THE WOMEN DON'T LIKE IT...

AH, HERE'S A LITTLE SPY...

WAIT!

I DON'T SEE A BOTTLE BUT THE MINUTE I GO IN, I CAN SMELL IT! AND I CAN SEE IT'S NOT JUST THE MATCH OR THE STRAWBERRIES MAKING MY DAD'S EYES SHINE LIKE THAT.

MY UNCLE OPENS THE SIDEBOARD AND TAKES OUT SOMETHING THAT HE SLIPS INTO MY HAND.

HERE...

SO?!

THEY'RE WATCHING THE MATCH...

i GO OUTSIDE UNDER THE PRETEXT OF PLAYING WITH MY DOG, AND i DISCOVER THE PRICE OF MY SILENCE...

A CHOCOLATE-COVERED BONBON!! A REAL DELICACY...

i'M TOO EASY TO BUY OFF...

SUNDAY iS OUR ONLY DAY OF REST, BUT THERE ARE STILL ANIMALS TO FEED...

THEY AREN'T FARM MACHINERY THAT CAN BE ABANDONED FOR 24 HOURS.

AFTER MASS, WE HAVE LUNCH. MY AUNT MAKES A BOUILLON WITH YESTERDAY'S CHICKEN AND ADDS PASTA. i LOVE HER PASTA! SHE CUTS iT BY HAND AND EVERY STRAND iS DIFFERENT.

A SECOND COURSE FOLLOWS. MASHED POTATOES, VEGETABLES, AND CHICKEN, ALL SERVED WITH TEA.

OUR USEFULNESS HAS COME TO AN END. WE RETURN TO THE CiTY IN THE AFTERNOON. MY PARENTS' "VACATION" iS OVER.

BUT TOMORROW NIGHT, AFTER THEY GET HOME FROM WORK, THEY'LL TAKE ME TO SKOWiERZYN, TO MY DAD'S FAMiLY...

BECAUSE MY VACATION, MY TRUE HOLIDAY (WITHOUT PARENTS OR STRAWBERRiES) iS JUST BEGINNING!

LAST STOP, SUMMER. EVERYBODY OFF!

IN SKOWIERZYN, YOU CAN'T SAY I DON'T DO MY PART. I GO PICK PARSLEY OR CHIVES FOR SALAD IN THE HERB GARDEN...

OR PLUMS IN THE ORCHARD FOR THE "PAMUŁA" (A FRUIT SOUP), I ALSO TAKE CARE OF THE COWS...

THE VILLAGE IS WELL-ORGANIZED. EACH HOUSEHOLD OWNS AT LEAST 2 COWS. EVERY MORNING, THE PEOPLE LET THEIR COWS OUT ONTO THE ROAD.

TWO FAMILIES, WHO'VE BEEN PREVIOUSLY DESIGNATED, LEAD ALL THE COWS TO A LARGE PASTURE. IT MAKES FOR QUITE A HERD!!

THE VOLUNTEERS STAY WITH THEM AND THEN LET THEM OUT AT MIDDAY. THE COWS KNOW THEIR OWN STABLES, AND QUITE OFTEN MAKE IT HOME ALONE.

EVEN SO, WE COME BY BICYCLE TO PICK THEM UP.

AROUND 2 O'CLOCK, THEY GO BACK OUT ONTO THE ROAD. THE SAME PEOPLE LEAD THEM TO PASTURE AND SEND THEM HOME AROUND 7 O'CLOCK.

THE NEXT DAY, TWO OTHER HOUSES WILL BE IN CHARGE. IT'S SO INGRAINED IN THE HABITS OF THE VILLAGERS THAT THEY ALWAYS KNOW WHOSE TURN IT IS.

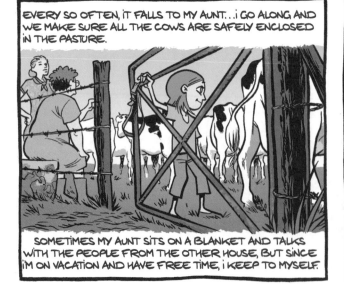

EVERY SO OFTEN, IT FALLS TO MY AUNT... I GO ALONG AND WE MAKE SURE ALL THE COWS ARE SAFELY ENCLOSED IN THE PASTURE.

SOMETIMES MY AUNT SITS ON A BLANKET AND TALKS WITH THE PEOPLE FROM THE OTHER HOUSE, BUT SINCE I'M ON VACATION AND HAVE FREE TIME, I KEEP TO MYSELF.

I REIGN OVER AN IMMENSE HERD, IT'S IMPRESSIVE! BUT THE COWS DON'T CARE. THEY CHEW THEIR CUD AS THEY IDLY LOOK ME OVER.

THERE'S NOT MUCH DISCIPLINE IN MY RANKS AND LITTLE HOPE I'LL REMEDY THE SITUATION. BUT SINCE COWS ARE PRETTY DOCILE, I DON'T WORRY TOO MUCH...

IT'S FUNNY HOW THE COWS KNOW WHEN IT'S TIME TO GO. JUST BEFORE 7 THEY GRADUALLY BEGIN TO GATHER NEAR THE GATE.

HOWEVER A FEW CAN ALSO BE FOUND AT THE OTHER END OF THE PASTURE AND I TAKE PLEASURE IN GOING TO SCOLD THEM!

A COW RUNNING IS A SPECTACULAR SIGHT, ENOUGH TO GIVE YOU THE WILLIES. IT LOOKS LIKE IT'S RUSHING FORWARD BLINDLY WITHOUT ANY CLUE HOW IT'LL STOP!

I ONLY SPEND THE DAY WITH THEM ABOUT ONCE A VACATION. BUT I'M USUALLY THE ONE WHO GOES TO MEET THEM IN THE EVENINGS.

AS SOON AS I'M ON THE ROAD, I FIND MYSELF SURROUNDED BY A STREAM OF COWS RUSHING HOME TO BE MILKED.

HEY?! WHAT ARE YOU DOING WITH THOSE COWS?

UM... THEY'RE MY AUNT'S, I'M TAKING THEM HOME!

NO NO!! THOSE ARE MY COWS!

HA HA! CITY FOLK DON'T KNOW A COW UNTIL IT'S A STEAK ON THEIR PLATE!

I DON'T LIKE STEAK!

HUMILIATED, I GO BACK TO FIND THE RIGHT COWS. BUT THEY ALL LOOK THE SAME TO ME.

I RIDE BY ALL THE SURROUNDING PASTURES IN VAIN...

WHAT AM I GOING TO TELL MY AUNT? I LOST YOUR COWS! SORRY, I'LL BUY YOU SOME NEW ONES TOMORROW, WOULD THAT BE OKAY? WILL YOU GET OVER IT?

IF ONLY...A COW COSTS A FORTUNE. AND SHE'S HAD THESE TWO SINCE THEY WERE BORN. SHE HELPED THE MOBILE VETERINARIAN GET THEM OUT OF THEIR MOTHER.

HEY! WHAT ARE YOU DOING THERE?

I'M WAITING FOR THE COWS...

THE COWS ?!?

THEY'VE BEEN HOME FOR MORE THAN AN HOUR, YOUR AUNT'S HALFWAY THROUGH MILKING THEM!

SHE WAS WONDERING WHERE YOU WERE?!

THE BEST THING ABOUT SKOWIERZYN AS COMPARED TO KAMIEŃ IS THAT IT'S FULL OF FRIENDS!

KASIA LIVES NEXT DOOR. OUR GRANDMOTHERS ARE HALF-SISTERS.

KRZYSIEK, ANIA AND GOSIA LIVE JUST ON THE OTHER SIDE. GOSIA IS ALREADY PRETTY OLD, SHE DOESN'T REALLY PLAY WITH US. KRZYSIEK SAYS SHE ONLY TALKS ABOUT BOYS AT HOME.

SŁAWEK, A NICE CHUBBY KID, IS TWO HOUSES FURTHER DOWN AND MAŁGOSIA, WHO'S EXACTLY MY AGE, LIVES BEHIND MY GRANDMOTHER'S HOUSE.

DURING THE DAY, WE MOSTLY GET AROUND BY BICYCLE. I KNOW EVERY NOOK AND CRANNY OF THE VILLAGE...

AND ALSO THE TRAPS, WHICH WE TRY TO AVOID... LIKE WIESIEK.

THAT GUY IS OFF HIS ROCKER. BUT SINCE HE WANDERS FREELY THROUGH THE STREETS, WE INEVITABLY STUMBLE UPON HIM.

GESTAPO!!

GET THE HELL INTO THE OVEN!

AAAAHH !!!

WE TURN AROUND INSTINCTIVELY, EVEN THOUGH THERE'S NO OTHER ROAD...OTHERWISE YOU HAVE TO GO REALLY FAR, CUT THROUGH SEVERAL VILLAGES...

SKOWIERZYN 12

BUT IT'S BETTER THAN ENDING UP IN THE CLUTCHES OF THIS RAVING LUNATIC.

THERE'S ALSO ONE HOUSE WE AVOID LIKE THE PLAGUE. AS SOON AS WE GET CLOSE, WE SPEED UP. CZARNA JULKA (BLACK JULIET), THE TERROR OF THE VILLAGE, LIVES THERE.

WE'VE NEVER SEEN HER, BUT WE SENSE HER PRESENCE.

SHE'S THERE, BEHIND THE YELLOWED CURTAINS OF HER DILAPIDATED WINDOWS. SHE'S WATCHING...

AT DUSK, WE SOMETIMES RIDE BY AS A CHALLENGE.

WE EACH HAVE TO CIRCLE THAT SIDE OF THE VILLAGE. NO CHEATING ALLOWED, WE HAVE TO RIDE IN FRONT OF HER HOUSE.

ONCE WE'VE COMPLETED OUR MISSION, WE COME BACK SMILING AND FEELING LIKE HEROES.

THE CURTAIN MOVED!

I HEARD THE DOOR CREAK!!

I SAW A BIRD TAKE OFF!

I SAW HER!

YOU SAW HER?!

UHH, NO NOT REALLY, BUT I'M SURE SHE SAW ME!

SHE'S A WITCH! SHE USED TO LIVE IN FRANCE!..

SHE MARRIED A POLE. THEY LIVED THERE BUT THEN HE DIED...

AND AFTER THAT, SHE STOPPED GOING OUT...

SHE WANTED CHILDREN. BUT THEY DIDN'T HAVE TIME...

NOW SHE HOLDS BLACK MASSES!

WE DON'T REALLY KNOW WHAT THAT MEANS BUT IF IT'S BLACK IT'S SCARY AND INCREASES THE MYSTERY AROUND HER.

I TRY TO BRING US BACK DOWN TO EARTH.

ARE YOU SURE SHE'S THERE?

OF COURSE, YOU'RE NOT FROM HERE, YOU CAN'T KNOW!

BUT THERE'S NO LIGHT ON!?

SHE DOESN'T NEED LIGHT, SHE CAN SEE IN THE DARK...

NOW ANY SOUND AT ALL CAN SCARE US TO DEATH. MY GRANDMOTHER FOR EXAMPLE...

MARZi!

IT'S LATE...

EVER SINCE HER HUSBAND DIED, SHE'S BECOME STRANGE...

SHE LIVES ALONE, THEY DIDN'T HAVE CHILDREN. THAT'S REASON ENOUGH TO GO CRAZY!!

BUT IF SHE STILL LIVES THERE, WHY AREN'T THERE EVER ANY LIGHTS ON?

OH, I DON'T THINK SHE HAS ELECTRICITY. SHE MUST USE CANDLES.

I WENT TO HER HOUSE, ONCE...

I NEEDED SOMETHING CHIC TO WEAR TO A DANCE. I'D HEARD THAT SHE'D BROUGHT BACK FANCY DRESSES FROM PARIS WHEN SHE WAS YOUNG.

AND ?

BAH! THEY WEREN'T AS PRETTY AS ALL THAT...

ADMIT IT, YOU WERE TOO FAT FOR THEM...

WELL...IN ANY CASE, SHE'S THIN AS A RAIL. IT'S FRIGHTENING TO SEE!

WITH HER LONG BLACK HAIR, SHE LOOKS LIKE A WITCH.

PFF!

THIS YEAR, MY AUNT'S SON JANUSZ MOVED INTO MY GRANDMOTHER'S WITH HIS GIRLFRIEND AND THEIR SON MATEUSZ.

MY COUSIN IS A MECHANIC. HE GOES TO WORK EVERY DAY WHILE HIS GIRLFRIEND TAKES CARE OF THEIR SON BUT TO TELL YOU THE TRUTH, MATEUSZ MOSTLY LIKES SPENDING TIME WITH ME.

IT'S LIKE HAVING A LITTLE BROTHER. THOUGH LITTLE BROTHERS SOMETIMES GET IN THE WAY.

NO, YOU'RE NOT COMING WITH ME! WE'LL SEE EACH OTHER LATER.

I NEED TO BE ON MY OWN!

TAKE ME WITH YOUUUU!

LUCKILY, HE DOESN'T KNOW HOW TO RIDE A BIKE YET.

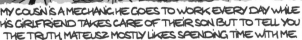

I DON'T OFTEN ESCAPE SO RUTHLESSLY.

HA HA! HER COUSINS DID THE SAME THING TO HER WHEN SHE WAS LITTLE...

HISTORY REPEATS ITSELF!

BUT ANYWAY, IT'S GREAT WHEN I DO, BECAUSE AS SOON AS I'M BACK, HE STICKS TO ME LIKE GLUE!

ON WEEKENDS, MY AUNT TAKES US TO THE BANKS OF THE SAN RIVER TO SWIM. IT'S VERY CROWDED.

THAT'S WHERE MY GRANDMOTHER DROWNED.

SHE WAS WASHING CLOTHES AND WENT TOO FAR OUT TO RINSE THEM.

SHE DIDN'T KNOW HOW TO SWIM, THE CURRENT SWALLOWED HER UP...

DURING THE WEEK, IT'S DESERTED, EXCEPT FOR MAYBE A FISHERMAN HIDDEN IN THE BUSHES, WHO WE ONLY SENSE BECAUSE WE CAN SEE HIS STICK DIVING INTO THE CLOUDY WATER.

WE GO THERE WITHOUT ANY ADULTS. WE SWIM AWHILE AND THEN GO HOME.

SINCE OUR GOING THERE IS STRICTLY FORBIDDEN, I ALWAYS HAVE TO DISPOSE OF THE EVIDENCE.

MY BATHING SUIT DRIES VERY QUICKLY, BUT I THROW THE TOWELS INTO THE TALL NETTLES GROWING ALONG THE ROADSIDE. THEY DISAPPEAR LIKE MAGIC.

HOWEVER, WITH MATEUSZ AROUND THINGS ARE NEVER THAT SIMPLE...

I KNOW WHAT YOU'RE DOING!

YOU'RE NOT PLAYING HIDE AND SEEK!!

I CAN SEE SMOKE ABOVE THE CORN...

YOU'RE SMOKING CIGARETTES !!

KASIA STOLE SOME CIGARETTES FROM HER DAD. MY DAD SMOKES TOO. IT STINKS, IT'S NOT GOOD FOR YOUR HEALTH, AND MY MOM IS ALWAYS GIVING HIM GRIEF ABOUT IT!

BUT IT MAKES US FEEL GROWN-UP.

I WANT TO SMOKE TOO!

NO, IT'S NOT FOR CHILDREN...

IN FACT, MATEUSZ, WHAT DID WE DO TODAY?

WE WENT HUNTING FOR SNAILS!

VERRRRY GOOD!

DO YOU WANT ANOTHER ONE?

UHH, NO THANKS, YOU?

ME NEITHER.

WE QUICKLY ABANDON THE CIGARETTES. THE ONES KASIA'S DAD SMOKES ARE REALLY AWFUL AND NOW WE STINK HORRIBLY...

THE VILLAGE FAIR IS THIS WEEKEND AND MATEUSZ'S MOM INVITED HER SISTER BEATA AND BEATA'S HUSBAND. THEY SPEND HOURS AT THE TABLE IN THE EVENINGS.

WHEN I'M NOT WITH MY FRIENDS, I JOIN THEM.

BEATA'S HUSBAND TELLS HORRIFIC STORIES. HE WORKS AT THE MORGUE, PREPARING THE CADAVERS.

AND WHEN I WENT TO DRESS HIM, HE WAS SO SWOLLEN IT TOOK A SUPER-HUMAN EFFORT JUST TO GET UNDERWEAR ON HIM!!

AH! AH! AH!

HE LAUGHS TO HIMSELF WHILE EVERYONE WATCHES HIM, HORRIFIED.

ON SATURDAY, AUNT NIUSIA LETS ME GO TO THE FAIR. I THINK SHE'D HAVE A GOOD TIME THERE, BUT NOT MY UNCLE.

WHAT'S IT TO YOU, OLD BAG, IT'S FOR YOUNG PEOPLE!

WE GO IN A GROUP, I STICK WITH MAŁGOSIA...

IT'S MOSTLY LITTLE KIDS OUT ON THE DANCE FLOOR. WE'RE A LITTLE INTIMIDATED AND DANCE ON THE GRASS NEARBY.

SUDDENLY, WE HEAR SHOUTING.

THE PEOPLE AROUND US ARE LAUGHING. SOMEONE'S ALREADY DRUNK. SUDDENLY I FREEZE... IT'S MATEUSZ'S UNCLE.

GET A LOAD OF HIM!

HE'S NOT FROM THE VILLAGE!

HE'S SMASHED. HE'S STILL WALKING BUT IT WON'T BE LONG BEFORE HE CRASHES.

HE'S SINGING AT THE TOP OF HIS LUNGS, COMPETING WITH THE ORCHESTRA.

ISN'T HE STAYING WITH YOU?

I DON'T KNOW THAT MAN...

BUT MY CHEEKS CAN'T LIE... AND THEN MY COUSIN COMES TO GET HIM.

THE FAIR CONTINUES AND WE'RE HAVING A GOOD TIME WHEN SUDDENLY.

HEY!! WHAT ARE YOU STILL DOING HERE, MISSY!!

IT'S MAŁGOSIA'S GRANDMOTHER. SHE'S USUALLY ADORABLE, BUT NOT TONIGHT.

WHAT TIME DID I TELL YOU TO GET HOME BY?

10 O'CLOCK...

AND WHAT TIME IS IT?!

BAM! BAM! BAM!

AND WHY DID WE GIVE YOU A WATCH FOR COMMUNION?

WHY?!

THAT HURTS!!

AND YOU, DON'T LAUGH!!!

...I WASN'T EVEN LAUGHING.

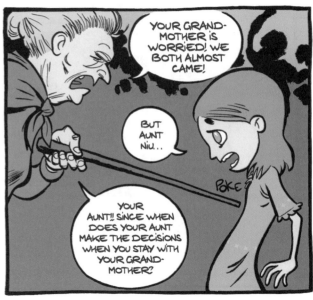

YOUR GRANDMOTHER IS WORRIED! WE BOTH ALMOST CAME!

BUT AUNT NIU...

POKE

YOUR AUNT!! SINCE WHEN DOES YOUR AUNT MAKE THE DECISIONS WHEN YOU STAY WITH YOUR GRANDMOTHER?

A LITTLE ANNOYED, WE WALK IN FRONT OF HER WHILE SHE CONTINUES TO MUTTER UNDER HER BREATH.

PFF... THESE SHOW-OFFS!! HAVE YOU EVER SEEN ANYTHING SO...

THEY'RE SO DOLLED UP!!

DO YOU THINK EVERYONE SAW US?

MY SOCIAL LIFE IS RUINED!

WHEN I GET HOME, SOMEONE IS ASLEEP ON THE LAWN AND THE DOOR IS LOCKED.

KNOCK KNOCK

GRANDMA... IT'S ME.

NO!

OH! THERE YOU ARE!! OH MY, YOU MISSED QUITE A SPECTACLE!

IS THAT BEATA'S HUSBAND OUTSIDE?

SHE DIDN'T WANT TO LET HIM INTO THE HOUSE DRUNK.

THEY MADE A SCENE! HE CRIED, SHE BEAT HIM...

WE HAD TO PULL HER OFF HIM, SHE WAS SO WORKED UP!!

POOR GUY, IT'S NO SURPRISE HE PREFERS THE COMPANY OF THE DEAD!

THERE'S ALREADY SOMETHING CADAVERISH ABOUT HIM, HE PROBABLY NEEDS ALCOHOL TO WASH AWAY EVERYTHING HE'S SEEN!

IT'S GOT TO BE A LIVING HELL FOR HIM...

COME ON! GO TO BED!!

THEY LEFT THE NEXT DAY. MY VACATION ENDS QUIETLY.

MY PARENTS WILL BE HERE SOON TO TAKE ME HOME.

THE DAYS PASS AND THEY'RE STILL NOT HERE.

YOU MISS THEM, DON'T YOU?

THEY'LL BE HERE SOON, DON'T WORRY. YOU STILL HAVE A LITTLE VACATION LEFT AND THEY MUST BE VERY BUSY.

BUT IT DOESN'T FEEL NORMAL.

IN THE WINTER, I WOULD UNDERSTAND. THE ROADS ARE SOMETIMES VERY SNOWY. SOMETHING MUST BE KEEPING THEM FROM COMING.

BEEP BEEP BEEP

MAŁGOSIA'S DAD, WHO WORKS IN THE SAME FACTORY AS MY DAD, BREAKS THE NEWS...

THE FACTORY IS ON STRIKE. THE MACHINES HAVE BEEN STOPPED FOR SEVERAL DAYS!

MOST OF THE WORKERS AREN'T LEAVING THEIR JOBS...

IT'S THE END OF SUMMER AND THE END OF INNOCENCE...

MORE STRIKES AND MORE PROBLEMS...

GRANDMA!

THE WORLD OF ADULTS IS BEYOND ME. I'D LIKE TO BE ONE SO I WOULD HAVE A BETTER GRASP...

BUT SEEING THEM LIKE THIS, POWERLESS, EXHAUSTED, I TELL MYSELF IT'S BEYOND THEM TOO.

184

ELEVEN DAYS AND ELEVEN NIGHTS

MOM IS TIRED OF THE LONG LINES, OF THE DAILY TRIPS TO AND FROM THE STORES.

SHE'S TIRED OF SPENDING HOURS WAITING FOR EVERYTHING AND COMING HOME WITH NOTHING.

WITH HER HANDS SHAKING, SHE CAREFULLY CUTS THE ONION INTO LITTLE PIECES. VERY LITTLE. THAT WAY IT'LL SEEM LIKE THERE'S MORE IN THE SOUP.

MOM'S CRYING, IS IT THE ONION? IF I ASK, THAT'LL BE HER ANSWER...ON DAYS LIKE THIS I DON'T DARE REMIND HER I HATE COOKED ONION.

THE STRIKE OF THE SUMMER OF '88 SURPRISED EVERYONE...EVEN THE STRIKERS.

THAT WAS ITS GOAL: TO NOT PREPARE FOR ANYTHING, TO ACT UNEXPECTEDLY, TO SURPRISE.

AS USUAL, MY MOTHER WAS WAITING FOR MY DAD TO COME HOME FROM WORK, BUT HE DIDN'T. THE NEWS SPREAD QUICKLY: "HUTA STRAJKUJE"! THE FACTORY'S ON STRIKE!

IT WILL END UP BEING THE BIGGEST STRIKE IN OUR CITY, ONE OF THE MOST IMPORTANT IN MY COUNTRY. BUT I DON'T KNOW THIS YET. NO ONE KNOWS IT.

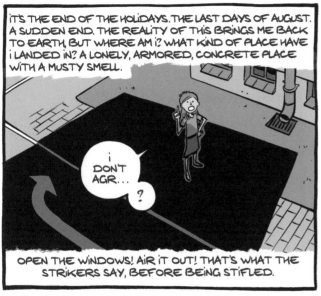

IT'S THE END OF THE HOLIDAYS. THE LAST DAYS OF AUGUST. A SUDDEN END. THE REALITY OF THIS BRINGS ME BACK TO EARTH, BUT WHERE AM I? WHAT KIND OF PLACE HAVE I LANDED IN? A LONELY, ARMORED, CONCRETE PLACE WITH A MUSTY SMELL.

I DON'T AGR... ?

OPEN THE WINDOWS! AIR IT OUT! THAT'S WHAT THE STRIKERS SAY, BEFORE BEING STIFLED.

WHAT KIND OF PLACE IS THIS WHERE YOU HAVE TO PROTEST JUST TO EAT? WHERE FREEDOM HAS TO BE ASKED FOR? WHERE YOU HAVE TO MARCH IN THE STREETS JUST FOR THE RIGHT TO SAY NO?

EEEEK!

ARE THERE MANY COUNTRIES LIKE THIS, WHERE YOU CAN'T SAY NO?

IT ACTUALLY SEEMS LIKE IT'D BE COOL TO HAVE A COUNTRY WITH NO "NO." WHERE EVERYONE ALWAYS AGREED. YES, WE LOVE EACH OTHER! YES, WE'RE HAPPY! YES, WE HAVE EVERYTHING WE WANT, YES!...UH, NO.

NIE! NIE! NIE! NIE! NIE! NIE! NIE! NIE! NIE!

IT'S AGAINST THE LAW IN POLAND. WE USED TO THINK NO. THEN WE WHISPERED IT. WE NEVER SHOUTED IT, BUT NOW WE'RE JUST BEGINNING TO SAY IT FIRMLY. IT'S ALREADY A LOT FOR THE AUTHORITIES. MAYBE TOO MUCH.

IN THIS COUNTRY, EVERYONE IS SUPPOSED TO SAY YES, TO SMILE EVEN IF IT HURTS, SMILE EVEN THOUGH YOU'RE SUFFERING. LIVE UNHAPPILY BUT PUT ON A HAPPY FACE TO BE OKAY WITH THAT.

I LOVE WAITING IN LINE!! AND ESPECIALLY WHEN, THE MOMENT I GET TO THE COUNTER, THERE'S NOTHING LEFT TO BUY! IT'S SIMPLY A NEW CHALLENGE FOR ME! I'M THRILLED!! I'M HAVING A GREAT TIME!

IT DOESN'T MATTER WHAT I SAY, IT HAS NO BEARING ON REALITY

STRAJK STALOWA WOLA

THE STRIKE BEGAN ON THE MORNING OF AUGUST 22ND. THE WORKERS WENT TO WORK AND THAT'S WHEN THEY LEARNED ABOUT IT. THOSE WHO WANTED TO PARTICIPATE DIDN'T GO HOME. MY DAD WAS ONE OF THEM.

WHEN HE DISAPPEARED IN THE SPRING AND I DIDN'T KNOW WHERE HE WAS, I PROMISED MYSELF I'D NEVER LET HIM DO THAT AGAIN. I KNOW HE LOVES ME, HE'LL LISTEN TO ME, I THOUGHT NAIVELY.

BUT REALLY, WHAT WAS I HOPING TO DO? STAND IN HIS WAY? IF YOU LOVE ME, YOU'LL STAY? WHAT WAS I THINKING?

HE'D SAY: I'M DOING THIS BECAUSE I LOVE YOU. SO THAT YOU CAN LIVE IN A FREE COUNTRY, SO THAT YOUR LIFE CAN BE BETTER THAN MINE.

I'M SCARED TO DEATH AND PROUD ALL AT THE SAME TIME. I WONDER WHETHER ONE DAY I'D ABLE TO MAKE THE SAME KIND OF SACRIFICES FOR SOMEONE?!

MY MOM IS SCARED TOO. EVER SINCE THE EVENTS OF LAST SPRING, SHE'S BEEN SAYING THAT ACTUALLY THINGS REALLY AREN'T THAT BAD. LOOK AT AFRICA, IT'S WORSE THERE, WE HAVE NO RIGHT TO COMPLAIN. NEXT TO THEM, WE'RE IN PARADISE.

HER WORDS AREN'T CONVINCING. SHE'S JUST SCARED OF LOSING EVERYTHING SHE'S BUILT UP TO NOW WITH MY DAD.

WHERE ARE WE TODAY? OUR FUTURE? AN INEXPERIENCED TIGHTROPE WALKER... ANXIETY HANGS IN THE AIR. LIKE WITH RAIN, YOU CAN FEEL IT BEFORE IT COMES.

YOU ALREADY KNOW, IT'S ALREADY THERE. IT'S SINGULAR, INEXPLICABLE. ANXIETY IS THE SAME. YOU BREATHE IT IN...

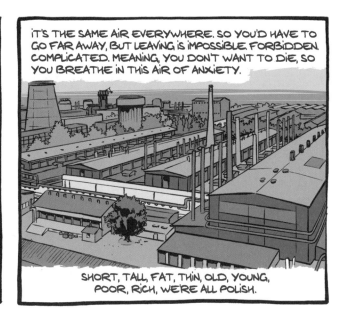

IT'S THE SAME AIR EVERYWHERE. SO YOU'D HAVE TO GO FAR AWAY, BUT LEAVING IS IMPOSSIBLE. FORBIDDEN. COMPLICATED. MEANING, YOU DON'T WANT TO DIE, SO YOU BREATHE IN THIS AIR OF ANXIETY.

SHORT, TALL, FAT, THIN, OLD, YOUNG, POOR, RICH, WE'RE ALL POLISH.

WE'RE ALL IN THE SAME BOAT, SAY THE ADULTS, AND WE'RE BEGINNING TO FEEL SERIOUSLY SEASICK. WE NEED MORE ARMS TO SPEED UP OUR PROGRESS, TO REACH LAND.

AND NOT JUST ANY LAND, BUT ONE THAT'LL SUIT ALL OF US. ONE THAT'S THE WAY WE WANT IT TO BE. OPEN AND FREE, A REAL HOME!

THIS IS ONE OF THE REASONS FOR THE STRIKE. THE WORKERS PARTICIPATING IN IT DON'T NEED TO SPEAK UP. THEIR PRESENCE SAYS ENOUGH.

MY DAD LIVES AT THE FACTORY. HE SLEEPS AND EATS THERE BUT DOESN'T WORK. AND I MUST ACCEPT IT. FOR HOW LONG? NO ONE KNOWS.

DOES HE HAVE A BED? WHAT DOES HE EAT? WHAT DOES HE DO WITH HIS DAYS? DOES HE HAVE SOMEWHERE TO BATHE?

I'M TAKING HIM SOME CLEAN CLOTHES, DO YOU WANT TO COME?

WE CAN GO THERE?!?

NOT LONG BEFORE, THE WORKERS HAD RETAKEN THE ENTRANCE TO THE FACTORY. THAT MAKES IT SOUND LIKE WAR. I IMAGINED BLOODY BATTLES BUT THERE WAS APPARENTLY NOTHING LIKE THAT.

THE CITY IS DESERTED, IT FEELS DEAD. WHERE DID THE PEOPLE GO?

I UNDERSTAND SOON ENOUGH. THEY'RE ALL IN FRONT OF THE FACTORY.

PEOPLE COME TO GREET THE STRIKERS, TO SUPPORT THEM, TO BRING THEM FOOD, DRINK, BLANKETS, SHEETS TO MAKE BANNERS, TO WRITE SLOGANS ON.

HOW DO WE GET TO THE GATE THROUGH THIS CROWD?

EVERYONE GETS A TURN. OFTEN, IT'S HER TURN. LET US THROUGH! IT'S EASY FOR ME TO SLIP BY. SOMETIMES BEING SMALL IS HANDY.

MY MOM SHOUTS OUT MY DAD'S NAME. THEY'RE GOING TO CALL HIM, TO LOOK FOR HIM INSIDE THE FACTORY.

IT TAKES A LONG TIME.

THE MAN COMES BACK EMPTY-HANDED...

IT'S NOT SO EASY. THERE ARE A LOT OF PEOPLE INSIDE. COME BACK TOMORROW, HE MIGHT BE IN ANOTHER PART OF THE FACTORY.

IT'S VERY BIG...

IT'S TRUE, DAD DOESN'T KNOW WE'RE HERE. WE THINK HE'S INSIDE. WE CLING TO THIS IDEA.

WHAT IF HE'S NOT THERE?

WHERE DO YOU THINK HE IS?!

I REMEMBER MY THEORY ABOUT HIS HAVING ANOTHER FAMILY. IT SEEMS SILLY NOW. A CHILD'S REASONING. I DON'T SAY ANYTHING TO MY MOM, I FEEL RIDICULOUS. I MUST BELIEVE HE'S IN THE FACTORY. I BELIEVE IT!

I FEEL RESTLESS AT HOME. HIS ABSENCE IS EVERYWHERE. HIS SLIPPERS ARE WAITING FOR HIM, THE ARMCHAIR DOESN'T CREAK THE SAME WAY WHEN I'M THE ONE SITTING IN IT. I EVEN MISS THE SMELL OF HIS CIGARETTES.

EVERYONE IN THE FAMILY SAYS OF MY FATHER "DO RANY PRZYLÓŹ", PUT HIM ON A WOUND AND HE'LL HEAL IT! NOW, HIS ABSENCE IS A WOUND.

MY MOM SENDS ME TO FIND PRESERVES IN THE BASEMENT. SHE WANTS TO BAKE HIM A CAKE FOR TOMORROW.

THE SPACE WHERE HE KEEPS HIS BICYCLE IS EMPTY. USUALLY, HIS BICYCLE BUGS ME TO REACH A JAR, YOU HAVE TO SLIDE YOUR HAND BETWEEN EITHER THE FRAME OR THE SPOKES.

AND IN THE DARK I ALWAYS THINK ABOUT ALL THOSE LITTLE MONSTERS WATCHING ME AND WAITING FOR THE PERFECT MOMENT TO JUMP ON MY OUTSTRETCHED HAND.

I JUST HAVE TO BE FASTER THAN THEM AND THE BIKE GETS IN MY WAY. BUT TODAY I DON'T BELIEVE IN MONSTERS ANYMORE. I'D LOVE TO SEE MY DAD'S BIKE...

THE MEDIA DON'T COVER THIS STRIKE MUCH SO THE OTHER FACTORIES WON'T GET ANY "BAD" IDEAS.

OUR BROTHERS REFUSE TO BE SLAVES TO A LIE...

THEY SPEAK OF A SMALL REBELLION. EASY TO CONTROL. BUT THE DAYS PASS AND THE GOVERNMENT ISN'T CONTROLLING ANYTHING. THE REBELLION CONTINUES AND GROWS BIGGER.

THE FOLLOWING SUNDAY, WE CELEBRATE MASS IN FRONT OF THE FACTORY. THE CHURCHES ARE EMPTY. EVERYONE'S HERE. THE SISTERS HAVE PREPARED SOUP FOR THE STRIKERS.

THEY REFUSE TO KNOW ONLY WHAT THEY ARE ALLOWED TO KNOW, SAY WHAT THEY ARE TOLD TO SAY, HEAR WHAT THEY ARE ALLOWED TO HEAR...

THEY ARE STRIKING BECAUSE THEY WANT TO LIVE LIKE FREE PEOPLE. THEY AND THEIR CHILDREN.

THEY WANT TO BE RESPONSIBLE. TO NOT BE MANIPULATED ANYMORE, TO DECIDE BY THEMSELVES, FOR THEMSELVES, FOR THEIR HOMELAND...

WE FINALLY REACH THE GATE. HE'S COMING THIS TIME.

HE'S THERE ALREADY IN FACT. HE LOOKS TIRED, THIN, HE SPORTS A BEARD, BUT HE'S SMILING. HE'S SERENE.

DAD...WHAT CAN I SAY? ALL THESE PEOPLE AROUND US WILL HEAR EVERYTHING. I JUST WANT TO SLIDE BETWEEN THE BARS AND BURY MY HEAD IN HIS ARMS.

I'D LIKE TO MELT INTO HIM. PLACE MYSELF IN HIS POCKET. BECOME A STICKER A TATTOO, JUST TO BE AS CLOSE TO HIM AS POSSIBLE. I'M THIN, BUT NOT ENOUGH TO SLIP IN..

WHEN ARE YOU COMING HOME?

SOON.

THAT'S ALL I MANAGE TO GET OUT.

WHY ARE YOU CRYING? LOOK, IT'S BEAUTIFUL OUT, WE'RE TOGETHER. THESE ARE YOUR LAST FEW DAYS OF VACATION. ENJOY THEM!

YOU CAN CRY WHEN SCHOOL STARTS, THAT I'D UNDERSTAND BETTER.

DAD...

I BROUGHT YOU A RAZOR AND SOME TOWELS. AND SOME CHANGES OF CLOTHES.

DO YOU HAVE WATER?

EVERY-THING'S OKAY?

EVERY-THING'S OKAY.

DAD AND MOM. THEY'RE ALL I HAVE, THEY'RE MY HOME. THE DOG A LITTLE BIT TOO. AND NOW IT'S BROKEN UP. I FEEL A PROFOUND SADNESS. IT'S IN MY STOMACH.

MY MOM SAYS IT'S YOUR SOUL THAT SUFFERS. MAYBE MY SOUL IS IN MY STOMACH.

MY DAD'S EYES ARE TIRED AND WRINKLED. WERE THEY LIKE MINE ONCE? WIDE OPEN? DID THEY WANT TO SEE EVERY-THING, UNDERSTAND EVERYTHING, HOLD EVERYTHING TOO?

DOES AGE AFFECT THE SIZE OF YOUR EYES? THE SIZE OF YOUR CURIOSITY?

MAYBE WE'RE NOT AS SURPRISED BY THINGS WHEN WE GET OLDER. OR MORE SIMPLY, THERE ARE THINGS WE DON'T WANT TO SEE ANYMORE?

IN MY DAD'S CASE, IT MUST BE EXHAUSTION. THE BAGS UNDER HIS EYES CONFIRM IT. THEY'RE REALLY PUFFY TODAY AND NOT ONLY HIS. ALL THE GROWNUPS WEAR THE SAME LOOK.

THEIR BAGS ARE WHERE THEY PUT EVERYTHING THAT'S WRONG, ALL THE THINGS THAT PREOCCUPY THEM, ALL THEIR WORRIES. I LOVE MY DAD'S EYES. LAUGHING AND SAD AT THE SAME TIME.

EVERYONE SAYS: YOU HAVE YOUR DAD'S EYES. WHATEVER! IF I HAD MY DAD'S EYES, HOW WOULD HE SEE THE WORLD?

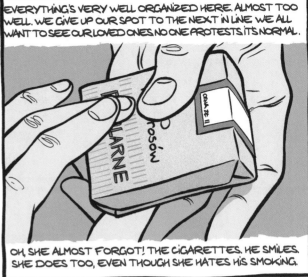

EVERYTHING'S VERY WELL ORGANIZED HERE. ALMOST TOO WELL. WE GIVE UP OUR SPOT TO THE NEXT IN LINE WE ALL WANT TO SEE OUR LOVED ONES NO ONE PROTESTS IT'S NORMAL.

OH, SHE ALMOST FORGOT! THE CIGARETTES. HE SMILES. SHE DOES TOO, EVEN THOUGH SHE HATES HIS SMOKING.

DAD TAKES ME BY THE HANDS. THEY DISAPPEAR IN HIS BIG AND ROUGH ONES.

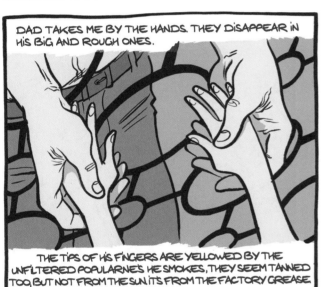

THE TIPS OF HIS FINGERS ARE YELLOWED BY THE UNFILTERED POPULARNE'S HE SMOKES, THEY SEEM TANNED TOO, BUT NOT FROM THE SUN. IT'S FROM THE FACTORY GREASE.

HIS NAILS ARE DIRTY AND WILL ALWAYS LOOK THAT WAY. THE DIRT DOESN'T COME OUT ANYMORE. IT'S A PART OF HIM.

STILL, HIS HANDS ARE CLEANER AND SMOOTHER THAN I'VE EVER SEEN THEM.

THE MILITIA IS ALWAYS AROUND. THEY KEEP WATCH. WE DON'T CARE, WE MANAGE TO FORGET ABOUT THEM. THERE ARE MORE OF US.

THE HELICOPTERS ARE TRYING TO DRIVE US AWAY, BUT THEY JUST DESTROY THE TOPS OF THE SURROUNDING TREES.

IT'S TIME TO GO. EVERYTHING'S OKAY. I REPEAT IT TO MYSELF, EVERYTHING IS GETTING BETTER IT'S GOING TO BE FINE

NIGHT IS FALLING...

VERY EARLY IN THE MORNING, THE CITY IS VIOLENTLY AWOKEN. DOZENS AND DOZENS OF THE TRUCKS THEY USE TO TRANSPORT "REBELS" ROLL THROUGH THE CITY, SIRENS BLARING!

BUT WE SOON LEARN: THEY WERE EMPTY!

OUR FEAR DECREASES, OUR ANGER MOUNTS: THEY'RE TRYING TO FRIGHTEN US. THEY DIDN'T SUCCEED. WE WON'T CALL FOR THE STRIKE TO END.

THEY SPEAK OF PACIFICATION BUT DON'T DARE ACT.

THE ZOMO ARE ON THE ALERT. THERE ARE MORE AND MORE STRIKERS. THE WHOLE CITY IS BEHIND THEM.

THE FACTORY'S MANAGEMENT IS GETTING ANGRY. NOT A SINGLE PIECE OF WEAPONRY IS BEING PRODUCED. THE WORKERS DON'T WANT TO SUPPORT THE BUSINESS OF WAR ANYMORE.

THE DAYS PASS. SEPTEMBER 1ST IS APPROACHING AND WITH IT, THE START OF SCHOOL. BUT SCHOOL IS IN THE BACKGROUND. LIFE IS GOING ON ELSEWHERE, IN FRONT OF AND INSIDE THE FACTORY.

EVERYONE WONDERS WHETHER THE WORKERS WILL GET WHAT THEY'RE DEMANDING. I JUST WONDER WHEN IT WILL END.

THE CHURCH SUPPORTS THE STRIKE. THE PRIEST IS THERE WITH THE STRIKERS EVERY DAY. THEY SET UP A BIG METAL CROSS IN THE FACTORY. THEY PRAY IN FRONT OF IT.

PEOPLE NEED TO BELIEVE. IN GOD AND IN THEIR IDEALS.

ON THE ELEVENTH DAY, THE STRIKE COMMITTEE RECEIVES A PHONE CALL FROM LECH WALESA.

HE SAID WE DID GREAT! THE GOVERNMENT WANTS TO TALK WITH THE TRADE UNION.

BUT WE HAVE TO END THE STRIKE. THAT'S THEIR CONDITION!

WHAT ABOUT AMNESTY FOR THE WORKERS WHO TOOK PART IN THE STRIKE?

THERE ARE NO GUARANTEES FOR THOSE WHO PARTICIPATED, BUT THE COMMITTEE STILL DECIDES TO END THE WORK BLOCKAGE. PEOPLE ARE PERPLEXED AND WORRIED.

ON THE AFTERNOON OF SEPTEMBER 4TH, THE WHOLE CITY COMES TOGETHER. AN ENORMOUS CROWD CHANTS IN FRONT OF THE FACTORY, GREETING AND ENCOURAGING THE STRIKERS WHO EMERGE DEFEATED, BUT ONLY BY EXHAUSTION.

SO IT'S OVER? WE LOOK FOR MY DAD. I HEAR HIS VOICE, OR AM I IMAGINING IT?

MARZI TUTAJ!

HERE!

GOD, WHY AM I SO TINY? I WANT TO BE TALL, RIGHT NOW!

DAD!

I DON'T THINK ABOUT THE FIVE THOUSAND OTHER CHILDREN AROUND ME WHO ARE SHOUTING THE SAME THING AT THE SAME TIME. SOMEONE GRABS ME ROUGHLY BY THE ARMS AND LIFTS ME UP.

I'M ANNOYED BUT DON'T HAVE TIME TO PROTEST. IT'S DAD, HE PICKED ME OUT OF THE CROWD.

A NEEDLE IN A HAYSTACK... IN SPITE OF HIS TIRED EYES, HE SAW ME!

WE CAN'T TALK, EVERYONE'S SHOUTING. WE FIND OUR NEIGHBORS AND THEIR KIDS. WE ALL SHOUT TOGETHER WITH GREAT ENTHUSIASM.

SO-LI-DARNOŚĆ
LI-DARNOŚĆ

IT'S FUN TO PROTEST WHEN YOU'RE PART OF A GROUP. IT'S MUCH MORE IMPRESSIVE!

PRECZ Z KOMUNĄ!

DOWN WITH COMMUNISM!

OUT WITH JARUZELSKI!!!

THEY'D TAKE ME MORE SERIOUSLY AT HOME IF I HAD THIS MANY PEOPLE BEHIND ME: PRECZ Z JAJECZNICĄ! DOWN WITH SCRAMBLED EGGS! SOLIDARNOŚĆ! A DREAM!!

THE CROWD'S EUPHORIA INFECTS US!

KOMUNA NA KSIĘŻYC!

SEND COMMUNISM TO THE MOON!!!

HEY! WE'RE NOT GOING TO POLLUTE THE MOON TOO!

WE ALL FEEL CARRIED AWAY BY THE SAME IDEA AND MOVE LIKE A TIDE THAT SWEEPS EVERYTHING ALONG WITH IT.

TONIGHT WE'RE ALL LIKE LITTLE WAVES BOUND TOGETHER.

WE'LL FLOOD THE CITY WITH THIS FEELING. THE SCALE MAKES IT FEEL LIKE MAY 1ST, BUT WITH TWO IMPORTANT DIFFERENCES...

WE ARE ALL PARTICIPATING OF OUR OWN FREE WILL, AND THE AUTHORITIES DON'T APPROVE. EVEN SO, WE PASS IN FRONT OF THE POLICE STATION.

MILICJA

RZUĆCIE PAŁY, CHODŹCIE Z NAMI!

THROW DOWN YOUR BATONS! COME JOIN US!!

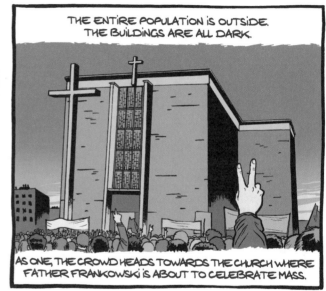

THE ENTIRE POPULATION IS OUTSIDE. THE BUILDINGS ARE ALL DARK.

AS ONE, THE CROWD HEADS TOWARDS THE CHURCH WHERE FATHER FRANKOWSKI IS ABOUT TO CELEBRATE MASS.

THE FEELING IS INDESCRIBABLE. THERE'S NO MORE WORRY IN THE AIR, BUT THE SWEETNESS OF A PERFECT END OF SUMMER, JOYFUL LIKE MY DAD'S EYES, LIKE HAPPINESS.

IT DOESN'T MATTER HOW LONG IT LASTS, ELEVEN DAYS OR ONE MINUTE, IT'S WORTH EXPERIENCING!

I'LL NEVER FORGET THIS FEELING OF SHARED JOY...

THIS END OF SUMMER. FULL OF HOPE. PROMISES. A BEAUTIFUL FALL OF GOLDEN LEAVES.

CHEATING NATURE

MY PARENTS DON'T USUALLY GO TO THE ORCHARD IN THE MIDDLE OF THE WEEK. IT'S EVEN MORE UNUSUAL FOR ME TO GO WITH THEM.

BUT IT DOES HAPPEN, AND SOMETIMES THINGS TAKE QUITE AN EXTRAORDINARY TURN THERE...

THIS PARTICULAR DAY, WE'RE BARELY OUT OF THE CAR BEFORE MY AUNT RUSHES OVER TO US, ALL IN A TIZZY!

DON'T TURN OFF THE ENGINE!

WE HAVE TO GO TO RADOMYŚL!!

THE VIRGIN MARY HAS APPEARED ON ONE OF THE SCHOOL'S WINDOWS!

MY DAD THINKS IT'S FUNNY BUT IS CATEGORICALLY OPPOSED TO THE IDEA.

I'M NOT GOING ANYWHERE. I CAME TO WORK IN THE ORCHARD, NOT TO PRAY IN FRONT OF A SCHOOL. I SEE WHAT YOU'RE THINKING...

MY MOM IS ALL ENTHUSIASTIC. SHE WANTS TO— SHE MUST—GO THERE. SHE CAN'T MISS THIS.

MY GRANDMOTHER, EVEN THOUGH SHE'S A STRONG BELIEVER, LOSES PATIENCE WITH THE TWO OF THEM.

HERETICS! THAT'S WHAT YOU ARE!

BUT MY AUNT AND MY MOM WON'T LISTEN TO ANYONE. THEY DECIDE THEY'LL GO ON THEIR OWN.

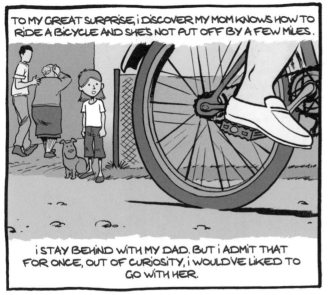

TO MY GREAT SURPRISE, I DISCOVER MY MOM KNOWS HOW TO RIDE A BICYCLE AND SHE'S NOT PUT OFF BY A FEW MILES.

I STAY BEHIND WITH MY DAD. BUT I ADMIT THAT FOR ONCE, OUT OF CURIOSITY, I WOULD'VE LIKED TO GO WITH HER.

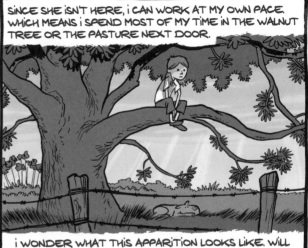

SINCE SHE ISN'T HERE, I CAN WORK AT MY OWN PACE, WHICH MEANS I SPEND MOST OF MY TIME IN THE WALNUT TREE OR THE PASTURE NEXT DOOR.

I WONDER WHAT THIS APPARITION LOOKS LIKE. WILL THE POPE COME? IT'S THRILLING ANYWAY. THIS DOESN'T HAPPEN EVERY DAY!

I QUESTION MY DAD, BUT HE HAS NO DESIRE TO TALK ABOUT IT.

SOMEBODY DID A BAD JOB WASHING ONE OF THE SCHOOL'S WINDOWS AND SOMEBODY ELSE THOUGHT THEY SAW THE OUTLINE OF THE VIRGIN MARY IN IT.

YOU KNOW, PEOPLE HERE NEED TO HOLD ON TO THE LEAST LITTLE SIGN, BUT YOU SHOULDN'T BELIEVE EVERYTHING.

COME ON, I'M GOING TO SHOW YOU SOMETHING...

SOMETHING TRULY MIRACULOUS!

HE WANTS TO SHOW ME HOW TO GRAFT A TREE.

I GO ALONG TO MAKE HIM HAPPY. SOMETIMES, I TELL MYSELF HE SHOULD HAVE HAD A SON INSTEAD OF A DAUGHTER. WHAT GOOD IS IT FOR A DAUGHTER TO KNOW HOW TO GRAFT A TREE?

A GIRL PREFERS TO DO MORE REMARKABLE THINGS. AT LEAST, I DO.

ARE YOU LISTENING TO ME?

YOU'RE MILES AWAY!

WE HAVE A LOT OF APPLE TREES IN OUR ORCHARD. HE WANTS TO CHANGE THE APPLE TREES INTO PEAR TREES. AND IT'S ACTUALLY POSSIBLE! IT'S CRAZY, BUT POSSIBLE!

WILL THE VIRGIN MARY BE ON THAT WINDOW FOR A LONG TIME? I'D REALLY LIKE TO SEE HER...

NOW THIS IS THRILLING!

BUT WE WON'T SEE ANY FRUIT ON IT UNTIL NEXT YEAR, IF ALL GOES WELL.

THIS DOESN'T INTEREST YOU AT ALL...

NO, NO, IT DOES.

I DON'T KNOW HOW TO LIE...

MY MOM AND MY AUNT REAPPEAR LATE THAT AFTERNOON. THEY'RE BOTH VERY MOVED.

IT'S A MIRACLE!

SHE WAS CRYING.

BECAUSE OF THE GOVERNMENT!!

THE CATECHISM MUST RETURN TO THE SCHOOLS... THAT'S WHAT SHE'S TRYING TO TELL US.

THINGS MUST CHANGE.

IT'S GETTING LATE. WE HAVE TO GET BACK TO THE CITY, GET HOME. BUT MY MOM'S INSISTENT, WE ABSOLUTELY HAVE TO GO BACK BY THE APPARITION. SHE'S PRESSURING MY DAD.

DON'T BE IMPIOUS!

HE FINALLY CAPITULATES. I'M REALLY HAPPY. I WANT TO SEE GOD SO MUCH. FINALLY.

I REALLY LIKE GOING TO RADOMYŚL. THE TWO VILLAGES ARE SEPARATED BY THE SAN RIVER. WE HAVE TO TAKE A FERRY ACROSS IT.

THERE'S NO GUARDRAIL. MY MOM FORBIDS ME FROM GETTING OUT OF THE CAR, BUT IF I STARTED PAYING ATTENTION TO ALL HER INTERDICTIONS, I'D STOP BREATHING!

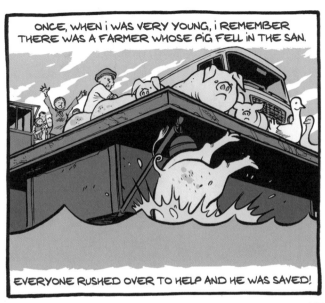

ONCE, WHEN I WAS VERY YOUNG, I REMEMBER THERE WAS A FARMER WHOSE PIG FELL IN THE SAN.

EVERYONE RUSHED OVER TO HELP AND HE WAS SAVED!

HE HAD MANAGED TO SWIM AROUND THE FERRY.

IT WAS A MIRACLE.. ANOTHER ONE.

TONIGHT THERE ARE NO ANIMALS ON THE FERRY. JUST PEOPLE ON BICYCLES, ON FOOT. EVERYONE WANTS TO WITNESS THIS STRANGE PHENOMENON.

THE FERRYMEN DON'T HAVE A SINGLE MINUTE TO THEM-SELVES. ON THE OTHER BANK A NEW CARGOLOAD IS ASSEMBLING.

THERE ARE DOZENS OF PEOPLE AT RADOMYŚL, BUT NO SIGN OF MARY. NOT ON THE WINDOW, NOT ANYWHERE.

WHY ARE SOME PEOPLE KNEELING? DO THEY SEE SOMETHING WE DON'T?

MY DAD FINALLY GETS OUT OF THE CAR.

SO? WHERE'S YOUR HOLY VIRGIN?

SHE'S THERE. LOOK AT EVERYONE. THEY SEE HER.

YOU HAVE TO REALLY BELIEVE TO SEE HER. NOT EVERYONE IS GRANTED THE PRIVILEGE...

MAYBE YOU HAVE TO STAND IN A PARTICULAR PLACE, TRY...

THE SUN IS AT A BAD ANGLE NOW, WE CAN'T SEE AS CLEARLY AS BEFORE.

I BEND DOWN, CRANE MY NECK, TWIST MYSELF IN KNOTS. I REALLY WANT TO SEE HER, BUT I STILL DON'T SEE ANYTHING.

SHE MUST HAVE LEFT...AND OUR TIME HAS COME TOO!

REGRETFULLY, MY MOM FOLLOWS US TO THE CAR. SHE COULD STAY HERE, FOREVER AND EVER.

THAT MUST BE FAITH...THOSE WHO BELIEVE, SEE. OR BELIEVE THEY SEE...BUT DON'T I BELIEVE? I'M SURE IF I'D SEEN HER, I'D BELIEVE.

LIKE NEXT YEAR I'LL BELIEVE IN THE PEARS THAT ARE GROWING ON TWO APPLE TREES IN OUR ORCHARD.

THE KNIGHTS OF THE ROUND TABLE AND TWO KAYAKS

DAD DOESN'T BRING BACK GOOD NEWS FROM THE FACTORY. AFTER THE SUMMER STRIKES, THE PARTICIPANTS ARE BEING PUNISHED. THEY FEARED AS MUCH, AND NOW IT'S HAPPENING.

PEOPLE START GETTING FIRED, OR SENT TO MILITARY TRAINING CAMPS.

MY DAD'S TURN HASN'T COME YET, BUT WE LIVE IN FEAR. ESPECIALLY BECAUSE HE NEVER DID HIS MILITARY SERVICE.

SO THEY COULD TAKE HIM NOW...I WOULDN'T WANT HIM TO BE GONE FOR TWO YEARS.

AROUND 3:30, WHEN HE'S SUPPOSED TO BE GETTING HOME, MY STOMACH STARTS TO ACHE. A BIG KNOT TAKES ROOT. IT DOESN'T DISSOLVE UNTIL THE MOMENT I HEAR MY DAD'S FOOTSTEPS ON THE DOORMAT.

THEY WON'T TAKE ME, DON'T WORRY!

WHY NOT?

BECAUSE I HAVE BUNIONS ON MY FEET, THAT'S WHAT SAVED ME BEFORE.

YOU DON'T THINK THEY'D DO IT NOW OUT OF VENGEANCE?

AND WHY DO YOU HAVE BUNIONS ON YOUR FEET?

BECAUSE I WORE SHOES THAT WERE TOO SMALL WHEN I WAS A KID...

THEY'LL NEVER GO AWAY?!

THEY'RE FOR LIFE, I THINK.

MY MOM SAYS NOTHING. SHE COULD SAY SHE WAS RIGHT, THAT SHE WARNED HIM...BUT, NOTHING. LIKE MY DAD, LIKE THE WHOLE CITY PROBABLY, LIKE MAYBE ALL OF POLAND, SHE'S DISAPPOINTED.

ALL THIS ACTIVISM, ALL THIS SOLIDARITY, AND THIS IS THE RESULT.

SOLIDARNOŚĆ PROMISED TALKS WITH THE AUTHORITIES. FOR SOME TIME, THEY'D BEEN HAVING MEETINGS TO SET THE DATE, WHICH WOULD THEN GET POSTPONED.

AT FIRST, THE TALKS WERE PLANNED FOR MID-SEPTEMBER MID-OCTOBER? NO. LATER? YES, AND THEN IN THE END, NO. IMPORTANT DECISIONS MUST BE MADE BEFOREHAND...

WHO'S GOING TO TAKE PART IN THE ROUND TABLE? HOW MANY PARTICIPANTS? THE AUTHORITIES ARE PLAYING FOR TIME, SAY THE ADULTS. THEY'RE SCARED OF SOLIDARNOŚĆ AND THEY THINK THE LONGER THINGS GO, THE ANGRIER THE PEOPLE WILL BE WITH WAŁĘSA, WHO WON'T BE ABLE TO RECOVER.

HE'S DEMANDING THE LEGALIZATION OF HIS PARTY. IT'S THE SUBJECT ON THE TABLE, BUT THE GOVERNMENT'S AGAINST IT.

THE LINES ARE STILL LONG AND WE HAVE RATION CARDS FOR EVERYTHING. SOON THEY'RE EVEN GOING TO RATION THE AIR WE BREATHE! THEY'RE ALREADY BLOWING HOT AIR...

THE PEOPLE CONTINUE TO PROTEST, THEY DON'T WANT TO BE FORGOTTEN. THIS WHOLE THING CAN'T TURN INTO A BOONDOGGLE! NIE ROZEJDZIE SIĘ PO KOŚCIACH!!

ON NOVEMBER 30TH, THE TELEVISION STATION AIRS A LIVE DEBATE WITH WAŁĘSA. THE PRESENTER'S GOAL IS CLEARLY TO MAKE HIM LOOK RIDICULOUS, TO SHOW HIM TO BE IRRATIONAL.

BUT HE DOESN'T SUCCEED. ON THE CONTRARY, AFTER HAVING SEEN WAŁĘSA THAT NIGHT, ANYONE WHO HAD STARTED TO DOUBT HIM BECAME A FAN ONCE AGAIN.

AS LONG AS THE AUTHORITIES CONTINUE TO BE AFRAID OF THEIR PEOPLE, YOU, SIR, ARE WALKING, STEP BY STEP, WHILE THE REST OF THE WORLD IS RIDING IN CARS!

IF YOU CONTINUE TO WALK, YOU'LL SEE THE RESULTS IN 200 OR 300 YEARS!!

IT WAS "40 MINUTES OF FREEDOM" IN EVERY LIVING ROOM.

WHAT'S "BIG BROTHER" GOING TO SAY? OUR WORRIED EYES TURN TO THE EAST.

THE RUSSIAN ARMY IS LEAVING AFGHANISTAN DEFEATED AND EXHAUSTED. GORBACHEV HAS ALREADY PLANNED TO REMOVE SOME OF HIS SOLDIERS FROM CZECHOSLOVAKIA, HUNGARY, AND EAST GERMANY. HE'S PROVING SIGNIFICANTLY LESS VIRULENT THAN HIS PREDECESSORS.

ANGER AND FATIGUE WELL UP ALL OVER THE COUNTRY.

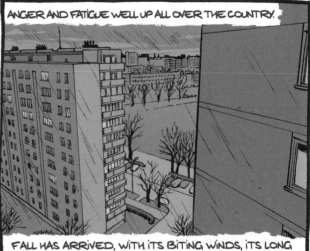

FALL HAS ARRIVED, WITH ITS BITING WINDS, ITS LONG RAINY EVENINGS. THE GLOOM MATCHES OUR OVERALL MOOD. IT MIRRORS THE MINDS OF THE ADULTS.

AND WE CHILDREN ABSORB EVERYTHING, ANYONE NOTICING, UNTIL THE MOMENT WE GET SQUEEZED.

WE'RE BABY SPONGES, YOU CAN'T JUST WRING US OUT, YOU HAVE TO BE CAREFUL WHAT YOU SOAK US IN. EVEN WASHED, RINSED, DRIED A HUNDRED TIMES OVER, TRACES STILL REMAIN IN US.

I DON'T KNOW WHO STILL LIKES WAŁĘSA AND WHO DOESN'T LIKE HIM ANYMORE. I DON'T KNOW IF I'M STILL SUPPOSED TO LIKE HIM OR IF IT'S OVER.

IT'S ALL A LITTLE MURKY. MY DAD'S ANSWERS AREN'T VERY CLEAR.

AND FINALLY THE LONG-AWAITED NEWS COMES... THERE WILL BE A ROUND TABLE ON FEBRUARY 6TH, 1989. EVERYONE WATCHES IT, THEIR TELEVISIONS ON.

OUR APARTMENTS TURN BLUE, YOU'D THINK THAT POLAND IS SCARED. BUT GREEN DESCRIBES US BEST, BECAUSE WE ARE FULL OF HOPE.

HERE WE ARE, LAUNCHED ON OUR QUEST FOR LIBERTY. WE'RE COUNTING ON WAŁĘSA. IF HIS HEART IS PURE, HE'LL BRING HOME THIS HOLY GRAIL.

BEFORE OUR VERY EYES, EUROPE AND THE REST OF THE WORLD ARE DEVELOPING RAPIDLY...

WHILE WE'RE LEFT EYEING MODERNITY IN THE WINDOWS OF STORES WHERE WE HAVE TO PAY IN FOREIGN CURRENCY!

NOTHING HAPPENS NORMALLY, THE RESULT OF A BAD SYSTEM AND OUR LACK OF FREEDOM.

WE FEEL STALIN'S BREATH ON OUR BACKS CONSTANTLY!

THE TABLE IS DIVIDED INTO SUB-TABLES, THERE ARE GROUPS AND GROUPS WITHIN GROUPS, I GET CONFUSED. I CAN'T FOLLOW THE DEBATES, IT'S TOO COMPLICATED AND DISCOURAGING. I WAIT FOR IT TO BE OVER AND ESPECIALLY FOR THE OUTCOME.

SINCE THEY AREN'T ABLE TO RESOLVE CERTAIN CONFLICTS, THEY RETREAT TO MAGDALENKA, AN ISOLATED LOCATION NEAR WARSZAWA.

THERE ARE NO CAMERAS OR JOURNALISTS THERE. ONLY THE CHURCH'S PRESENT, TO ACT AS A BUFFER BETWEEN THE OPPOSING PARTIES.

THE STRIKES AND PROTESTS CONTINUE. IN SPITE OF THE WINTER WEATHER, FEBRUARY IS HOT IN KRAKÓW, WARSZAWA, POZNAŃ, GDAŃSK. PEOPLE ARE PROTESTING, STUDENTS ARE DEFYING THE STATE, IT'S BEAUTIFUL TO SEE.

I WOULD SO LOVE TO HAVE BEEN BIG AND TO HAVE TAKEN PART IN THE PROTESTS! MY DAD IS HAPPY: THE YOUNG PEOPLE ARE ENGAGED, THEY WON'T LET THEMSELVES BE DECEIVED. THEY KNOW WHAT THEY WANT AND THEY'RE NOT SCARED.

SOME PEOPLE ARE CALLING THE ROUND TABLE "THE RED TABLE"... IT'S TAKING TOO LONG AND PEOPLE ARE GETTING IMPATIENT.

ON TOP OF THE STRIKES, PRICES ARE GOING UP AND THE COUNTRY IS DESTABILIZED, SHAKEN. THE EMPTY STORES, THE LONG LINES AND THE "NIE MA" ARE MULTIPLYING. WE DON'T KNOW WHAT'S HAPPENING ANYMORE, NO ONE SEEMS TO BE RUNNING ANYTHING, AND THEY'RE STILL IN TALKS...

DESPITE HIS PRESENCE AT THE ROUND TABLE, WAŁĘSA IS TRAVELING ACROSS POLAND TO REASSURE EVERYONE. HE EVEN COMES TO STALOWA WOLA TO SEE THE WORKERS AT THE BLOCKED FACTORY.

WE ALL WANT THE SAME THING. MAYBE THE YOUNG PEOPLE ARE RIGHT. MAYBE THERE'S NO AVOIDING A FIGHT.

BUT I'VE BEEN AWARDED THE NOBEL PEACE PRIZE...

I ACT WITH PEACE!

THEIR JOY IS DAMPENED, BUT THEY ARE ALL THERE TO HEAR HIM.

GIVE THIS ROUND TABLE A CHANCE! WE'LL FIGHT LATER IF IT BECOMES NECESSARY!!

LOTS OF PEOPLE FEEL WE SHOULD NEVER HAVE SAT DOWN AT THE SAME TABLE WITH OUR TORMENTORS, WITH THOSE RESPONSIBLE FOR MARTIAL LAW. TALKING WITH THE COMMUNISTS MEANS ACCEPTING COMMUNISM IN POLAND.

THE DEBATES LAST TWO MONTHS...

IT'S JUST THE FIRST STEP ON THE ROAD TO DEMOCRACY.

THE COMPROMISE WE'VE ARRIVED AT IS JUST A MEANS TO AN END.

SOLIDARNOŚĆ, TO EVERYONE'S JOY, IS LEGALIZED. THERE WILL BE ELECTIONS TO THE DIET, BUT THEY WON'T BE ENTIRELY DEMOCRATIC. WE WILL BE A LITTLE BIT FREE. ABOUT 35%. WE WILL ONLY HAVE COMPLETE FREEDOM IN THE SENATE.

ELECTIONS ARE HURRIEDLY ORGANIZED.

THEY'RE HOPING TO PUSH US INTO 5TH GEAR, WHICH OUR FIATS DON'T EVEN HAVE!

THEY EXPECT TO PULL ONE OVER ON US AGAIN, SINCE WE BARELY KNOW THE CANDIDATES!

BUT THE DIRECTOR ANDRZEJ WAJDA, WHO IS VERY COMMITTED TO THE CAUSE, HAS AN IDEA.

THE OPPOSITION CANDIDATES SHOULD BE PHOTOGRAPHED WITH WAŁĘSA THAT WAY, EVERYONE WILL KNOW WHO THEY ARE.

JUNE 4TH IS A SUNDAY; AFTER MASS WE HURRY TO THE VOTING BOOTHS. FOR THE FIRST TIME IN 40 YEARS, THE POLISH PEOPLE COULD VOTE!

BUT WE HEAR A CHILLING PIECE OF NEWS THAT QUELLS OUR ENTHUSIASM: THE COMMUNISTS IN CHINA ARE MASSA-CRING STUDENTS IN TIANANMEN SQUARE, THE GATE OF HEAVENLY PEACE. IT LEAVES US FEELING VERY STRANGE.

PEOPLE ARE WORRIED BUT AT THE SAME TIME THEY BECOME EVEN MORE DARING IN THEIR OPPOSITION TO COMMUNISM. IT HAS TO STOP!

I CAN ONLY WATCH AND WONDER, WHO ARE THEY VOTING FOR? THE RESULTS ARE UNANIMOUS. SOLIDARNOŚĆ HAS MADE A STUNNING VICTORY!

THERE'S ONLY ONE BIG QUESTION REMAINING: THE PRESIDENTIAL ELECTION.

THE PARLIAMENT, MEANING THE DIET AND THE SENATE TOGETHER, WILL BE RESPONSIBLE FOR THIS DECISION ON JULY 19TH. THIS IS WHEN THE POLISH PEOPLE LEARN WHAT THE ROUND TABLE HAS COOKED UP FOR THEM. . ONE SOLE CANDIDATE IS PUT FORWARD: THE GENERAL.

CERTAIN PEOPLE FEEL THAT IF JARUZELSKI IS NOT ELECTED, WE RISK A CIVIL WAR AND INTERVENTION FROM MOSCOW.

WE UNDERSTAND IT'S PART OF THE PRICE THAT THE OPPOSITION HAD TO PAY DURING THE TALKS. MANY CONSIDER IT A NATIONAL BETRAYAL, BUT THAT DOESN'T CHANGE THE FACT THAT THE ACCORDS WILL GO DOWN AS THE BEGINNING OF THE CHANGES.

THE BEGINNING OF THE FALL OF COMMUNISM.

POLAND BECOMES THE FIRST COUNTRY IN THE COMMU-NIST BLOC TO HAVE A NON-COMMUNIST PRIME MINISTER.

WE'RE AT THE START OF A NEW ERA, A NEW CHAPTER IN POLAND'S HISTORY.

WE'RE GOING TO TRY TO PULL OUT OF THIS PERIOD OF DEPRESSION.

HIS NAME IS TADEUSZ MAZOWIECKI.

OTHER GOOD NEWS WAS AROUND THE CORNER. CHANGES IN HUNGARY, CZECHOSLOVAKIA, ROMANIA, AND THE MOST SHOCKING OF ALL: THE WALL COMING DOWN...

THE WALL HAS FALLEN!

WHAT WALL?

WHAT DO YOU MEAN, WHAT WALL!? THE BERLIN WALL!!

IT WAS SUPPOSEDLY TORN DOWN BY MISTAKE!

NO, BUILDING IT WAS THE MISTAKE!

THEY REPEATED THE NEWS ON THE RADIO, ON TV. EVERYONE WAS TALKING ABOUT IT. WE WERE TRAPPED IN A NIGHTMARE, BUT IT'S OVER NOW AND WE HAVE TO LEARN TO TALK ABOUT IT AS THE PAST!

THAT NIGHT IT WAS LIKE ALL THE WALLS IN MY BUILDING HAD COME DOWN TOO. AS IF ALL THE APARTMENTS WERE REALLY ONE BIG ONE.

THE WALL HAS FALLEN!

BOOM BOOM BOOM

ALL THE DOORS STAYED OPEN. HERE IT IS, WE'RE INVITING FREEDOM OVER. WE'RE WELCOMING IT IN TOGETHER. WITH OPEN ARMS AND WARM HEARTS.

HOW'S THIS GOING TO CHANGE OUR LIVES?!

IT WON'T...

BUT IN OUR HEADS, EVERYTHING HAS CHANGED. AND FOR FUTURE GENERATIONS, FOR MY GENERATION, IT MEANS FREEDOM! A BIG WORD, A BIG IDEA. IS IT POSSIBLE? WILL IT BE MORE THAN A WORD? WE ARE FULL OF HOPE.

WITH THE ROUND TABLE, POLAND FINALLY FEELS LIKE IT'S OURS. WITH THE FALL OF THE WALL, WE'RE FINALLY IN EUROPE, AND FRANCE FEELS CLOSER ALL OF A SUDDEN.

WE SENSE OUR ROUND TABLE HASN'T GARNERED MUCH ATTENTION WEST OF OUR BORDERS.

SOLIDARNOŚĆ

THEY'LL ONLY REMEMBER KING ARTHUR'S ROUND TABLE. OUR POLISH KNIGHTS WILL NEVER TAKE UP SPACE IN THE MINDS OF THE WEST.

OUR COMMUNISM'S FALL WASN'T SPECTACULAR. THERE WAS NO SPLAT! NO BOOM!

THE FALL DIDN'T HARM ANYONE, NOT EVEN THE "BAD GUYS," WHICH DIDN'T MAKE SOME OF THE "GOOD GUYS" VERY HAPPY. BUT ARE THEY REALLY GOOD IF THEY WANT OTHERS TO SUFFER?

IT WASN'T LIKE THE BERLIN WALL. BLAM! SLAM! CRACK! CLEAR OUT, IT'S COLLAPSING!

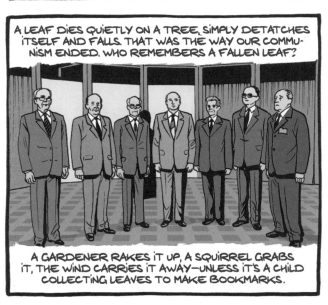

A LEAF DIES QUIETLY ON A TREE, SIMPLY DETATCHES ITSELF AND FALLS. THAT WAS THE WAY OUR COMMUNISM ENDED. WHO REMEMBERS A FALLEN LEAF?

A GARDENER RAKES IT UP, A SQUIRREL GRABS IT, THE WIND CARRIES IT AWAY—UNLESS IT'S A CHILD COLLECTING LEAVES TO MAKE BOOKMARKS.

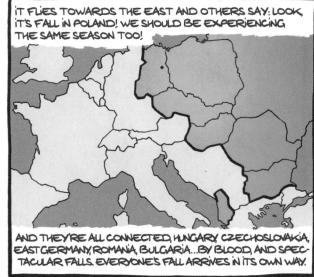

IT FLIES TOWARDS THE EAST AND OTHERS SAY: LOOK, IT'S FALL IN POLAND! WE SHOULD BE EXPERIENCING THE SAME SEASON TOO!

AND THEY'RE ALL CONNECTED, HUNGARY, CZECHOSLOVAKIA, EAST GERMANY, ROMANIA, BULGARIA...BY BLOOD, AND SPECTACULAR FALLS. EVERYONE'S FALL ARRIVES IN ITS OWN WAY.

OURS WAS VERY NATURAL.

WE WERE THE FIRST LEAF.

IN THE MIDST OF ALL THESE UPHEAVALS, I WAS GOING THROUGH MY OWN PERSONAL TRANSFORMATION, ON MY SCALE. MY FEET GREW WITHOUT MY NOTICING.

I WAS TRYING TO BE INTERESTED IN POLITICS, AND I ENDED UP WITH TWO KAYAKS INSTEAD OF FEET.

ARE THEY THE RIGHT SIZE?

I DON'T KNOW.

DO YOU HAVE THE NEXT SIZE?

YOU ALWAYS HAVE TO HURRY BECAUSE THE LAST PAIR COULD BE SNATCHED UP BY SOMEONE ELSE ANY SECOND.

NO, NO, THESE FIT!

ARE YOU SURE?

YES...

I HAD ONLY TRIED ON ONE OF THE SHOES. THE OTHER FOOT TURNED OUT TO BE TOO SMALL, BUT HOW COULD I SAY ANYTHING NOW?

IN ANY CASE, I THOUGHT THESE SHOES LOOKED SO BIG, I HAD ENORMOUS FEET! WHAT BETTER THAN KAYAKS TO EQUIP THEM WITH?

ALMOST IMMEDIATELY, A HOLE FORMS AROUND THE BIG TOE OF ONE OF MY SNEAKERS.

WE BOUGHT THOSE THREE DAYS AGO! YOUR FEET COULDN'T HAVE GROWN IN THREE NIGHTS!!!?

WHAT CAN I DO IF I HAVE A TOE THAT'S BRANCHING OFF?

WE TRY TO RETURN THEM BUT THE SALES LADY SAYS IT WAS MY FAULT, AND THAT I SHOULD HAVE CUT MY TOE-NAILS. MY MOM GETS ANNOYED AND ASKS ME TO TAKE OFF MY SHOES.

THOSE ARE YOUR FEET!!

I'D LOVE TO HAVE ANSWERED NO...

SHE HAS BIG FEET. THIS ONE'S BIGGER THAN THE OTHER. AND SHE'S PREDISPOSED TO GETTING A HALLUX VALGUS... A BUNION.

AT LEAST I KNOW WHO'S RESPONSIBLE FOR THAT...

IN ANY CASE, THE OTHER SHOE IS STILL IN GOOD CONDITION.

AND AS YOU CAN SEE, THERE'S NOTHING LEFT TO BUY...

I DO MY BEST TO HIDE MY FEET.

EVEN IN GYM CLASS, THEY STAND OUT.

YOU'VE GOT FUNNY FEET...

UM, YEAH, DON'T YOU KNOW FEET ARE ALWAYS FUNNY?

AT LEAST MINE DON'T STINK, FATSO!

REFERENCES TO MY FEET BRING OUT MY AGGRESSIVE SIDE.

REMAINING HOPEFUL THE STORES WILL SOON BE FULL OF SHOES IN MY SIZE, I PLAY IN SOCKS IN GYM CLASS.

AH! WHAT FEET!!

I DON'T RESPOND TO THE TEACHER. I JUST THINK IT. LIKE POLAND, 35% FREE.

NOW-ALL WE HAVE TO DO IS BE PATIENT.

AND KEEP GROWING.

GROWING INTO WHAT AWAITS US - FREEDOM...

...AND IN MY CASE, MY FIRST NON-COMMUNIST SHOES...

HOMEMADE CHEWING GUM

I LOVE CHEWING GUM. MY PARENTS DON'T SHARE MY INFATUATION.

WE USED TO HAVE TO PAY DOLLARS FOR IT AT PEWEX. GETTING YOUR HANDS ON SOME WAS DIFFICULT AND RARE.

NOW THAT IT'S FREELY AVAILABLE, MY PARENTS FIND OTHER EXCUSES TO KEEP ME FROM CHEWING IT! THEY SAY IT RUINS MY APPETITE.

SO I FOUND ANOTHER SOLUTION...

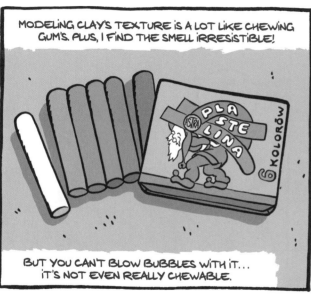

MODELING CLAY'S TEXTURE IS A LOT LIKE CHEWING GUM'S. PLUS, I FIND THE SMELL IRRESISTIBLE!

BUT YOU CAN'T BLOW BUBBLES WITH IT... IT'S NOT EVEN REALLY CHEWABLE.

IT MELTS IN YOUR MOUTH AND THE COLOR BLEEDS ONTO YOUR TEETH. AN ALMOST INSTANTANEOUS STOMACHACHE CONVINCES ME TO STOP.

SO RECENTLY WE'VE BEEN USING WINDOW PUTTY FOR CHEWING GUM. IT'S MUCH MORE RELIABLE THAN MODELING CLAY.

I READ ABOUT IT IN FERENC MOLNAR'S NOVEL "THE PAUL STREET BOYS". THE BOOK'S HEROES FIGHT EACH OTHER WITH PUTTY BALLS, BUT TO KEEP THEM FROM HARDENING TOO QUICKLY THEY HAVE TO TAKE TURNS CHEWING THEM.

CLEARLY, I'M NOT THE ONLY ONE WHO DOES IT.

WE UNWRAP THE PACKAGE OF PUTTY SQUARES AND MAKE A BALL IN OUR MOUTHS. IT'S LIKE CHEWING GUM BUT TASTELESS. SOMETIMES, TO MAKE IT LOOK MORE EXOTIC AND ORIGINAL, WE GRATE A COLORED PENCIL INTO IT.

AFTER A FEW CHEWS, IT CHANGES COLOR, LIKE MAGIC!

WE PERFORM A FEW EXPERIMENTS. WE GRATE IN RED AND BLUE AND ARRIVE AT PURPLE CHEWING GUM. IT'S LIKE BLUEBERRY GUM. WELL, JUST THE COLOR, NOT THE TASTE...

BUT EVERYONE ELSE'S EYES BURN WITH JEALOUSY! WE HAVE THE RECIPE, WE CAN'T GIVE AWAY OUR SECRET.

IT'S EASIER TO PULL THE PUTTY OFF WINDOWS IN THE COUNTRY THAN IT IS IN THE CITY, IN OUR APARTMENTS. BUT WE MAKE DO WHEREVER

AND WE DON'T FIGHT WITH IT, WE JUST PULL IT OFF AND SHARE IT.

ONE DAY, OUR PARENTS FIND OUT WHAT WE'RE UP TO AND WASTE NO TIME BUYING US A PACKAGE OF GUMBALLS THAT LAST US OVER A WEEK EACH.

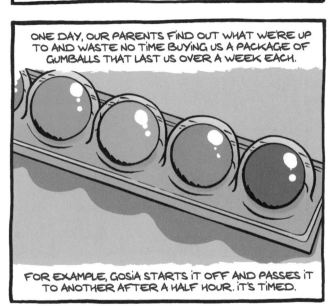

FOR EXAMPLE, GOSIA STARTS IT OFF AND PASSES IT TO ANOTHER AFTER A HALF HOUR. IT'S TIMED.

I DON'T LIKE CHEWING AFTER SOMEONE ELSE, BUT I DON'T ALWAYS HAVE A CHOICE IF I WANT SOME...

IT'S ALREADY BEEN IN SEVERAL MOUTHS...

ONE TIME, ONE OF US THREW IT AWAY, THINKING IT WAS ALL USED UP. ONE GIRL IN OUR CLASS WHO HADN'T HAD HER TURN RACED TO FISH IT OUT OF THE GARBAGE...

SHE RAN IT UNDER WATER AND SAID IT WAS STILL GOOD!

WE ALSO DISCOVERED THAT REALLY WELL-CHEWED OLD CHEWING GUM MAKES A GOOD ERASER. AND YOU CAN STILL CHEW IT AFTERWARDS.

GOOD CHEWING GUM NEVER GOES BAD!

AUNT GIENA

A VERY DISTANT BRANCH OF OUR FAMILY LIVES NEXT DOOR TO MY GRANDMOTHER IN SKOWIERZYN. AND A LITTLE WHILE AGO, THEY WERE JOINED BY A NEW MEMBER.

SHE'S NOT A BABY, QUITE THE CONTRARY, SHE'S AN OLD PERSON. SHE JUST ACTS MORE AND MORE LIKE A BABY.

EVERYONE CALLS HER AUNT GIENA. SHE AND HER HUSBAND LIVED A FEW VILLAGES AWAY. BUT NOW HE'S DEAD AND SHE'S BEEN SICK RECENTLY. SHE ABSOLUTELY HAS TO BE TAKEN CARE OF.

SINCE SHE DOESN'T HAVE CHILDREN, HER COUSINS DECIDED TO BRING HER TO LIVE WITH THEM.

AUNT GIENA HAS LOST HER MIND. I THINK IT'S A FUNNY EXPRESSION. TO LOSE YOUR MIND, TO BE OUT OF YOUR MIND. I SCATTER PIECES OF MY MIND HERE AND THERE.

BUT I KNOW THERE'S NOTHING FUNNY ABOUT IT IN HER CASE.

SHE'S OFTEN BORED AND HANGS OUT IN FRONT OF THE HOUSE. SOMETIMES SHE COMES OVER TO MY GRANDMOTHER'S, THEY TALK A LITTLE.

SHE'S ALWAYS VERY SERENE AND SMILING. HER EYES ARE INCREDIBLY BLUE, LIKE A SUMMER SKY. IT'S CONTINUALLY SUNNY INSIDE HER HEAD.

ONE DAY, SHE ACTS VERY EXCITED TO SEE ME.

OH MY! LOOK HOW PRETTY YOU ARE! YOU MUST BE ON TELEVISION!!

SHE SAYS EXACTLY THE SAME THING THE NEXT TIME. I EVENTUALLY FIGURE OUT SHE SAYS IT TO A LOT OF OTHER PEOPLE.

WHAT AUNT GIENA DOES MOST OFTEN IS GO BACK TO HER OWN HOUSE. SHE HEADS OUT ON FOOT AND OUR COUSIN FINDS HER ON THE ROAD BECAUSE HER HOUSE IS 12 MILES AWAY AND IT'S ALREADY BEEN RENTED TO ANOTHER FAMILY.

IF SHE KEEPS RUNNING AWAY, WE'LL HAVE TO SHUT HER IN!

IT'S IMPOSSIBLE TO WATCH HER ALL THE TIME!!

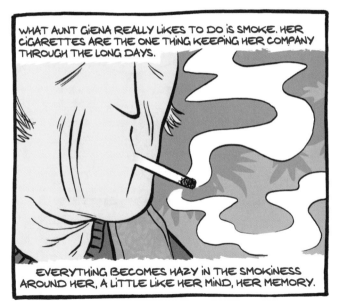

WHAT AUNT GIENA REALLY LIKES TO DO IS SMOKE. HER CIGARETTES ARE THE ONE THING KEEPING HER COMPANY THROUGH THE LONG DAYS.

EVERYTHING BECOMES HAZY IN THE SMOKINESS AROUND HER, A LITTLE LIKE HER MIND, HER MEMORY.

KASIA, OUR COUSIN'S YOUNGEST DAUGHTER, TAKES HER FOR A BIT OF A RIDE. I HAVE TO ADMIT, I PLAY A ROLE IN IT TOO.

I'M GOING TO THE STORE... DO YOU WANT CIGARETTES?

HER EYES LIGHT UP AS SOON AS YOU SAY THE WORD CIGARETTE: PAPIEROS. HER HANDS SHAKE AS SHE RUMMAGES IN HER POCKETS FOR SOME CHANGE.

THIS ISN'T ENOUGH. DON'T YOU KNOW THEY'RE EXPENSIVE?

SHE SMILES, A LITTLE EMBARRASSED, BUT THAT'S ALL SHE HAS. I FEEL ILL AT EASE. I KNOW SHE HANDED OVER ENOUGH FOR THREE PACKS, EVEN THOUGH I NEVER BUY THEM.

AT THE STORE, KASIA BUYS CIGARETTES... AND CANDY. BUT LATER, SHE CHANGES TACK...

I BOUGHT SOME CANDY AND A PTYS...

WHAT ABOUT THE CIGARETTES FOR AUNT GIENA?!

DON'T WORRY, SHE'LL FORGET!

YOU'RE HEART-LESS...

YOU TOO, YOU'RE WITH ME...

AH! THERE YOU ARE. WHAT DO YOU WANT TO EAT TONIGHT?

NOTHING... I HAVE A STOMACH-ACHE.

BUT I STILL SEE KASIA AGAIN. I'M HAPPY TO HEAR SHE'S NOT CHEATING AUNT GIENA ANYMORE, BUT SHE STARTS EXPLAINING WHY RIGHT AWAY.

SHE DOESN'T HAVE ANYTHING ON HER NOW. MY PARENTS ARE MANAGING HER MONEY AND HER CIGARETTES.

BESIDES, THEY DON'T BUY THEM FOR HER ANYMORE. SMOKING ISN'T GOOD FOR YOU!

I DON'T SAY ANYTHING. EVEN THOUGH I KNOW HER PARENTS BOTH SMOKE LIKE CHIMNEYS.

MY DAD GOES OVER TO TALK TO AUNT GIENA SOMETIMES. HE SHARES HIS CIGARETTES WITH HER. HER CHEEKS ARE THINNER BUT HER EYES ARE JUST AS BLUE. SHE STILL SMILES.

THE ONLY GOOD THING ABOUT THIS ILLNESS IS THAT YOU NEVER REALIZE YOU'RE SICK.

YOUR CIGARETTES AREN'T ANY GOOD.

WHAT DO YOU USUALLY SMOKE? TELL ME, I'LL GO GET SOME FOR YOU.

SHE KEEPS SMOKING BUT DOESN'T ANSWER. SHE'S ALREADY SOMEWHERE ELSE. I HOPE THAT WHEREVER SHE GOES WHEN SHE'S LIKE THAT, SHE'S HAPPY.

MY DAD TELLS ME THAT WHAT SHE SAYS MAKES LESS AND LESS SENSE. LIVING WITH SOMEONE LIKE HER CAN'T BE EASY.

DON'T THINK THEY'RE PHILANTHROPISTS BECAUSE THEY TOOK HER IN. THEY HAVE HER HOUSE AND HER MONEY...

SMOKING WAS HER LAST PLEASURE. THE ONE THING NOT TAKEN AWAY...

WHAT ELSE DOES SHE HAVE LEFT?

KASIA AND HER NEIGHBOR KRZYSIEK HAVE A NEW GAME. WHEN I COME FOR THE WEEKEND, THEY INSIST ON SHOWING ME.

THEY DRESS THEMSELVES IN WHITE, GO INTO GIENA'S ROOM —WHERE OUR COUSINS HAVE FINALLY SEQUESTERED HER— AND PRETEND TO BE DOCTORS. SHE BELIEVES THEM AND LETS HERSELF BE LISTENED TO, EXAMINED, AND UNDRESSED. THEY TELL ME ABOUT IT AS IF IT WERE NO BIG DEAL.

THIS TIME THEY CAN TELL IMMEDIATELY IT'S NOT A GOOD IDEA. AS SOON AS WE GO IN, A TERRIBLE SMELL MAKES US RECOIL.

THERE'S A BUCKET NEXT TO HER BED WHERE SHE'S SUPPOSED TO DO HER BUSINESS, BUT THE CONTENTS ARE EVERYWHERE. ON THE WALLS, ON HER HANDS, ON HER MOUTH. GIENA SEEMS COMPLETELY DISORIENTED...

WHAT HAPPENED TO HER?

SHE DOESN'T SEEM HUMAN. SHE'S MORE LIKE A CAGED ANIMAL.

I GO BACK TO MY GRANDMOTHER'S AND RECOUNT THE WHOLE STORY. EVERYONE IN MY FAMILY IS INDIGNANT. THE TWO HOUSES STOP SPEAKING TO EACH OTHER. ONE DAY WHEN MY AUNT NIUSIA WANTED TO SEE AUNT GIENA, THEY EVEN ALMOST CAME TO BLOWS.

YOU HAVE NO IDEA WHAT IT'S LIKE TO TAKE CARE OF SOMEONE LIKE HER!

DO YOU THINK IT'S EASY?!

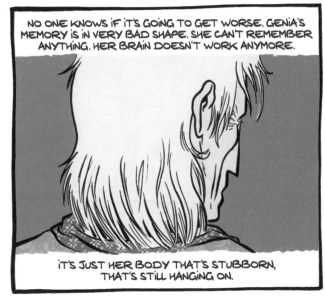

NO ONE KNOWS IF IT'S GOING TO GET WORSE. GENIA'S MEMORY IS IN VERY BAD SHAPE. SHE CAN'T REMEMBER ANYTHING. HER BRAIN DOESN'T WORK ANYMORE.

IT'S JUST HER BODY THAT'S STUBBORN, THAT'S STILL HANGING ON.

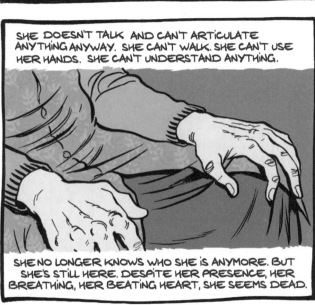

SHE DOESN'T TALK AND CAN'T ARTICULATE ANYTHING ANYWAY. SHE CAN'T WALK. SHE CAN'T USE HER HANDS. SHE CAN'T UNDERSTAND ANYTHING.

SHE NO LONGER KNOWS WHO SHE IS ANYMORE. BUT SHE'S STILL HERE. DESPITE HER PRESENCE, HER BREATHING, HER BEATING HEART, SHE SEEMS DEAD.

I THOUGHT WE DIED QUICKLY. WHEN WE GOT OLD. I THOUGHT WE DIED VERY SIMPLY.

I DIDN'T THINK YOU COULD DIE AND STILL LIVE...

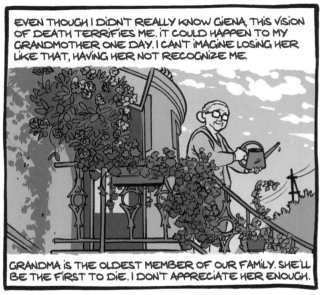

EVEN THOUGH I DIDN'T REALLY KNOW GIENA, THIS VISION OF DEATH TERRIFIES ME. IT COULD HAPPEN TO MY GRANDMOTHER ONE DAY. I CAN'T IMAGINE LOSING HER LIKE THAT, HAVING HER NOT RECOGNIZE ME.

GRANDMA IS THE OLDEST MEMBER OF OUR FAMILY. SHE'LL BE THE FIRST TO DIE. I DON'T APPRECIATE HER ENOUGH.

SHE TELLS ME STORIES ABOUT THE WAR, ABOUT HER CHILDHOOD, WHILE I'M THINKING ABOUT GOING OFF TO PLAY.

YOU KNOW, BACK THEN WE LIVED IN ANOTHER HOUSE THAT WAS WHERE THIS ONE IS NOW.

IF YOU HAD TO TEAR DOWN THE FIRST ONE TO BUILD THE NEW ONE, WHERE DID YOU SLEEP?

ON THE STRAW IN THE STABLE, NEXT TO THE COWS...

HA HA HA!

I WAS WRONG, I KNOW THAT NOW. LUCKILY, IT'S NOT TOO LATE FOR EITHER OF US.

IN MY CLASS, THERE ARE FIVE GIRLS WITH THE SAME FIRST NAME. FIVE ANIAS...

YES?

YES?

ANIA.

YES?

YES?

YES?

SO TO AVOID CONFUSION, WITH THE PRINCIPAL'S PERMISSION, THE TEACHER DECIDED TO CHANGE FOUR OF THE GIRLS' NAMES.

THEY'RE ALL DIFFERENT BUT BESIDES THEIR NAMES, THEY ALL HAVE ONE THING IN COMMON: NO ONE WANTS TO BE CALLED ANYTHING ELSE. EXCEPT IT'S UP TO THE TEACHER.

WHAT'S YOUR MIDDLE NAME?

IWONA.

MAGDA.

MAGDA, TOO.

I DON'T HAVE ONE.

ME NEITHER!

IT'S NOT GOING TO BE EASY...

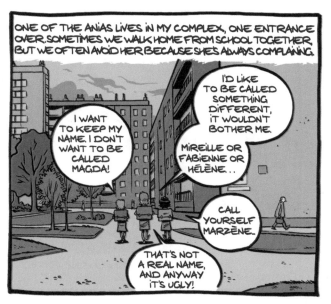

ONE OF THE ANIAS LIVES IN MY COMPLEX, ONE ENTRANCE OVER. SOMETIMES WE WALK HOME FROM SCHOOL TOGETHER, BUT WE OFTEN AVOID HER BECAUSE SHE'S ALWAYS COMPLAINING.

I WANT TO KEEP MY NAME. I DON'T WANT TO BE CALLED MAGDA!

I'D LIKE TO BE CALLED SOMETHING DIFFERENT, IT WOULDN'T BOTHER ME.

MIREILLE OR FABIENNE OR HÉLÈNE...

CALL YOURSELF MARZÈNE.

THAT'S NOT A REAL NAME, AND ANYWAY IT'S UGLY!

CAN YOU IMAGINE BEING LUCKY ENOUGH TO CHANGE YOUR NAME?

IT'S LIKE BECOMING SOMEONE ELSE, LIKE STARTING A NEW LIFE!

YEAH, WELL... IF I CALL YOU ZUZIA, HOW DOES THAT CHANGE YOUR LIFE?

YOU STILL LIVE IN THE SAME PLACE, YOU HAVE THE SAME PARENTS, YOU GO TO THE SAME SCHOOL...

YOU JUST HAVE ANOTHER NAME AND THE BOYS WILL STILL FIND A WAY TO TEASE YOU ABOUT IT.

IT'S TRUE... AND WHY BE SO SET ON CHANGING THEIR NAMES? THE NAME ANIA HAS SO MANY NICKNAMES THAT EACH ANIA COULD HAVE HER OWN.

ANNA

ANIA

ANKA

ANULKA

ANECZKA

ANUSIA

...

BUT WE'RE STILL TALKING ABOUT THE SAME PERSON. THEY WON'T GO FOR IT, THE NAMES ARE TOO SIMILAR AND THEY'RE EACH USED TO BEING ADDRESSED BY ALL THOSE NICKNAMES...

IN LIGHT OF THE PARENTS' VOCIFEROUS PROTESTS, IT WAS FINALLY DECIDED THAT ALL THE ANIAS WOULD STAY ANIAS. TO INDICATE WHO WAS BEING ADDRESSED, YOU SIMPLY HAD TO ADD THEIR LAST NAME.

ANIA WRZESZCZO-WICZYŃSKA...

TO THE BLACK BOARD!

WE HAVE NAMES FOR THEM ALL (BUT THEY'RE JUST BETWEEN US)

PIEGUSKA FRECKLES

ŚNIEŻYNKA SNOWBALL

GAPISZON BUGEYES

ANIA-NIA-NIA THE ONE EVERYONE AVOIDS...

PIJAWA LEECH

IT'S STRANGE THAT THEY'RE ALL SO ATTACHED TO THEIR NAME, I'VE NEVER LIKED MINE. THERE ARE SO MANY PRETTY ONES, I DON'T UNDERSTAND WHY MY PARENTS CHOSE THIS ONE.

MARZI!

IT'S ALSO VERY UNUSUAL, I'M LUCKY TO ALWAYS BE THE ONLY MARZI IN MY CLASS.

FRANKLY, I THINK EVEN IF YOU COUNTED THE WHOLE SCHOOL, IT'D BE PRETTY RARE. I SHOULD FEEL UNIQUE, THAT'S WHAT MY PARENTS SAY. BUT I DON'T LIKE BEING SET APART, I'D RATHER BE ONE OF THE CROWD.

MARZI

ANIA

I DON'T LIKE FEELING DIFFERENT BECAUSE I SENSE THE DIFFERENT ONES ARE ALWAYS KEPT AT A DISTANCE.

MY MOM AND DAD SAY: "WHY ARE YOU SO UPSET ABOUT THIS? IT'S ONLY A NAME!!" YES, BUT I HAVE TO BEAR IT MY WHOLE LIFE, THEY HAVE NO IDEA!

MARZI

THEY HAVE NAMES FROM THE BIBLE, MARIA AND JOZEF SHOULD I BE UNIQUE LIKE JESUS?! I DON'T WANT TO BE HIS REINCARNATION, I DON'T WANT TO SUFFER FOR OTHERS, I WASN'T MADE FOR IT. I SUFFER ENOUGH FOR MYSELF!

MY NICKNAME, "MARZENIA", MEANS "DAYDREAMS." IS THAT WHY MY PARENTS CHOSE THIS NAME?

THEY DIDN'T KNOW WHAT SEX I'D BE BEFORE I'D STUCK MY HEAD OUT OF MY MOTHER. THEY TOLD ME THEY DIDN'T HAVE A NAME READY. BUT AS SOON AS THEY SAW ME, THEY CHOSE "DAYDREAMS."

SOMETIMES YOU DON'T NEED TO LOOK AT THE CALENDAR TO KNOW WHAT'S GOING TO HAPPEN. THE SUN SETS, NIGHT FALLS. ONE EVENT LEADS TO THE NEXT.

COMMUNION GIVEN OUT AT CHURCH SIGNALS THE END OF MASS. I'M HUNGRY, IT MUST BE CLOSE TO MEALTIME (EVEN IF IN MY CASE IT'S MEALTIME MORE OFTEN THAN I'M HUNGRY).

IT'S THE SAME FOR SUMMER. I KNOW EXACTLY WHEN IT'S GOING TO ARRIVE. THANKS TO THE BEETLES...

THEY SHOW UP WITHOUT WARNING. ANY PLACE THERE'S A SPECK OF GREEN: LAWNS, WEEDS, TREES, BUSHES, FLOWERBEDS. THEY ALWAYS COME OUT IN THE EVENING.

AND THEY START TO TWIRL IN THE AIR. HONESTLY, THE WAY THEY MOVE IS TOTALLY CHAOTIC, IT LOOKS LIKE A FURIOUSLY WILD DANCE.

THEY LOOK NERVOUS AND IMPART NERVOUSNESS TO THOSE IN THEIR WAY. ESPECIALLY TEENAGE GIRLS WHO DON'T GENERALLY TOLERATE INSECTS WELL!

THE BEETLES GET TANGLED IN THEIR HAIR AND IF THEY'RE WEARING SKIRTS THEY ALWAYS MANAGE TO GET LOST IN THEM.

WHEN I WITNESS THIS KIND OF SCENE, I CAN'T MAKE OUT THE LITTLE INSECTS FROM THE HEIGHT OF MY WINDOW. SO IT LOOKS LIKE THE GIRLS ARE POSSESSED!

EVERY SO OFTEN A BEETLE GETS AS HIGH AS MY FLOOR, BUT ONCE HE ARRIVES HE'S SO EXHAUSTED HIS FURY IS SPENT.

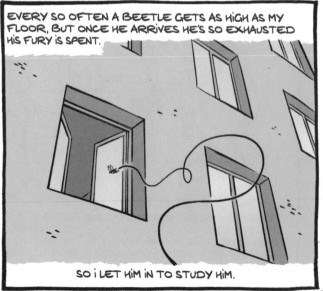

SO I LET HIM IN TO STUDY HIM.

IT'S COMPLETELY DIFFERENT IN THE COUNTRY.

THERE, VEGETATION IS EVERYWHERE— AND SO ARE THE BEETLES!

IN THE EVENINGS, AFTER THE COWS ARE IN, KRZYSIEK, KASIA, SŁAWEK AND I GO HUNTING FOR BEETLES.

WE EACH COME EQUIPPED WITH A JAR OR A BOTTLE AND WE IMPRISON A VAST QUANTITY OF THESE RED INSECTS.

THIS IS OUR CHANCE TO LOOK AT THEM UP CLOSE.

THERE ARE SO MANY OF THEM THEY WALK ON TOP OF EACH OTHER AND SKATE ALONG WIGGLING FRANTICALLY. IT GROSSES ME OUT, MY ENTIRE BODY STARTS TO ITCH ALL OVER!

TODAY, WE'RE JOINED BY SOME OTHER KIDS. THEY'RE THE BOYS FROM THE OTHER SIDE OF THE VILLAGE.

I DON'T KNOW THEM, BUT I DON'T MIND PLAYING WITH THEM.

THE BEETLES COME UP OUT OF THE GROUND, THEY FALL FROM THE TREES, IT'S TOTAL CRAZINESS! FROM A DISTANCE, WE CAN SEE INDOMITABLE SWARMS OF THESE BEASTS AND WE RUSH INTO THEM!

WE CHASE EACH OTHER, EMPTYING OUR CONTAINERS ONTO EACH OTHER'S HAIR OR BACKS.

SŁAWEK'S QUITE FAT AND NEVER RUNS FAST ENOUGH TO CATCH ME. BUT I HAVE NO PROBLEM CATCHING HIM!

HA HA HA HA HA

KASIA'S DIFFERENT. SHE RUNS VERY FAST WHEN I CHASE HER, BUT AS SOON AS IT'S A BOY, IT'S LIKE SHE SLOWS DOWN ON PURPOSE!

IF THE BOYS EMPTY THEIR BOTTLES ON HER, SHE SHAKES WITH LAUGHTER. WHEN I DO IT, SHE SHOUTS AT ME, ANNOYED!

WHAT'S WRONG WITH YOU!?!

WHATEVER!...

KASIA LIKES ONE OF THEM. WE TALK ABOUT IT AFTERWARDS, AS SOON AS WE'RE ALONE AGAIN.

DO YOU THINK HE LIKES ME? DID YOU SEE HOW HE LOOKED AT ME?

I MOSTLY SAW HOW YOU LOOKED AT HIM...

BUT THERE'S NOTHING SPECIAL ABOUT HIM, MACIEK IS MORE HANDSOME!

YEAH, DEFINITELY MORE HANDSOME.

HA! YOU SEE, EVEN KRZYSIEK THINKS HE'S HANDSOME!

YEAH, BUT ŁUKASZ IS MY FAVORITE.

YOUR FAVORITE?! YOU SOUND LIKE A GIRL!

HEY, IT'S JUST A MANNER OF SPEAKING...

BUT YOU GIRLS DON'T GET IT!! KRZYSIEK IS A FAIRY!!

HE LOOKS LIKE A BOY, BUT HE'S A GIRL AND THAT'S WHAT A FAIRY IS!!

YOU CAN SMELL IT AND YOU CAN SEE IT!

AND, LOOK AT THAT LITTLE SISSY, HE'S CRYING!! WAA, WAA, WAA, SŁAWEK WAS MEAN TO ME... WAAA!

A REAL MAN DOESN'T CRY!!

YOU CAN SMELL IT?

OF COURSE YOU CAN! HE WEARS MORE PERFUME THAN THE TWO OF YOU PUT TOGETHER!

HE TAKES CARE OF HIMSELF, THAT'S ALL...

A REAL MAN DOESN'T WEAR PERFUME! HE DOESN'T EVEN BATHE VERY OFTEN!

HUNH?!

WELL I DON'T WANT A REAL MAN. I'D RATHER HAVE ONE WHO SMELLS GOOD!

KEEP DREAMING! KRZYSIEK WOULD NEVER BE INTERESTED IN YOU!

HE MIGHT FIND ME ATTRACTIVE, BUT NOT YOU! THAT'S WHAT IT MEANS TO BE A FAIRY.

YOU! ATTRACTIVE?! HAVE YOU SEEN YOURSELF? YOU LOOK LIKE MY GREAT-GRANDFATHER'S ASS!

I'M SURE THE MINUTE YOU SET FOOT IN THE CEMETERY, THE DEAD SINK DOWN TWO STORIES LOWER!!!

ATTRACTIVE! HA HA!

VACATION COMES AFTER THE BEETLES. THAT I KNOW.

IT'S NOT MY STORY ANYMORE, IT'LL BE HIS...

GOODBYE DOLLY

OF ALL MY MOM'S BROTHERS AND SISTERS, THERE'S ONLY ONE AUNT THAT I DON'T KNOW: CIOTKA STEFKA. THIS YEAR, I'M FINALLY GOING TO MEET HER. HER AND HER WHOLE FAMILY.

SHE LIVES VERY FAR AWAY FROM US, IN MAZURY, THE LAKE COUNTRY IN THE NORTH OF POLAND.

IN THE BEGINNING OF THE 1950S, SHE LEFT THE SOUTH WITH HER HUSBAND WŁADEK TO FIND A PLACE TO LIVE.

THEY MOVED INTO THE AREA THE GERMANS HAD OCCUPIED AND THEN ABANDONED AT THE END OF THE WAR. IT HAD REMAINED UNCLAIMED EVER SINCE.

STEFKA AND WŁADEK HAVE SEVERAL CHILDREN, WHO EACH HAVE CHILDREN... WHO ARE APPROXIMATELY MY AGE. I DIDN'T KNOW ANY OF THESE RELATIVES.

BEFORE, I THOUGHT OF OUR FAMILY TREE AS AN AVERAGE-SIZED APPLE TREE WHERE I HAD HAPPILY FOUND MY PLACE. NOW, I FEEL LIKE A PEAR TREE HAS BEEN GRAFTED ONTO OUR TREE WITHOUT THE APPLES' KNOWLEDGE.

IT'S FUNNY TO BE STAYING WITH FAMILY YOU DON'T KNOW. IT'S LIKE WE SHOWED UP AT A STRANGER'S HOUSE AND TOLD THEM: "WE'RE RELATIVES, I'M ONE OF YOUR GREAT-GRANDMOTHER'S SISTER'S DAUGHTERS, THE YOUNGEST ONE WHO LIVES IN THE SOUTH..."

WE MOVE IN, WE EAT FROM THEIR FRIDGE, WE SLEEP IN THEIR BEDS...

THEY WELCOME US WITH WIDE-OPEN ARMS.

MY MOM AND MY AUNT LOOK ALIKE. AS FOR THE REST, I'M KEEPING MY FINGERS CROSSED.

MY UNCLE AND AUNT LIVE WITH ONE OF THEIR SONS, HIS WIFE AND THEIR BABY ON A BIG FARM. THEY LIVE OFF THE LAND.

EDYTA, ANOTHER GRANDDAUGHTER OF MY AUNT'S, HAS COME TO STAY FOR THE SUMMER. SHE'LL BE MY COUSIN-FRIEND.

WE SLEEP TOGETHER IN A CORNER OF THE LIVING ROOM. A THICK VELVET CURTAIN PROTECTS US FROM THE LIGHT AND NOISE IN THE REST OF THE ROOM. WE SHARE AN ENORMOUS FOUR-POSTER BED.

WE FEEL LIKE PRINCESSES.

WE'RE IN AN ENCHANTED UNIVERSE WHILE ON THE OTHER SIDE OF THE CURTAIN, THE ADULTS ARE CELEBRATING THEIR REUNION MORE AND MORE LOUDLY.

THE CURTAIN IS VERY HEAVY AND VERY SOFT. YOU HAVE ONLY TO PULL IT CLOSED TO ENTER INTO ANOTHER WORLD.

IT ALSO PROVES THAT BORDERS EXIST AND WILL ALWAYS EXIST. THAT'S SOMETHING I LEARNED THIS VACATION.

WHAT ARE YOU DOING?

SHH, I'M LISTENING.

WHAT ARE THEY SAYING?

THAT THE WORLD HAS CHANGED.

THEY'RE FIGHTING. AH, GOOD OLD REUNIONS! EVEN SO, THE LAST TIME THEY SAW EACH OTHER WAS BEFORE I WAS BORN. SO MANY THINGS HAVE HAPPENED SINCE...

ALCOHOL LOOSENS TONGUES. THE ADULTS REVISIT HISTORY, THEY RELIVE THE PAST INSTEAD OF STAYING IN THE PRESENT AND ENJOYING THIS RARE MOMENT OF TOGETHERNESS.

JARUZELSKI DID WHAT NEEDED TO BE DONE AT THE TIME! HE SPARED US ALL A BLOODBATH!

SO YOU THINK THE STATE OF WAR DIDN'T SHED BLOOD?

A BLOODBATH...YIKES!?

THE RUSSIANS WOULD HAVE ENTERED THE COUNTRY AND OCCUPIED US...

SO OUR OWN LEADERS DID IT INSTEAD!! THAT'S WHAT HAPPENED!

AND THEN HE TRIED TO CLIP SOLIDARNOŚĆ'S WINGS!

YOU'RE AN IDEALIST, JÓZEK, YOU AND ALL THE OTHER UNION MEN. WAŁĘSA WAS BOUGHT...

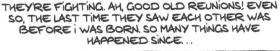

HERE THEY ALWAYS CALL IT "YOUR SOLIDARNOŚĆ".

WHAT ARE THEY TALKING ABOUT? IS IT INTERESTING? DO YOU UNDERSTAND ANY OF IT?

THAT NOTHING IS BLACK AND WHITE...

OF COURSE NOT! LOOK, YOU'RE A REDHEAD, I'M BLOND, THE CURTAIN IS BURGUNDY!

ONLY OLD FILMS ARE BLACK AND WHITE, AND SOME OLD TVS.

DO YOU WANT TO TELL ME A STORY?

IN COLOR OR IN BLACK AND WHITE? WAIT, I KNOW! I'LL BE A BLACK AND WHITE TELEVISION FOR YOU!

DO I HAVE TO TAP YOU TO GET AN IMAGE?

EDYTA HAS A HARD TIME GETTING TO SLEEP EVERY NIGHT. SHE ASKS ME TO MAKE UP STORIES. I LIKE DOING IT. THIS PLACE LENDS ITSELF TO IT WONDERFULLY.

IT WILL BE CALLED: THE LITTLE GIRL WHO DREAMED IN COLOR...

A LITTLE GIRL WAS LIVING IN A BLACK AND WHITE WORLD...SO SHE COULDN'T WAIT FOR THE MOMENT SHE FELL ASLEEP...

BECAUSE HER DREAMS WERE SO MUCH PRETTIER THAN THE WORLD IN WHICH SHE LIVED OUT HER SAD DAYS.

ONE DAY, JUST BEFORE SHE DRIFTED TO SLEEP, SHE SAID TO HERSELF: "I HAVE TO STAY CONSCIOUS I'M DREAMING SO I CAN BRING BACK SOMETHING FROM THAT OTHER WORLD"...

AFTER THAT, EVERY MORNING SHE WOKE UP WITH ONE OBJECT: A YELLOW TOWEL, A BLUE DRESS, AN ORANGE UMBRELLA...

AND LITTLE BY LITTLE, SHE FILLED THE REAL WORLD WITH THESE COLORS!

IN HER NEW UNIVERSE THAT NOW LOOKED LIKE HER DREAMS, SHE WAS HAPPY...

AND?

AND?

GO ON!!

BUT IT DISPLEASED THE AUTHORITIES WHO TOLD HER SHE DIDN'T HAVE THE RIGHT TO KEEP COLOR ALL TO HERSELF, SO THEY FORBADE HER FROM SLEEPING...

I DON'T KNOW...

OKAY, LET'S SAY THAT SINCE SHE COULDN'T SLEEP ANYMORE, SHE DIED OF EXHAUSTION AND RETURNED TO HER COLORFUL WORLD...

WHAT?! THAT'S HORRIBLE! THAT'S NOT THE REAL ENDING, IS IT?!?

I DON'T LIKE ENDINGS!

IF YOU'D RATHER, WE COULD SAY THAT SHE CONTINUES TO BRING BACK NEW OBJECTS, IN NEW COLORS, AND THANKS TO HER THE WORLD BECOMES MORE AND MORE BEAUTIFUL...

BUT HOW'S THAT POSSIBLE? SHE ALREADY CLEARED OUT HER DREAMS, RIGHT?

NO, EVERYTHING GROWS BACK, YOU SEE...

OBJECTS GROW BACK?

LIKE PLANTS? LIKE HAIR?

YES... I MEAN NO... IT'S A STORY I MADE UP. I DON'T KNOW. IT'S POSSIBLE THEY GROW BACK. IN MADE-UP STORIES, ANYTHING CAN GROW BACK, RIGHT?

YOUR STORY IS VERY STRANGE, IT'S PRETTY FARFETCHED.

WHY DON'T YOU FETCH YOURSELF TO A FARAWAY PLACE THEN AND SLEEP? I'M TIRED. GOOD NIGHT!

EDYTA FINALLY SHUTS UP... I WONDER IF SHE'LL BRING SOMETHING BACK FROM HER DREAMS TONIGHT...

EVERY MORNING, IT'S THE SAME THING...

SLEPT WELL? WHAT DID YOU DREAM ABOUT?

TEETH...

AUNT STEFKA INTERPRETS EVERYTHING.

TEETH?! HOW HORRIBLE! WHAT WERE THEY LIKE?

I HEARD A NOISE AND THEN I SAW ONE UNDER THE COUCH...

WAS IT MOVING?!

YEAH, IT WAS JUMPING AND SHOUTING "I'M HUNGRY, I'M HUNGRY"

HOW CAN YOU DREAM ABOUT TEETH?

ONCE UPON A TIME THERE WAS A LITTLE TOOTH THAT DIDN'T WANT TO BEHAVE. SHE COULDN'T SIT STILL, SHE WOULD SAY, I'M BORED!

BUT THE OTHER, BIGGER TEETH, DIDN'T PAY ANY ATTENTION TO HER...

SO SHE WOULD DREAM: AS SOON AS I'M BIG, I'LL LEAVE! I'LL PULL MYSELF OUT OF HERE, I DON'T WANT TO END UP LIKE YOU, YELLOWED AND SET IN MY WAYS. I DON'T WANT TO SMELL ROTTEN!

AND ONE NIGHT SHE ESCAPED AND FOUND HER WAY INTO EDYTA'S DREAM!

SHE WANTED EDYTA TO TAKE CARE OF HER, SHE THOUGHT SHE'D BE A GOOD PERSON FOR IT.

WHAT AN IMAGINATION!

HMPH, WHAT NONSENSE!

HOW STRANGE TO THINK THAT DREAMING ABOUT TEETH MEANS BAD LUCK. STEFKA EXPLAINS TO US SERIOUSLY THAT SO DOES WATER, BABIES AND HORSES...

ALMOST EVERY DAY WE GO VISIT ANOTHER BRANCH OF THE FAMILY. THEY DON'T LIVE VERY FAR FROM EACH OTHER. BUT SINCE WE DON'T KNOW THE WAY, WE FOLLOW THE TRAIN TRACKS.

AFTER A GOOD HALF AN HOUR OF WALKING, YOU'LL SEE A VERY BIG MIRABELLE TREE, TAKE A LEFT JUST AFTER IT...

IT'S A TRACK THAT ISN'T USED ANYMORE. IT ONCE CONNECTED GERMANY AND THE USSR, BUT COMMUNISM DOESN'T EXIST HERE ANYMORE, THERE'S NOTHING LEFT TO CONNECT.

IS THIS ONE BIGGER THAN THE ONE WE JUST PASSED?

HOW LONG HAVE WE BEEN WALKING?

MORE THAN HALF AN HOUR?

THAT'S BECAUSE WE STOPPED TO PICK MIRABELLES. AND THEN YOU HAD TO PEE, REMEMBER.

AND WHAT DOES A GOOD HALF AN HOUR MEAN? IS THERE SUCH A THING AS A BAD ONE?

STOP TALKING! SAVE YOUR BREATH FOR WALKING.

ARE YOU SURE WE'RE GOING THE RIGHT WAY?

WE'VE BEEN WALKING AND WALKING, MAYBE WE'RE IN THE USSR ALREADY? I DON'T THINK THESE MIRABELLES ARE AS GOOD.

AND THERE ARE MORE MOSQUITOES, DON'T YOU THINK?

VISITING FAMILY WEARS ME OUT. THEY PINCH MY CHEEKS, THEY CHECK ME OUT HEAD TO TOE...

WHAT A GOOD GIRL SHE IS!

SHE'S NOT VERY TALKATIVE!

WHAT CAN I SAY? THAT THEY'RE BORING AND I'M DYING TO GO BACK TO EDYTA? ODDLY, THE ONLY PEOPLE WE DON'T VISIT ARE HER PARENTS.

STILL, A FEW OF THE VISITS LEAVE ME WITH SOME GOOD MEMORIES. ONE OF MY MOM'S COUSINS RECEIVES A LOT OF PACKAGES FROM AMERICA THANKS TO HER HUSBAND'S FAMILY.

COFFEE, COCOA, STOCKINGS...AND TOYS FOR HER THREE SONS.

AMAZING ONES...CARS, CHARACTERS, I'M FASCINATED BY THEM. THERE'S A BOX FULL OF THEM.

THE THREE BOYS WOULD RATHER PLAY OUTSIDE. THEY HAVE TOY GUNS AND RUN AROUND SHOOTING THEM OFF. THEY DON'T SEEM INTERESTED IN THE BOX ANYMORE.

I RUMMAGE AROUND IN IT, ADMIRINGLY. WHY DOESN'T ANYONE SEND US A BOX LIKE THIS? BURIED NEAR THE BOTTOM I FIND A DOLL JUST LIKE THE ONE I'VE SPENT SO MANY YEARS DREAMING ABOUT! SHE LOOKS NEGLECTED, DINGY, DUSTY.

YOU CAN KEEP HER IF YOU LIKE...

I DON'T KNOW WHY HE SENT A DOLL!?

I STAND OPEN-MOUTHED...IT'S THIS EASY?!

SHE'S GIVEN TO ME JUST LIKE THAT, AFTER I'VE BEEN ASKING MY PARENTS FOR HER FOR SO LONG?! I CAREFULLY PUT HER AWAY IN MY MOM'S PURSE.

IF IT TURNS OUT ONE OF THE BOYS LOVES HER AND SEES ME WITH HER, HE'LL SAY "PUT HER BACK, SHE'S MINE!" BUT WHAT DOES HE NEED HER FOR? BOYS DON'T PLAY WITH DOLLS

I IMAGINE A DOZEN SCENES ALONG THESE LINES. EVERY 5 MINUTES I CHECK TO MAKE SURE SHE'S STILL THERE. THAT I'M NOT DREAMING. QUICK, LET'S GET OUT OF HERE BEFORE MY AUNT CHANGES HER MIND!

OH, WHAT'S THIS??

I PUT HER THERE SO I WOULDN'T FORGET HER...

RIGHT, SHE'S THE LAST THING I'D EVER FORGET!

I TURN RED, I'M SURE THE BOYS THINK I STOLE HER.

DID YOU ASK THEM IF THEY WANTED TO GIVE HER TO YOU?

I REFUSED TO PLAY WITH THEM (I DIDN'T WANT THEM TO KILL ME!). IT'S THE FIRST TIME WE'VE MET, I MUST BE MAKING A BAD IMPRESSION...

MY AUNT SAID I COULD...

OF COURSE SHE CAN! RIGHT BOYS, YOU DON'T PLAY WITH HER?

A MOMENT OF SILENCE...IT'S OBVIOUS THEY PLAY WITH HER SOME. BUT LUCKILY FOR ME, THEY WON'T ADMIT IT. ON OUR WAY OUT, ONE OF THEM CORNERS ME: "SHE HAS SOME OTHER OUTFITS." HE GIVES THEM TO ME!

BACK AT THE HOUSE, I DON'T SHOW HER TO ANYONE. I STASH HER AT THE BOTTOM OF MY PARENTS' SUITCASE. BUT I CAN'T SLEEP, I'M SO OVERWHELMED WITH EMOTION.

I CAN'T BELIEVE IT.

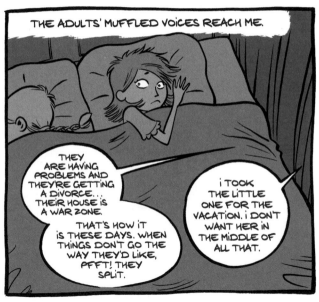

THE ADULTS' MUFFLED VOICES REACH ME.

THEY ARE HAVING PROBLEMS AND THEY'RE GETTING A DIVORCE... THEIR HOUSE IS A WAR ZONE.

THAT'S HOW IT IS THESE DAYS. WHEN THINGS DON'T GO THE WAY THEY'D LIKE, PFFT! THEY SPLIT.

I TOOK THE LITTLE ONE FOR THE VACATION. I DON'T WANT HER IN THE MIDDLE OF ALL THAT.

OH, WHAT FACES! DIDN'T YOU TWO GET ANY SLEEP? WHAT DID YOU DREAM ABOUT?

ABOUT A GIANT SEA WITH TINY TEETH-SHAPED FISH SWIMMING AT THE BOTTOM OF IT. AND ON THE BEACH, A HERD OF BABIES CHASING AFTER GALLOPING HORSES...

HA! THE BABIES WERE TOOTHLESS, MAYBE THAT'S A POINT IN MY FAVOR?

OH WELL! IF THE SKY DOESN'T FALL ON YOUR HEAD TODAY, IT'LL BE A MIRACLE.

MY UNCLE OWNS THIRTY COWS, AN ENORMOUS COW SHED. HE DOESN'T MILK THEM BY HAND.

I LIKE MY AUNT NIUSIA'S METHOD BETTER, BUT SHE ONLY HAS TWO. HERE, THE WHOLE FAMILY WOULD HAVE TO TAKE IT ON!

AT THE EDGES OF THE FARM THERE ARE BULLS IN BIG ENCLOSURES WITH ELECTRIC FENCES...A TINY LITTLE WIRE FOR SUCH BIG ANIMALS...

THEY NEVER TRY TO ESCAPE?

NO, THEY SENSE THE VOLTAGE.

I DON'T FEEL ANYTHING. CAN I TOUCH IT?

NOT WITH YOUR HAND. USE A STRAND OF GRASS, YOU'LL SEE.

I PLUCK A BLADE OF GRASS AND TOUCH THE WIRE WITH IT...

GNNNN

FOR A MOMENT I CAN'T SPEAK. THE CURRENT RUNS FROM MY ARM DOWN MY LEG, WHICH STARTS JUMPING ALL BY ITSELF. IT'S ALL VERY STRANGE. MY DAD AND EDYTA CAN'T STOP LAUGHING.

WE TAKE ADVANTAGE OF THE STRAW HARVEST BY RIDING ON THE WAGON. IT'S NEAT, LIKE FLOATING ON A CLOUD.

i CAN'T COMPLETELY RELAX BECAUSE SPIDERS LOVE HAY. YOU CAN'T SEE THE HARVESTMEN VERY WELL, THEY'RE LIKE WALKING STICKS. EVERY STRAW IS SUSPECT...

i SEE A WISP APPROACHING ME...

WHERE ARE YOU GOING, STRAW?

IF IT DOESN'T ANSWER IT'S BECAUSE IT'S REALLY A SPIDER THAT DOESN'T WANT TO END UP AS A COW BED. HE'S RIGHT, I WOULDN'T WANT TO END UP LIKE THAT EITHER! BUT I'M NO SHELTER FOR SPIDERS!

i JERK BACK A LITTLE TOO FORCEFULLY AND OUR CLOUD TIPS OVER! WE JUST MISS LANDING UNDER THE TRAILER WHEELS.

WHAT HAPPENED? DID I RUN YOU OVER?!?

A... A SPIDER WALKED ACROSS MY HAAAND!!!

TO FORGET THE SPIDERS, EDYTA AND I DISTRACT OUR- SELVES BY DARING EACH OTHER TO RUN IN FRONT OF MY UNCLE'S HIVES. i GET STUNG IMMEDIATELY.

MAKE A WISH!

THAT IT STOPS HURTING!!!

IN YOUR HEAD, NOT ALOUD. AND WHAT KIND OF A WISH IS THAT? MAKE A REAL WISH!!!

BUT IT WAS A REAL WISH...

STOP CRYING! ARE YOU SURPRISED IT STUNG YOU? YOU PRACTICALLY INVITED IT TO! RUNNING LIKE A FOOL IN FRONT OF THE HIVES, YOU MUST'VE MADE IT REALLY MAD!

BUT IF AN ELEPHANT RAN LIKE A FOOL IN FRONT OF MY HOUSE, I WOULDN'T GO ATTACK IT...

WHAT A DAY! i DIDN'T REALLY HAVE THOSE DREAMS, BUT I'M BEGINNING TO THINK MAYBE I SHOULDN'T HAVE SAID I DID!

WE SPEND THE NEXT FEW DAYS AT THE NEAREST LAKE. OTHER MEMBERS OF OUR FAMILY JOIN US.

UNCLES, AUNTS, COUSINS, NIECES, NEPHEWS, MOTHERS- IN-LAW...A TRIBE. JUST WHEN i THINK I'VE GOT A HANDLE ON THIS FAMILY, NEW MEMBERS ARRIVE.

I DON'T KNOW HOW TO SWIM, NEITHER DOES EDYTA. WE BOTH PRETEND TO SWIM BY MOVING OUR ARMS AND BREATHING LIKE FISH, BUT OUR FEET TOUCH THE BOTTOM.

OH, I JUST SAW A CREATURE!

A FISH?

NO, SOMETHING STRANGE, IT HAD LOTS OF FEET AND WAS CREEPING ALONG THE BOTTOM...

I... THINK IT JUST TOUCHED ME!

AHHHHH!

THAT'S HOW I LEARNED TO SWIM!

OUR LAST MORNING... IT FEELS LIKE AN ENDING. EVERYONE SEEMS A LITTLE SAD, ESPECIALLY EDYTA. AUNT STEFKA TRIES TO LIGHTEN THE MOOD.

SO? BEAUTIFUL DREAMS LAST NIGHT?!

HMM... I DREAMED OF BEES WITH ENORMOUS TEETH THAT WERE FLYING NASTILY, READY TO BITE!

HOW CAN YOU FLY NASTILY?

LIKE THIS, LOOK! BZZZZ...

HEE HEE

IS IT GOOD LUCK TO DREAM OF BEES? WE'LL SEE WHAT TODAY BRINGS...

EDYTA HAS A HARD TIME LETTING ME GO. I DON'T EVEN KNOW WHETHER WE'LL SEE EACH OTHER AGAIN. WE EXCHANGE ADDRESSES.

BUT THAT'S THE ADDRESS HERE!?

YEAH, I'M GOING TO LIVE WITH GRANDMA FOR A WHILE...

YOU KNOW, SOMETIMES I'D LIKE TO LIVE WITH MY GRANDMA TOO! IT'S LIKE BEING ON VACATION ALL THE TIME!

I'LL THINK OF YOU.

I'LL WRITE YOU STORIES.

WITHOUT ENDINGS?

YES! SHAGGY DOG STORIES!

FARFETCHED ONES, ABOUT BURSTING OUT LAUGHING IN A GLOOMY BUS FULL OF PEOPLE. ABOUT DREAMING WITH YOUR EYES OPEN, ABOUT ANYTHING ELSE YOU WANT.

SHE CRIES VERY HARD. SO HARD I DON'T KNOW WHAT TO DO.

I HADN'T REALIZED SHE WAS SO ATTACHED TO ME. WHAT CAN I DO? WHAT CAN I SAY TO COMFORT HER?

HERE!

SHE'S FOR YOU. SHE'S THE MOST PRECIOUS THING I OWN THAT I CAN GIVE YOU...

HAVE FUN WITH HER...

I DIDN'T KNOW YOU HAD A BARBIE!

HER EYES LIGHT UP. SHE'S STILL CRYING, BUT SMILING A LITTLE.

NOW I'M THE ONE WHO FEELS LIKE CRYING. BUT I SMILE, A LITTLE.

I REGRET MY GESTURE IMMEDIATELY. I SWALLOW. OH WELL, IT'LL STAY IN THE FAMILY.

AND HERE ARE HER CLOTHES...

THIS SEEMS TO MAKE HER HAPPY. ALL THE BETTER. EASY COME, EASY GO. BUT I'M GROWING UP. I DON'T NEED TOYS ANYMORE, RIGHT?

WE LEAVE, MY HEART IS HEAVY. ON THE FIRST BUS, I DECIDE TO WRITE STORIES FOR EDYTA. UNFORTUNATELY, THE NAUSEA TAKES HOLD OF ME RIGHT AWAY.

I PROPOSE TO MY PARENTS THAT I TELL THEM THE STORIES AND THEY CAN HELP ME RECREATE THEM LATER. BUT THEY DON'T LISTEN. ONLY THE PEOPLE AROUND US NOTICE THAT MY MOUTH NEVER CLOSES. I'M EITHER THROWING UP, OR TALKING...

I SHUT UP.

THE COUNTRYSIDE ROLLS BY SLOWLY. I TAKE IN THE TREES, THE HOUSES, THE PEOPLE...EACH ONE HAS ITS OWN STORY. YOU JUST HAVE TO PAY ATTENTION.

I READ THE STORIES IN THEIR EYES, THE WIND WHISPERS THEM TO ME IN THE LEAVES OF THE TREES.

THIS IS WHERE I'LL DRAW MY INSPIRATION FROM TO MAKE EDYTA LAUGH. TO PROTECT HER FROM THE WORLD OF ADULTS AS LONG AS I CAN. TO PULL CLOSED THE BEAUTIFUL VELVET CURTAIN AND LET HER DREAM IN COLOR.

A huge thanks to Edward and Nicole. They deserve a medal for their help.
Thanks to Anjali for being there whenever I needed her.
And thanks to Brigid for her Polish eyes.

Marzena Sowa

Karen Berger Senior VP – Executive Editor, Vertigo Sarah Litt Assistant Editor
Robbin Brosterman Design Director – Books Louis Prandi Publication Design Bob Harras VP – Editor in Chief

Diane Nelson President Dan DiDio and Jim Lee Co-Publishers Geoff Johns Chief Creative Officer
John Rood Executive VP – Sales, Marketing and Business Development Amy Genkins Senior VP – Business and Legal Affairs Nairi Gardiner Senior VP – Finance
Jeff Boison VP – Publishing Operations Mark Chiarello VP – Art Direction and Design John Cunningham VP – Marketing
Terri Cunningham VP – Talent Relations and Services Alison Gill Senior VP – Manufacturing and Operations David Hyde VP – Publicity
Hank Kanalz Senior VP – Digital Jay Kogan VP – Business and Legal Affairs, Publishing Jack Mahan VP – Business Affairs, Talent
Nick Napolitano VP – Manufacturing Administration Ron Perazza VP – Online Sue Pohja VP – Book Sales
Courtney Simmons Senior VP – Publicity Bob Wayne Senior VP – Sales

Cover Artist: Sylvain Savoia

MARZI: A MEMOIR
First American edition published in 2011 by DC COMICS. Published by arrangement with MEDIATOON LICENSING – France.

Marzi - L'Intégrale 1 - La Pologne vue par les yeux d'une enfant
© DUPUIS 2008, by Sowa, Savoia
Marzi - L'Intégrale 2 - Une enfant en Pologne
© DUPUIS 2009, by Sowa, Savoia
www.dupuis.com
All rights reserved

Printed in the USA.

ISBN:978-1-4012-2959-7

Certified Chain of Custody
60% Certified Fiber Sourcing and
40% Post-Consumer Recycled
www.sfiprogram.org

This label applies to the text stock
SGS-SFI/COC-US10/81072